SOUTHERN AF...

ANGOLA

ZAMBIA

MALAWI

• Lusaka

Zambesi R.

Umfuli R.

Mazoe R.

Shangani R.

• Harare

Okavango R.

ZIMBABWE

• Bulawayo

BOTSWANA

MOZAMBIQUE

Limpopo R.

NAMIBIA

Gaborones •

• Pretoria

• Johannesburg

Maputo

SWAZILAND

Orange R.

LESOTHO

SOUTH AFRICA

Cape Town

Port Elizabeth

The Mighty Nimrod

The Mighty Nimrod

A LIFE OF FREDERICK COURTENEY SELOUS
AFRICAN HUNTER AND ADVENTURER
1851–1917

Stephen Taylor

COLLINS
8 Grafton Street, London W1
1989

William Collins Sons and Co. Ltd
London . Glasgow . Sydney . Auckland
Toronto . Johannesburg

First published 1989
Copyright © Stephen Taylor 1989

Maps by Leslie Robinson

BRITISH LIBRARY CATALOGUING IN PUBLICATION DATA

Taylor, Stephen
The Mighty Nimrod: A Life of Courteney
Selous, African hunter and adventurer
1851–1917
1. Africa. Southern Africa. Selous,
Frederick Courteney, 1851–1917
I. Title
968.04'092'4

ISBN 0-00-217504-5

Photoset in Linotron Ehrhardt by
Wyvern Typesetting Ltd, Bristol
Printed and bound in Great Britain by
Mackays of Chatham PLC, Letchworth

For my parents

Contents

Illustrations

Acknowledgements

My thanks go to the following institutions for permission to use copyright material in their possession: The Zimbabwe National Archives, the Rhodes House Trust (for material in the Rhodes House Library), the Royal Geographical Society, the British Museum (Natural History section) and the Brenthurst Library. Many individuals helped with additional material and information, and I would especially like to thank Dr Terence Ranger of Manchester University, Mrs Paddy Vickery of the Bulawayo Library, Gavin Douglas of the Zimbabwe National Archives, Alan Bell of Rhodes House Library, Dr James Casada, Mrs M. Weiner of the Brenthurst Library, Miss M. De La Haye of the Société Jersaise, Mrs P. Cunningham of the Cullen Library, Alan and Lesley Windram, Mr Mark Horn and Mr Guy Pritchett. Organizations whose assistance was valuable included the Mendelssohn Library in Cape Town and the Landeshauptstadt of Wiesbaden.

Miss Ursula Maddy was extremely helpful with valuable information and memories about her family, and with photographs. Miss Victoria Ford contributed photographs and Commander Gerald Selous personal recollection.

My deep gratitude goes to my agent, Mary Bruton. So, too, to my family, for their advice on this work and tolerance of my long absences during its writing. Finally, it was my great good fortune to have a friend with an interest in the book's progress. Its failings would have been far greater without Tom Fort, who read the manuscript and whose meticulous eye and suggestions for its improvement were, quite literally, invaluable.

Foreword
by Wilfred Thesiger

As a boy I was enthralled by the books by Gordon Cumming, Baldwin, Newman, Powell-Cotton and other great African hunters. I was fourteen when I acquired a copy of Selous's *African Nature Notes and Reminiscences* – I immediately set about getting his other books. Selous was now my hero: in my eyes no other African hunter could compare with him, not only as a hunter but as a man. This is a view I still hold today – unlike so many of his contemporaries he was no ruthless killer. At first he shot elephants for a livelihood, but at heart he was essentially a naturalist, fascinated by every kind of animal, by butterflies and plants. He soon devoted himself to collecting specimens for the Natural History Museum in London, and for his exploratory travels in search of them he was awarded the Founder's Medal of the Royal Geographical Society.

In his books Selous was reticent about himself, and only after I had read this comprehensive and perceptive book by Stephen Taylor did I feel I had a full picture of Selous's life, and a real comprehension of his character, without, I am glad to say, any feeling of disillusionment.

Stephen Taylor traces Selous's life from his schooldays at Rugby, where he was captivated by the bird life of the surrounding country and resolved to travel and hunt in Africa, to his death in action in East Africa during the First World War. He was killed at the age of sixty-five after serving for eighteen months against Von Lettow-Vorbeck, the skilful and elusive German commander – a campaign in which the British forces were reduced by more than half through illness and casualties.

When I had read this book I understood why news of Selous's death had caused such widespread distress, even the regret felt by those of his German opponents who had known of him.

MAY, 1989

Preface

When I started researching this book, I expected to make discoveries that would disturb the conventional image that has been passed down of Selous as a Victorian *beau ideal*. The only previous biography, *The Life of Frederick Courtenay* [sic] *Selous*, published in 1918, was more in the nature of a personal tribute by a close friend, J. G. Millais. Moreover, perhaps because he feared that his hero might be soon forgotten amid the appalling toll of the Great War, Millais worked in great haste, and without benefit of the research that has been done since, on either the outstanding figures of the time, such as Rhodes, or on historical events, specifically the British advance into Central Africa. Furthermore, Millais's friendship with Selous was based on their common interests as sportsmen. Thus his account is long on detail of hunting incidents, most of which are provided in Selous's own writings, and less illuminating than might be expected on the most important episodes and crises of Selous's life, specifically the opening up of Mashonaland, the conflicts with the Matabele, and the Boer War. Millais described the first of these episodes, the accomplishment of which Selous was most proud, in eight pages, while devoting as much space to a relatively uneventful hunting trip to North America. In the nature of such a work, he specifically overlooked material which was not to the credit of his hero. None of this detracts from Millais's value as a source on Selous's background, from the rounded picture which he provides of Selous's activities from year to year, or from the insights into Selous's character provided in his final chapter, all of which I have drawn on.

My researches turned up facts which, while not debunking the conventional image, added a certain floridness to it. Like many of the early hunters and traders in what was known as the Far Interior, Selous was rumoured to have had an African mistress. Although this subject proved elusive, a document in the Zimbabwe Archives

xiii

eventually came to light which showed that before marrying a parson's daughter Selous had indeed had a long relationship with a woman, probably from the court of the Tswana chief Khama, and fathered two children by her. Other source material added further human dimensions to the portrait. As a youth, Selous was so wild that his parents despaired about his future, and allowed him to go to Africa only in the hope that it would keep him out of trouble with the law. In his early years in Africa, he was not simply a hunter, but a member of a circle of well-educated, Bohemian wanderers. Later he became a passionate advocate and agent of the British Empire, only to recoil in horror eventually at the voracity of his country's expansionism. Although a Darwinian and a rationalist, his experiences in the wilderness left him with strong beliefs in the spirit world.

Where I believe this book revises the record substantially is in the question of Selous's part in the activities of Cecil John Rhodes. In histories of the period, Selous is identified as the man of action who carried out the orders of Rhodes, the visionary, in the opening up of Central Africa. The general view has been that in the Mashonaland expedition, Selous was simply the guide who led the way, Buffalo Bill style, for the settlers. The archival evidence shows Selous's part to have been a good deal more important than this. It demonstrates that he was an instigator of British expansion in his own right, that he acted as a restraint on Rhodes when he was considering wild schemes to attack the warrior nation of the Matabele, and that he provided focus, depth and direction to Rhodes's vague notions about northward expansion, and a Cape to Cairo railway. It should be added that the evidence also reveals that Rhodes and the British South Africa Company later manipulated Selous to misrepresent to the British public the potential of Rhodesia when the new territory was in economic difficulty.

I cannot pretend that the portrait that emerges from these pages is a complete one. For a man of apparently simple tastes and values, Selous was a mass of paradoxes, and although he wrote extensively about hunting and natural history, he revealed little of himself in his published work. Not much of his correspondence survives. The letters to his mother, in the Zimbabwe Archives, give some insight into his emotional, moody nature, but with her he was a dutiful rather than a spontaneous correspondent. The one set of letters that might have cast a good deal more light on his personality and life were to his wife, Gladys. Sadly, these were destroyed, apparently burned after her death, either by their son Harold, or Gladys's sister Phyllis.

But in the end, I venture to hope, such gaps matter less than they would in most biographies. Even if Selous had accomplished nothing remarkable, his story would have been worth retelling simply as an adventure tale, as life lived at the gallop, packed with thrills and daring. It also illustrates a man who had neither envy nor malice, and who was ruled in most things by a sense of chivalry and duty. Of his death, both heroic and fitting, former US President Theodore Roosevelt wrote: 'I greatly valued his friendship; I mourn his loss; and yet I feel that in death, as in life, he was to be envied.'

PART ONE

1851–1888

CHAPTER ONE

A Veritable Tom Brown

In the final weeks of 1916, exhausted and fever-riddled British and Commonwealth troops trudged with heavy hearts and heavier boots through the quagmire of the German East African plains. Two years of guerrilla warfare in the tropics had left allied forces as demoralized in this forgotten corner of the war as the men engaged in the titanic struggle for Europe. Between disease and a vastly more skilled and resilient enemy, the combined British, Indian and South African forces had been reduced in two years to less than half their fighting strength.

One of the few making light of the conditions was a man who was not only the most celebrated of the British combatants, but also probably the oldest. On the last day of 1916, as he led his company in a new advance against the black askari troops and their white German officers, Captain Frederick Courteney Selous, DSO, celebrated his sixty-fifth birthday. Short but powerfully built, this remarkable figure marched at the head of his men with a slouch hat pushed back on his head, a handkerchief knotted around his neck and swinging a long native staff. Among the items in his kitbag was a small net, with which he pursued butterflies off duty. Despite his age, the impression he conveyed was one of youth and fitness. 'He was as cheerful as a schoolboy,' a colleague wrote. Although his unit, the 25th Battalion of the Royal Fusiliers, was reduced by 60 per cent through casualties and sickness, Selous had been on active service for eighteen months and seemed to revel in each new test of his constitution. Another officer, less than half his age, noted with awe his bearing, 'as straight as a guardsman', and the 'beautiful healthy look in his face'.

Selous had become a legend long before his arrival in East Africa.

3

By the popular press of the day he had been dubbed the 'Mighty Nimrod', a legacy of his early career as a hunter. To others he was 'Allan Quatermain', for he was widely held to have been the model on whom Rider Haggard had based the hero of his novel *King Solomon's Mines*. But elephant hunting with a muzzle-loader could not alone have established for Selous an enduring place in the history of the Victorian era and the Empire. This he won as a traveller and explorer in Southern and Central Africa; as the resourceful frontiersman who had guided British forces northwards in the occupation of Central Africa; and as the survivor of numerous daring exploits during the Matabele Wars. This romantic portrait, of a man who demonstrated the same dash and imperturbability at the point of an assegai as under the feet of an enraged bull elephant, was summed up by a friend's description of Selous as 'the hero of a thousand hair's-breadth escapes'.

Among the Victorians who left their mark on Africa, Frederick Courteney Selous was unusual for a youth that was notably lacking in hardship. David Livingstone, whose writings first turned the young Selous's thoughts to Africa, endured a childhood harsh enough to have crushed a less sturdy spirit. Henry Stanley was a product of acute emotional deprivation, while the young Cecil Rhodes was too sickly to mix with his fellows. No such trauma disturbed the comfort and emotional security of Selous's upbringing. He would come to embody, to a greater degree than many another imperial hero, the Victorian virtues of chivalry, courage and integrity. But he was spared the anvil on which the age often forged its great men.

Not that his youth was colourless or uneventful. He epitomized the spirit of pluck that the English public school system sought to foster, thriving in the rough, vigorous environment of Rugby. Among his contemporaries he stood out as a boy whom others hero-worshipped. One remembered him as 'a veritable Tom Brown'. Blessed with splendid physique and health, no young man could have embarked on a life of action in wild places better equipped physically.

His father was one of three remarkable brothers born in England of a Jersey couple who gave their sons a good education and a

4

distinctive family name, Slous, but not a great deal more. Neverthe-less, the brothers prospered in the rise of the nineteenth-century bourgeoisie, and each in his own way left a mark on the contempor-ary life of London: Frederick Lokes Slous, the father of our hero, as a businessman; Henry Courteney Selous as an artist and author, and Angiolo Robson Selous as a dramatist. Selous, the anglicized family name adopted by Henry and Angiolo in adulthood, became general in subsequent generations, but Frederick Lokes kept the name Slous to avoid confusion in the business world in which he had become established.

Most accounts have it that the family were of Huguenot descent, and that their forebears had taken refuge on Jersey in the great Protestant exodus from France after the revocation of the Edict of Nantes in 1685. Frederick Lokes, an animated and cultured man, more French than English in manner, was inclined to exclaim passionately: 'They turned us out! They turned us out!' The truth is more prosaic. The head of the line was an English soldier of the seventeenth century named Phillip Slow. Historians have noted that it was not uncommon for Channel Islanders of humble origin to claim Huguenot ancestry.

Whatever their antecedents, by the time our story opens the Selous family had acquired the bearing of what one who knew them called 'the cultured and well-to-do classes'. They were a close family, sharing the liberal convictions of the day, and cultivated tastes in the arts. Music, in particular, was a common bond, and all three brothers were creditable performers at amateur musical salons. When the time came to choose careers, Henry stood out for his talent as a painter and was admitted to the Royal Academy at the unusually young age of fifteen. His flair for the large canvases of historical and literary subjects so popular with the Victorians would establish him among the leading artists of the age. Frederick and Angiolo were directed towards the commercial world and joined the Stock Exchange, but it turned out that Angiolo was also artistic by temperament, and he soon left to work in the theatre. He too had a sense for what the Victorian public would find appealing, and wrote plays which won popular acclaim in productions by Charles Kean and Henry Irving. One work, *True to the Core – a Story of the Armada*, was the sensation of 1866, rousing a storm of patriotic fervour at the

5

Surrey Theatre in London and on a tour of provincial theatres. Meanwhile, Frederick, who had started at the Stock Exchange as a clerk, so prospered that he was made a partner, and finally rose to become chairman of the Stock Exchange committee. In time, the brothers were able to build substantial residences side by side in Gloucester Road, which at the time looked out in solitary splendour to Kensington Gardens and the Serpentine. Here the Selous clan flourished in untroubled gentility.

Frederick married three times. His first wife, Elizabeth Clipperton, bore him a son, Edrich. The second, Julia Mole, died childless. The third was Ann Sherborn, a strong-willed and impulsive woman of landed country stock, who was more than twenty years Frederick's junior. Ann, according to her second son, Edmund, had 'advanced views'. Just how unconventional these views were, or in what way, is not clear, but Ann was drawn throughout her life to the great romantic and liberal issues of the time, a trait that she passed on to her children. She also possessed more traditional feminine virtues, such as a love of nature and of poetry; she was particularly fond of Scott, who strongly influenced her in the composition of her own verses. Ann bore Frederick five children, the eldest, Frederick Courteney, being delivered at home on the last day of 1851.

It was a lively and somewhat eccentric circle: father an extravagantly impulsive figure, a witty talker, a fine chess player and musician; mother no less of a conversationalist, a woman drawn to new ideas, exuding vivacity and, a more rare quality, gladness; and, living on either side, uncles recalled by Selous's brother Edmund as 'out-of-the-canvas stepping personalities, carrying with them atmosphere and aroma'. Music was a focus for social activity in Gloucester Road. Frederick was widely regarded as the best amateur player of the clarinet in London. Uncle Henry was a cellist, while Angiolo sang and accompanied himself on the guitar. Though principally an artist, Henry also produced successful children's books under the pen-names Aunt Eleanor and Aunt Cae, and acted in amateur dramatics. Not to be outdone, Angiolo painted well enough to invite comparison with his brother.

The odds would have been long against such a home producing a young man who would earn his living by killing dangerous animals.

But young Fred – as he was known to his family – was always different. Certainly he had little in common with his father, who for years was alternately baffled and disturbed by the conduct of his eldest son. Edmund, who was a few years younger than Fred, but had a perceptive eye for the quirks of his elders, said it was as if he came into the world with a mind already made up about his place in it, and that he remained untouched through childhood and youth by any home influence. That this was possible in so stimulating an environment is an indication of Selous's single-mindedness, and of a self-sufficiency which, while it would be crucial to survival in Africa, was almost chilling in the way it enabled him to isolate himself. 'So far back as I can remember,' Edmund wrote, 'he was always just himself, with a settled determination that in its calm unobtrusive force had in it something elemental.'

Edmund, unlike Fred, was a delicate boy. They seem never to have been close and corresponded rarely, which is interesting in itself as a fascination with nature and its creatures was common to both; Edmund was, in fact, generally accepted by contemporary experts as the superior field naturalist, and his work as an ornithologist was far more significant than any of his brother's better known nature writings. It is possible that another shared interest accounted for the coolness between them: both fell in love when in their twenties with a lass named Fanny Maxwell, the daughter of a romantic novelist. Fanny married Edmund but once confided that she had actually found Fred the more attractive.

To his three sisters – Florence, Ann and Sybil – Fred was an affectionate if distant and somewhat awesome figure. After childhood, he was seen only during fleeting visits when he came home with astonishing stories and cluttered by the savage paraphernalia of the hunter. Fred himself thought Florence the most like him in temperament. In a rare outburst of intimate reflection, he wrote to Sybil in 1891: 'You alone of all of us have what may be called a sunny disposition. Edmund and Tottie [Ann] are both melancholic, and Florence and I are not always good tempered; though my temper, originally bad, has been subdued a good deal by the life I have led.'

A stream of visitors made their way to the Selous residences during Fred's childhood. Apart from the musical activity which was so much a part of home life, Frederick enjoyed entertaining friends such as Baron Bramwell, a judge, with whom he played chess. Holidays were spent at a farmer's country home on the Isle of Wight and it was on an early visit here, when he was aged about six, that Fred discovered the outdoor world, through rambles during which Ann Selous drew his attention to plant life and to species of birds and butterflies. During the same holiday he had his first experience of bird-nesting, climbing a larch to take a pigeon's eggs. Over the next two years, before going away to boarding school, Fred plundered every nest he was able to find in Kensington.

It was the young Selous's fate to grow up during the heroic age of African exploration. England had recently awakened, after centuries of indifference, to the vast potential and challenge of the so-called Dark Continent. In 1856 two young army officers, Richard Burton and John Speke, led the first expedition of what became a British quest to resolve the riddle of the White Nile's source. A sense of mission, to cast light and to save souls as well as to explore, seized the national consciousness.

The incarnation of this romantic spirit, and Selous's boyhood hero, was David Livingstone. Between 1853 and 1856, the missionary-explorer had tramped across the continent, from the west coast to the east, and on a magical stretch of the Zambesi river 'discovered' the great cataracts which he called the Victoria Falls. His exploit was acclaimed by Sir Roderick Murchison of the Royal Geographical Society as 'the greatest triumph in geographical research in our times', and was described by Livingstone himself in his first book, *Missionary Travels and Researches in South Africa.*

Published in 1857, this volume made a profound impression on Fred, as much as a tale of adventure in exotic lands as for its description of the author's spiritual mission. One image in particular, a line drawing of Livingstone sprawled under a snarling lion which had just mauled him, exerted a fearful fascination in the boy's mind for years. He could feel the horror of the moment, could see, only too vividly, the brute's gaping jaws, and found astonishing Livingstone's statement that a man being bitten by a lion feels no pain. This assertion continued to occupy Selous as a man, even after a few uncomfortable experiences of his own with lions.

It was Ann Selous, with her ardent nature and love of the heroic, who introduced Fred to Livingstone's writings. Ann had a touch of explorer's blood herself, being descended from James Bruce, who in 1770 was the first Briton to reach the source of the Blue Nile in Abyssinia. This remote genealogical link would later be invested with significance to explain Selous's career. But the influence of his mother, and the enthusiasm with which he took to books on Africa, were the compelling factors. Her second daughter, Ann, remembered evenings when the five children would cluster round to hear her spin a story. 'She was a true raconteuse and we drank with delight the tales from the old mythologies of romance and adventure. She would tell us of deeds of derring-do and all that was inspiring in the way of freedom and love of country.'

At the same time, she was stimulating young Fred's interest in the wilderness. While Frederick had the incomprehension of the cultured city-dweller for nature, Ann not only understood but encouraged her son's fascination with living creatures. It was only natural that a fixation about Africa developed. His sister Ann remembered that as a child he played with a toy wagon and for school prizes invariably chose books on Africa, while the perceptive Edmund recalled: 'He may not have lisped Africa but, if not, he at least came so near to it as to have made us all remember that he did.'

It had started with Livingstone, but another figure on the African landscape had an even more critical influence on Selous's life. Had it not been for William Charles Baldwin he might have gone to Africa anyway. After he read Baldwin's *African Hunting and Adventure* there was never any further doubt, certainly in his own mind. Livingstone had impressed him, but Baldwin's exploits were a revelation.

W. C. Baldwin, the son of a Lancashire vicar, was one of the earliest and most eccentric of the men who ventured to Africa for sport. A diminutive figure, almost hidden behind the magnificence of his beard, he was a reasonable shot and a jovial companion. He was also, however, incompetent in matters of bushcraft and reckless to a degree beyond folly. That he survived a decade in the wilderness to write his classic account of early hunting is one of the minor miracles of African adventure. In one splendidly characteristic passage he recounts stepping up to a twenty-foot crocodile for which he had conceived an animus with the intention of giving it a good kick in the ribs ('I was shod with heavy English shooting boots,' he hastened to assure his readers) only to be dragged back by an astonished companion.*

This volume came into Fred's hands before he reached his teens. Baldwin wrote racily of the pursuit of the whole range of African wildlife. The immense slaughter for which he and other early hunters, like William Cornwallis Harris and Roualeyn Gordon Cumming, were responsible seems appalling now. (On Baldwin's last expedition, in 1860, his party killed 61 elephant, 23 rhinoceros, 11 giraffe, 30 buffalo and innumerable antelope and smaller animals besides 70 quagga, a form of zebra which, hardly surprisingly, is now extinct.) But the contemporary view was that Africa contained a limitless supply of game, and to a youngster, fascinated by the wild, stalking and shooting dangerous creatures sounded nothing less than thrilling. The line drawings in the Baldwin book were even more dramatic than those in Livingstone's, and the narrow escapes from crocodiles, buffalo and elephant held young Fred in thrall. Livingstone had made Africa sound like a vast continent of limitless opportunity for young Englishmen. Baldwin had populated it with animals beside which the creatures of the English countryside paled. Henceforth Fred had only one objective: to get there as soon as possible.

His first school was in a gloomy mansion in Tottenham, north London, called Bruce Castle. Years later he would recall his first assembly, a bewildered, miserable boy of nine on a dismal January day in the vast oak-panelled banqueting hall. A picture of Selous's schooldays is given by an unpublished manuscript, quoted by Millais, which he wrote when he was in his fifties, an established author on hunting but facing financial difficulties and making an attempt at the more lucrative line of popular fiction. Macmillan & Co. had encouraged him to write a boy's yarn similar to *Tom Brown's Schooldays*, for which he drew on his years at Bruce Castle and Rugby, but in the end it was left incomplete.

The escapades of John Leroux, Selous's name for his youthful

---

*Baldwin's journal frequently betrays his greenness; in one early entry he complains of being kept awake by 'lions, tigers and wolves'. The last two are not found in Africa.

alter-ego, form a standard account of public school life, all boyish-high-jinks and harmless fun. The boys are spirited and mischievous, the masters by and large sagacious and kindly. The countryside is idyllic, although policed by gamekeepers, a mean and stupid species with whom the hero comes regularly into conflict.

Young Selous was a considerable handful from the outset. On his first day at Bruce Castle he got into a fight with a boy who teased him about his frilly collar. Egg-collecting was to land him in more trouble. His audacity in climbing oaks and elms alarmed the headmaster who tried without success to curb him; unable to raid nests by day, Fred took to lowering himself from the dormitory by rope at night.

He became a bold prankster. One night he and a friend dangled a dummy from their dormitory window, to the consternation of a policeman on his rounds who summoned the headmaster to Fred's bedside. On another occasion, he locked a junior master in a cowshed. While this daring in a boy of eleven excited the admiration of his fellows, it put a strain on the tolerant regime at Bruce Castle, which was well in advance of its time in eschewing beating. Neighbouring landowners complained about a boy who was constantly seen trespassing; meanwhile, booty from these rambles, the skins of small animals like water rats, weasels and stoats, joined the birds' eggs in Fred's locker.

At this stage, Frederick no doubt regarded his eldest son's growing obsession with tolerant affection, though regretting that he did not yet more appreciate the finer things in life. After four happy years at Bruce Castle, he was still only thirteen and there was every reason to hope that he would take up more conventional interests in time. Though he was often in trouble with his masters, Fred worked diligently at his lessons and was clearly no dullard.

He demonstrated this by gaining a place at Rugby. The great public school for the landed families of the Midlands had, in recent years, started admitting boys from further afield, but such was its reputation that there were three times more applications than there were places. Fred would have to sit an entrance examination in Greek, which he had never studied. To remedy this deficiency, he was sent to the equivalent of a cramming college, an institution run by a clergyman in the village of Belton in Northamptonshire.

The Reverend Charles Darnell was stout, elderly and easy-going. His lessons were undemanding too, and the surrounding countryside seemed a vast playground for the dozen or so adventurous souls in his charge. At a nearby lake they fished for pike and occasionally downed a moorhen with an airgun owned by one of the boys. These prizes were taken to the cottage of a local woman renowned for her cooking. Years later, sitting around an African campfire, Selous would recall the scent of the English countryside and meals of baked pike, and skinned and roasted moorhen.

One story from the year he spent at Belton is well known in Selous lore. J. G. Millais, his friend and first biographer, was told it by Mr Darnell's daughter:

> One night my father, on going round the dormitories to see that all was in order, discovered Freddy Selous, lying flat on the bare floor clothed only in his nightshirt. On being asked the cause of this curious behaviour he replied, 'Well you see one day I am going to be a hunter in Africa and I am just hardening myself to sleep on the ground.'

This story would have a whiff of the apocryphal, but for the fact that it is supported by another from a school fellow of Selous's that, 'One of his preparations [for Africa] was sleeping next the dormitory window, which he opened wide on the coldest nights as the nearest approach he could get to "sleeping in the open". I was in the dormitory, and devilish cold it used to be.'

The cramming accomplished its purpose. Fred passed the Rugby entrance exam and in January 1866 arrived at the doors to Whitelaw House. Once again he was fortunate in coming under a benign regime. The school had a tradition of scholastic excellence and rigorous discipline. Thomas Arnold, its most renowned headmaster, had imposed his vision of moral idealism through regular employment of the birch and expulsion. His death caused an interregnum but under Frederick Temple, who became headmaster in 1858, Rugby was experiencing a liberal renaissance.

Temple, later to become Archbishop of Canterbury, was one of England's greatest schoolmasters. Kindly and informal, he once rebuked an over-zealous colleague: 'All your questions are too hard. Why do you frighten your boys so?' He was nevertheless an imposing presence, and just as formidable in his way as Arnold. One eminent contemporary said: 'It was because he was so great a man that he exercised such power as a teacher.'

In a decade of reform, Temple instituted one of the happiest periods in Rugby history. One boy described it as 'a fine, strong, rough, vigorous and completely self-confident society. We felt that we were breathing the air which makes strong, brave and efficient Englishmen, and I think we were right in the main.' Discipline was still strict, but usually fair. Crude bullying was uncommon. Although delicate and sensitive boys might still have found it a bruising environment, to Fred it was heaven.

He was greatly fortunate in his housemaster. His particularly energetic brand of high spirits could well have caused his expulsion on a number of occasions. But James Wilson, later headmaster of Clifton, was another great teacher of boys. One of the few masters at Rugby who was not then a clergyman, Wilson was still in his twenties when he first encountered Selous. A master at Bruce Castle had given him a good idea what to expect, writing: 'Take my advice and say your house is full; the boy will plague the life out of you.' A catalogue of Selous's misdeeds clinched the matter. 'Such were his crimes,' Wilson recalled, 'that of course I wrote back and said he was the boy for me.'

Fred was fourteen when he arrived at Rugby and over the next two and a half years he benefited greatly from being in the care of this good and tolerant man. At their introductory talk Wilson asked what he wanted to do with his life. 'I mean to be like Livingstone,' Fred replied. At Cambridge in 1857 Wilson had heard Livingstone deliver his ringing exhortation to young Englishmen to undertake a life of service in Africa, and though it is unlikely that even at this stage the young Selous had service in mind, he and the master had a long talk about Livingstone, Africa and natural history. Wilson was impressed. 'I soon saw he had the fire and modesty of genius, and was a delightful creature,' he recalled.

That first winter at Rugby in 1866, Livingstone was in Fred's mind a great deal. The explorer had returned to England eighteen months earlier from his disastrous journey along the Zambesi river, and had just had published the book *Narrative of an Expedition to the Zambesi and its Tributaries*. It was a low point in Livingstone's life; the

13

venture had failed in its principal objective, to open a riverine trade route to the African interior; it had killed his wife and damaged his reputation as the leading English explorer of the age. But as Fred pored over the book in his study he saw only the great river, a vast stretch of wilderness broken by magnificent cataracts and teeming with game. He wrote home: 'I am reading a new book by Mr Livingstone. It is very interesting and is about the discovery of two great lakes. Send me two catapults.'

Boys shared quarters, two or three to a room, and made their own tea and breakfast. Outside lessons there was free time for an hour before dinner and an hour afterwards. On half holidays boys played cricket or rugby or followed their own designs. In summer there was swimming in the Avon river. In 1867, the school's tricentenary, the Natural History Society was formed, Fred being a founder member. Wilson had from the outset taken an easy-going attitude towards his countryside ramblings after specimens. Now he gave the boy further latitude, sometimes allowing him to stay out after roll call, and stocking the library with a fine set of bird reference books for his use.

Wilson's indulgence was to save Selous time and again. For, as another Rugby boy recalled, Fred was naturally drawn to breaking the rules: 'What he loved best was a bit of mischief with field sport or natural history attached to it . . . Poaching of all sorts was dear to him; bathing in forbidden places had a charm; but besides all this, he was good at books, good at games, knew no fear, and was loved by everybody . . . No matter what scrapes he got into, he would never tell a lie.'

Attractive as this portrait is – of the public schoolboy of popular fiction, a trifle wild perhaps but entirely without malice or deceit – there was another side to the coin. Selous's wildness had a darker aspect, which took the form of intolerance of opposition and quickness to anger. Beneath the calm assurance remarked on by his brother, there lurked a capacity for volcanic rage which would erupt when he was balked. He had discovered that his open-faced manner gave him considerable powers to charm, and though honest he would resort to guile if it would help him wriggle out of trouble. Thus he ingratiated himself with those in authority while doing much as he pleased. A contemporary, C. K. Francis, who became a

14

London magistrate, wrote: 'The mere fact of anything being "verboten" was a kind of signal to Selous that it must be accomplished.'

Puberty brought new physical prowess. He had always been a strong and agile boy. Now his development was almost complete. His powers of sight and hearing were astonishing. Wilson recalled one occasion on which Fred eavesdropped on a conversation eighteen feet away above the hubbub of a house supper. Although on the short side, he was well muscled and wire-taut. He was fast on his feet as well as nimble and, having learnt to swim on holidays on the Isle of Wight, was the best swimmer in school.

Fred also distinguished himself at the great school game devised by William Webb Ellis. Rugby football, then in its infancy, had evolved none of the features of handling and skill seen in the modern game. Matches were played between houses and were characterized by one contemporary spectator as 'a sort of tribal warfare'. Indeed, the injuries caused by the practice of indiscriminate kicking, or hacking as it was called, so disturbed Temple that he eventually changed the rules to forbid it. Selous himself later described rugby as 'a chaotic and brutal affair of little science'. All the same, he threw himself into it with such zest that he became, at fourteen, the youngest boy ever to be honoured with a house cap.

This was all very well, but so far as Frederick Slous was concerned it was a long way from everything that he expected of his eldest son. Frederick thought of medicine or the law as being appropriate choices of career, and by now the suspicion must have started to form that Fred might not follow the path envisaged for him. Differences between father and son had widened as the boy matured. Now fifteen, Fred shone at athletics of all kinds: his father loathed sport. Back home from school, the boy showed indifference to the artistic activities dear to the family, and while his siblings participated enthusiastically at musical evenings, Fred yearned to be off on his own. He submitted dutifully, but without pleasure, to violin lessons, and while he could not be faulted on his school record, it was clear that he had no real interest in academic accomplishment. When the subject of the future came up, he invariably spoke of making his fortune in Africa, so much so that eventually the mere mention of the continent upset Frederick.

At the end of his first year at Rugby, Fred came home for a holiday which could have ended further speculation about his future then and there. The first of what would be many brushes with death was a very close shave indeed.

The winter of 1867 was a harsh one, and all over the country lakes were frozen into skating rinks. One of the most popular skating spots was Regents Park where, like hundreds of Londoners, Fred had taken his skates on the grim day of 15 January. He was out on the ice when it started to break up. As cracks appeared, with reports like pistol shots, there was a general dash for the bank.

Selous suddenly found himself stranded far out on a slab which would only support him if he lay out at full stretch. Any attempt to step to the bank would have tipped the ice, dumping him into the water. There was no doubt what that would have meant; a number of people had made desperate attempts to skate out of danger, only to slide off into the water and immediately disappear as the heavy slabs closed over them.

Despite the horror of this position – for anyone, let alone a boy of fifteen – what Fred felt was less fear than a determination not to die. He was in no immediate danger and, for the time being, thought it sensible to wait for rescue. An attempt to retrieve those stranded out on the lake was mounted from the bank but soon abandoned. Two men in the water near Fred gave up the struggle to stay afloat and disappeared. It came to him as the light faded that rescuers were either not aware of his plight, or had simply given him up as a hopeless case. If he was going to get off the ice alive, it would be by his efforts alone.

Cautiously, keeping his weight as widely distributed as he could, he crawled across the ice, inching his way from one slab to another. Choosing a path over the bigger pieces, which were more likely to support him, he made for a large slab of unbroken ice connected to the bank. It was a manoeuvre requiring sustained coolness amid peril. The urge to attempt a headlong scramble for safety must have been as pressing as it would have been suicidal. Once a slab all but turned over on him before he could get his weight properly distributed, but he managed to stay atop and continued to work his way to eventual safety.

The next day the newspapers were full of what came to be called the Regents Park Disaster: forty-nine people had perished beneath the ice. Fred, reading the report in *The Times* in the snug comfort of Gloucester Road, was shocked. He had observed the drama coolly, even dispassionately, and had had no idea of the scale of the tragedy. One thing he had learned however: he would not lose his nerve in a crisis. This ability to detach himself from an emergency, to maintain, *in extremis*, an eye for the way out, was to save his life time and again.

Back at Rugby, his education proceeded less eventfully. It did not escape the school's attention, however, as Fred passed through his second year, that he showed an ever-increasing inclination to flout authority. Wilson, who was prepared to close his eyes to some offences, was aware that Selous had returned from his holidays with a rifle and was keeping it hidden at a local farm, whence he set out on forays to collect specimens. Others were less indulgent. Mischievousness was one thing, but the apparently determined way Fred went about breaking every rule in the book was another. A fine lad he might be, manly and honest perhaps, but voices – notably in the Sixth Form – were heard muttering that young Selous was getting too big for his boots.

They were probably right. Adolescence had brought out new traits of bumptiousness and intolerance. The confidence of youth had become in Fred something more akin to arrogance. Behind the ingratiating manner he fulminated bitterly against anything that stood in his way. The fact that his conduct was not in any sense wicked did not help him with those who reasonably expected more conformity.

There was disgruntlement at home as well over his behaviour, and Frederick was considering drastic action to bring his son, as he saw it, to his senses. Ann Selous, though she better understood Fred's elemental nature, was also concerned at his lack of restraint and how he went his own way, contemptuous of opposition. He would be nearing middle-age before he brought under control his impatience with those who differed with his views.

The laws of trespass, in particular, aroused the demon in him, and many a time only his turn of pace saved him from the gamekeepers of estates nearby. He nearly lost his rifle after dropping it in one such flight, but had the audacity to write to the landowner who, admirably, returned it. Another time, he was apprehended in the grounds of Pilton Manor, and was dragged in front of the bailiff before managing to escape. While he was being thus manhandled, Fred considered attacking his captor, and forbore only on the grounds that it would get him into greater trouble at school. He would not always exercise the same self-control.

Ironically, it was the occasion of what he regarded as his greatest coup at Rugby which gave those who wanted to teach him a lesson their chance. In swimming a freezing lake, stark naked, in winter to pluck eight pale-blue eggs from a heronry at Coombe Abbey, he showed the lengths to which his determination would drive him; and for the first time he experienced the elation of triumph hard won. He believed he had got away without being spotted, but a complaint from the abbey reached Temple who, according to Wilson, 'warned the Natural History Society pretty plainly'. The offender suffered the ignominy of being summoned before the committee and officially denounced for what amounted to a straightforward act of poaching. The eggs were confiscated, and Fred was ordered to write out 500 lines of Virgil, though Wilson, soft-hearted as ever, arranged for the eggs to be returned to him.

A more painful come-uppance involved the Sixth Form, from whom the young Selous finally received the thrashing he merited but had so long escaped. He was in what was to be his last year at Rugby and, though only in the Fifth Form, had conceived a contempt for the senior boys, who were accorded special privileges, including the authority to discipline. One night Fred and an Australian boy named Foster tipped a Sixth Former out of his bed. The Sixth, who were described by Wilson as 'perhaps not very impressive, though virtuous', met the next day to consider retribution. The denouement was described by Wilson:

> In the evening they called up Selous and Foster into the library before them all, and the head of the house announced they were going to cane them both; no mere hand caning, but a good sound caning on the right place. Selous and Foster put their backs against the wall, and said they would make an example of anyone who touched them. They would take a licking from me or Temple; but not from such fools as the Sixth were.

The head of the house came to me for advice. I said he had better send them to me. They came; they pleaded guilty; but take a thrashing from those fools they would not. I said, of course, that it was a Sixth Form matter; that it was unheard of that I should be their executioner; that Temple would give them the same answer; they must submit or go. What would their fathers say when I wrote that their sons would not take a licking they had richly deserved? 'Not from such fools as those fellows.' A happy thought occurred to me. 'Suppose you go back and say that I had persuaded you that a licking was the very thing you both wanted, and to ask them to do it thoroughly, and thank them profusely when it is over.' They took the humour and improved on my idea. They went back with grave and long faces and said I had prayed with them and quite convinced them that a caning was what they wanted. So they bent over the table, and at each stroke said: 'Thank you, thank you, it's doing me good, it's doing me good.' The Sixth let in you may be sure; but it elicited nothing but gratitude.

That same year, 1868, Fred left Rugby. The reason is not recorded, but Frederick had been unhappy for some time with his son's education, and it seems the break represented a new initiative on the father's part. Fred's obsession with the countryside and its creatures had turned from a harmless hobby into a threat to his prospects, and far from providing a new direction, Rugby seemed only to have ingrained the problem. Fred would go to Europe to finish his education. Perhaps in Switzerland, Frederick's favourite country, the lad would learn something of the traditions and values of European culture. As for Africa, Frederick wanted to hear no more of it.

So at the end of summer Fred packed his trunk and said goodbye to his friends and to Wilson. His friendship with the master endured, and after Selous's death, Wilson wrote a tribute in the *Meteor*, the school paper, which concluded: 'One of his friends, Sir Ralph Williams, well said of him, "The name of Fred Selous stands for all that is best and straightest in the South African story," and I will venture to say that it stands for the same in Rugby annals.'

The school retained a place in Selous's affections. He would return to be fêted as an eminent old boy, and in time would send a son of his own there. But now he was bound for Europe.

CHAPTER TWO

Bismarck and Biedermeier

Selous spent almost three years on the Continent, in Switzerland, Prussia and finally Austria. It was an arrangement that many other young men would have envied. Still in his teens, he was living independently abroad with no material needs, in surroundings both beautiful and culturally stimulating. His father, who by now had prospered sufficiently at the Stock Exchange to buy a house at Wargrave in Berkshire for the family's weekend use, made sure he was comfortably provided for, and his studies were light enough to leave him ample leisure in what was a glittering and eventful era in European history.

He was first sent to Switzerland, where he stayed only briefly and was never happy. And while it would be wrong to say that he was impervious to the charm of Wiesbaden and the magic of Vienna, the attractions of continental life never persuaded him away from his intention to travel and find adventure, in Africa above all. Throughout his stay in Europe he assiduously played on the sympathies of his mother and sisters and, through them, sought to bring Frederick round. That he got his way in the end was due not only to his persistence, but to conduct which, if not in the full sense criminal, was still discreditable enough to appal his despairing father, and convince him that the boy was beyond control.

The first plan was that Fred should study medicine, French and music in Switzerland. Even his mother had chided him for irresponsibility and he accepted for the time being the idea of becoming a doctor. Medicine was not the worst path he could take, especially when he considered the alternative, a career in the City. In his cockiness, Fred regarded his father's profession with ill-concealed contempt, describing it as 'scribbling away on a three-legged stool in

21

a dingy office in London'. Although aged only sixteen, he was certain he would never be able to settle down quietly in England. As a doctor, he reasoned, he would at least be able to get abroad, perhaps serving on board ship or as an army surgeon.

In August 1868 he arrived in Neuchâtel in Switzerland where he enrolled at the Institution Roulet, a private establishment. It was to be a brief stay. Frederick had remarked grimly before his departure that it would be remarkable if he learned anything at all; that he would probably spend all his time shooting and fishing. In fact, and in fairness, Selous usually applied himself to his studies. But he felt restless in Switzerland, and dismayed by the task ahead. Within three months of arriving in Neuchâtel, he wrote to his mother: 'How glad I shall be when my education is finished and I have got into my profession. Five years more of it is something awful to contemplate.' If only he could take up sheep-farming in the colonies 'or something of that sort', he remarked, adding wistfully, 'but I suppose I must give up that idea.'

Only a month later he was back in London, and by the time Frederick accompanied him to Wiesbaden the following spring, all talk of medicine had been abandoned. What caused this turnaround can only be speculated upon, but something dramatic must have happened to terminate his career at the Institution Roulet so suddenly. No surviving evidence indicates what it was. Perhaps Fred just refused to go on with medical studies; perhaps he was expelled. It seems unlikely, whatever the reason, that Frederick approved; a letter written by Fred from Temple Bar in a tone of morose defiance to his sister Florence in April 1869, is suggestive of a family row:

> Many thanks for your spiritual letter which almost tempts me to commit suicide; if I can't get good shooting and fishing in this world I'll have it in the next, if what the Chinaman says is true; but by hook or by crook I will have some in this world too, and make some rare natural history collections into the bargain.

There was more in the same vein, with an account, no doubt intended to get back to his father, of the splendours of life in Natal, in South Africa, described to him by a couple of recent acquaintance. 'A perfect paradise ... lovely beyond description ... a wonderfully gay place . . . the society there is very good.' It was no coincidence that Natal was also the old stamping ground of his hunting hero, William Baldwin.

These tactics were to no avail. In September 1869, he was on his way back to Europe, to Wiesbaden in Prussia. There was no objective to his studies – which concentrated on German and the violin – other than a rounding of his education but, in some respects at least, Prussia was a change for the better. The forests to the north of the town were rich in birdlife, there was duck-shooting on the Rhine only a couple of miles to the south, and fishing in the smaller streams. Also living in Wiesbaden was an English family named Colchester including a boy, Charley, of Fred's age. They were charmed by Selous, invited him for Christmas and they threw a party for him on his eighteenth birthday. Kate Colchester, Charley's sister, was quite smitten and declared: 'He was a dear boy, and we all loved him.'

Wiesbaden was then in its heyday as a spa and popular resort for wealthy Europeans. The mineral springs and mild climate, the elegance of its buildings and surroundings, attracted the famous as well as the merely rich. Regular visitors during Selous's stay included Brahms and Dostoyevsky, and members of the royal families of Europe. He was in lodgings at the home of a junior official at the Chancellery, Eduard Knoch, in Röderstrasse. This was in the handsome old centre of the town which led up a hill to a church. In the afternoons, Fred liked to walk down to the Kursaal gardens, where a brass band played, and in the evening he would watch society at the gaming tables.

In these gracious surroundings he was happy enough, and in chatty, affectionate letters to his mother, recorded local incidents: a Prussian officer shot dead in a duel ('Serve him right'); and a Russian count losing a fortune at gambling ('What an April fool!'). One winter's day at the gardens, he was skating with Kate Colchester when there occurred a reminder of the Regents Park tragedy two years earlier. A crack in the ice opened up, precipitating Kate into the water. Without hesitation, Fred leaped in and supported her until they were helped out.

Germany in the 1860s was going through a period of epochal change that would transform the political geography and the balance of power in Europe. The principal features which in Prussia had so far marked this upheaval meant little to the English youth. Otto von Bismarck, an imperious conservative appointed head of government seven years before, had modernized the army and, with the ultimate objective of unifying Germany, successfully waged wars against Denmark and Austria.

But there was another side to Prussian life, and it was one which had no appeal for Selous. The reformist uprisings in Europe of 1848 produced a liberal movement in Prussia which Bismarck had just succeeded in crushing, with the encouragement of the Hohenzollern monarchy and by flagrant violations of the constitution. The Iron Chancellor's exercise of authoritarian powers saw the triumph of Prussian conservatism and, in the end, the extinction of France's opposition to German unification, but the cost to citizens' rights was high.

A correspondent wrote to the local newspaper, the *Wiesbadener Zeitung*: 'Whoever lives in Prussia feels at every step that the military and police state encloses him in its net, that he as a burgher has fewer rights than the haughty nobility, that a powerful and truly officious bureaucracy may defy unpunished every right of a burgher.'

The police had an intimidating range of powers to interfere in a citizen's private life, down to dictating what job he did and how he raised his children. Police permission was required to move to another district, as it was to hold any public assembly (from which women and apprentices were barred). Abuses were common. The only way for an individual to seek redress was by written complaint, which was commonly ignored. In short, the Prussia of the 1860s was the forerunner of the modern totalitarian state.

It may be imagined how the rebellious English youth, to whom authority of any sort was anathema, felt about this forbidding social environment. The character formed in a liberal home, and by the tolerance of Temple's Rugby, reacted sharply against the Bismarckian philosophy of 'blood and iron'. During the storm that was about to break over Europe, Fred would be vociferously anti-Prussian.

It should be added that by then he had another, and far less creditable, reason for disliking Prussian authoritarianism. An incident which took place in the Wiesbaden forest in the summer of

1870, causing his parents the most profound disquiet, was the inevitable outcome of his contempt for what he regarded as petty restrictions. Ironically though, it almost certainly speeded his departure for Africa.

He had become good chums with Charley Colchester, who was hardly less adventurous a spirit and who would call for Selous at his lodgings in Röderstrasse. From there they would sally forth on egg-collecting forays in the belt of forest that surrounded Wiesbaden. After years of disregarding the laws of trespass, the fact that the woods were protected made no difference to Selous, but he should have known that in Prussia even minor transgressions would be viewed seriously; he had already had a couple of brushes with authority, in the shape of an elderly forester named Keppel, who had warned him away from the woods.

The lure of a honey buzzard nest was his downfall. Fred and Charley were in the act of robbing the nest one summer morning when they were discovered by Keppel. What followed was described by Selous himself in a manuscript the bulk of which is now lost but parts of which were used by his biographer Millais to provide the following, apologist, version of the incident.

> 'Now I shall take you to prison,' [Keppel] roared, as he seized hold of the coat in which Selous had hidden the two eggs he had taken. By this time, however, the fighting spirit was aroused on both sides, for Selous had no intention either of being captured or resigning his treasures quietly. A fierce struggle ensued in which the coat was torn in half, when at last Selous, losing his temper, gave the old forester a right-hander on the jaw which dropped him like a felled ox.
>
> The boys were now alarmed and for a moment Selous thought he might have killed the man, but as he showed signs of recovering they took to their heels and ran home with all possible speed. Since complications were bound to follow Selous at once consulted a lawyer who advised him to leave Prussia.

The 'complications' were no small matter. Selous had in fact been to see the mayor of Wiesbaden, who warned him that he faced the virtual certainty of a prison sentence. After hurried consultations with the Colchesters, Selous fled by train to Salzburg in Austria, where the Prussian authorities would be unable to reach him. Charley also left Wiesbaden for an outlying town, hoping the affair would blow itself out, but the law was not to be deterred. He was traced and arrested, to serve a week in jail for poaching.

Selous's case was far more serious. The mayor had told him that stealing eggs was a trifle in Prussian law compared with assaulting an official, and an elderly one at that. If caught he could expect to be sentenced to between two and three months.

When news of Fred's flight to Austria reached London Frederick was predictably and understandably horrified. The worry of finding a suitable profession for his wayward son had weighed heavily on him for the past two years. Now he had to face the possibility that the boy, not yet out of his teens and a fugitive from the law, was not just rough and wilful, but actually bad. Frederick's first response was to order him back to Wiesbaden to face his punishment.

Far from being contrite, Selous was inclined to brazen out the affair. On arrival at Salzburg he had taken a room at a café for a month, and in June wrote to his mother in terms which, given the circumstances, were startling in their effrontery. After beginning with an apology for causing her 'a good deal of inquietude', he went on:

> I must say I was rather surprised at the very Prussian view Papa took of the affair. I think it was rather too much to expect me to go back to Wiesbaden, which I must emphatically refuse to do, but excepting this I will do anything else you wish. The only thing is, I wish you would not take on so about a trifle making a molehill into a mountain, which you seem to me to be doing.

Such bumptiousness provoked even Selous's ever-loving and tolerant mother, and by July he was taking a more circumspect line, although still hardly contrite. 'I hope you have forgiven me the "impertinent little remarks" whatever they were to which you alluded in your last letter.' For all his bold front, a spate of letters home indicates he realized he had misjudged his parents' mood, and was at pains to ingratiate himself again, at least with his mother.

'This morning I have been very busy choosing some new pieces for violin and piano with the help of my music master. Please tell Papa I have paid all my debts in Wiesbaden, even to the uttermost farthing,' he wrote.

And: 'I pity poor Charley, he will catch it from Mrs Colchester. It is a good thing he is too big for her . . . Mind you give me all the news in your next letter for you know that the last three or four have been principally full of fears and misgivings, which knowing your good sense as I do I think I may safely consider to have altogether disappeared, n'est ce pas?'

Ann Selous was never able to resist her first-born for long. Within a matter of weeks she was enclosing gifts with her letters, including a £5 note. She had also agreed to Fred's request to give Charley Colchester, who had just been released from prison, 'a berth down at Wargrave while future steps are decided'. A jail-bird Charley might be, but, Fred assured his mother, 'he would be a capital companion for Edmund.'

Frederick, who was evidently losing authority in his own household as he approached the age of seventy, was not impressed by his son's transparent efforts to regain favour, and tried to insist that if he would not go back to Prussia he should return home. Still Fred resisted. By now the reason was less fear of retribution, than because he was greatly taken with Austria.

The Habsburg Empire was in the midst of what Hermann Broch, a contemporary Austrian novelist, called 'the gay apocalypse'. Austria itself was witnessing a flourishing of social and intellectual life in which the war against Prussia, only four years earlier, was already a dim memory. The central social institution was the coffee house, a public salon of gaiety and wit.

This milieu represented a revival of the Viennese culture known as Biedermeier, which was characterized by good-humoured society and sentimental art. (The name came from Papa Biedermeier, a caricature of middle-class comfort.) The bourgeois soirée thrived, as did music, theatre and painting generally. A major public dispute concerned the relative merits of Brahms and Wagner, while at the same time the Austrian love of frivolity in music had come into its own, and the 'waltz king', the younger Johann Strauss, was at the height of his popularity. Vienna was the centre of the musical world, but Strauss's frothy concoctions were also being played in Salzburg, where they charmed the young Selous.

After the grey sternness of Prussia, the bonhomie and grace of these surroundings were immensely appealing, made more so by the discovery of an unexpected talent. Having plodded away at the violin for years without bringing enjoyment to anyone concerned, Fred found that he had a natural aptitude for the zither, a stringed Bavarian folk instrument. In the next year he picked up a repertoire which would serve him well, for Selous and his zither, on which he played Strauss waltzes and popular tunes, became a regular turn around the campfires of the African interior.

For the time being, he was still facing an ultimatum from Frederick to return to England, but in July, in one of the few letters he ever wrote to his father, he made a determined plea to be allowed to stay abroad:

My dearest Father,

I have just received a proposal that has overjoyed me. I have today told my landlord and everyone else concerned that I may have to leave Salzburg in a few days. Amongst others I told my old Hungarian friend of whom I spoke in one of my first letters. The old fellow has it appears taken a great fancy to me and on my telling him that I should very likely be forced to return to England and all the reasons and how much I objected to the same he made me a most kind proposition. I had already told him that in a couple of years or so I'm going to Natal and that in order to fit myself for a colonist I should have to study farming for a year . . . He is a large landowner and farmer in Hungary . . . and he offers to take me as a pupil and teach me farming . . . He says he will treat me like a son and personally look after my studies . . . Surely there is now no reason for my returning at once. It seems to me that if you do require me to return you will be doing me a positive wrong . . . And now I have done, and hoping you will consider this letter believe me

Ever your affectionate son,

Fred

A few days later events came to his rescue. On 2 August 1870, the French army crossed the Prussian frontier; a new war had started in central Europe.

The Franco-Prussian conflict had been in the making for years, indeed had been inevitable since the Austro-Prussian war four years earlier. But despite their proximity to events, most Austrians were happily oblivious of the storm. In one instance, a Viennese orientalist named August Pfizmaier only learnt of the war some weeks after it had broken out by reading a Chinese newspaper. Selous heard about it in a letter from his anxious mother, to which he replied: 'I was very much surprised to find that war had been declared. I was in the most sublime ignorance that there was any misunderstanding between the two countries.'

Opinion in England was naturally Francophobic and sympathetic to the ally of Waterloo; it was further influenced when Bismarck released to *The Times* details of a plan conceived by Louis Napoleon for annexing Belgium. At the Selous household in London there was a fear that the war might become a generalized European bloodbath, which would threaten Fred's safety and his father's investments.

Most Austrians were not only ignorant of, but indifferent to, what was happening on their border, but Fred, still lodging above a Salzburg café, took a fervently partisan view. His support of France had little to do with a mistaken belief in his own French ancestry, still less any liking for the Napoleonic tradition (his heroes from history were the parliamentary rebels Oliver Cromwell and John Hampden). Rather it was a reflection of his vehement anti-Prussianism.

'Vive la France, à bas la Prusse,' he wrote home. He also had the temerity to suggest that the poaching incident had been a blessing in disguise. Wiesbaden had been abandoned as soon as war was declared, he said, and 'after all it was lucky I left and came to Austria you see, for if I was anywhere within 100 miles of the scene of the war I suppose you would feel nervous, whereas now I am as far removed from it as you yourself in England. I wish that you would send me a few papers, for there is next door to nothing in these wretched little Austrian publications.'

By the end of summer, the military might of Imperial France had been destroyed, though resistance of a sort dragged on until the following January. Disruption of the European transport system helped Fred further to delay his return to England, while he closely followed the progress of the war, crossing the Bavarian frontier to speak to Prussian soldiers who had taken part in the battles of Worth and Sedan. Still his sentiments remained profoundly anti-German. On 20 October, after Louis Napoleon's surrender, he wrote home:

> I see a great deal said in the English papers about the 'Francs tireurs' [an irregular, guerrilla force] being little better than murderers. I think that the French ought to consider all the soldiers composing the German armies as so many burglers [sic], and shoot them down like rabbits in every possible manner: and moreover as the Germans are murdering the peasants, men, women and children, for such offences as being in possession of an old sword ... I think the French would be perfectly justified in shooting every German soldier they take prisoner.

Selous found inactivity 'torture in any environment', and even in the lovely surroundings of Salzburg he was rarely at rest. Near the town was a glade where he chased butterflies with a net, to the astonishment of local peasants who apparently believed he was a lunatic. In the course of his rambles he also struck up a friendship with a tough old hunter-cum-poacher. His new friend, like other older men, was attracted by his boyish energy and enthusiasm, and introduced him to the mountainous hunting grounds of Bavaria.

Together they made a trip to the Untersberg, where Fred shot a pair of chamois deer. It was a personal landmark, his first real game 'bag'. Thirty years later, when he was the most famous hunter in the world and the walls of his trophy room in Surrey were lined with tusks and lion skins, the first entry in the game book read: 'Oct '70 – Two chamois – Untersberg, Bavaria.'

This encounter only deepened his desire to hunt in Africa, though by now he was secure in the knowledge that it was only a matter of time before he got his way. He would stay in Salzburg until the following summer, savouring Austria in a way that may have encouraged Frederick to reflect that his son's European education had not, in the end, been a total waste.

On a visit to Vienna, Fred declared magnificent the palace of the Habsburg emperors, and the opera house, completed only two years earlier. He went to the opera three times. Wagner he disliked, and was at least in agreement with the influential Viennese critic, Eduard Hanslick, in finding *Tannhäuser* a bore. 'I couldn't understand the story at all, and there were no pretty airs in it,' Fred complained. Gounod's *Faust*, however, he thought 'splendid'.

His time in Europe was drawing to an end and, as Selous prepared to embark on his adventure, we should consider how, from afar, the notion of Africa struck the contemporary world.

Africa had fulfilled a need in the Victorians. Its unexplored mysteries and treasures, its barbarity and spiritual and physical challenges, provided the perfect testing ground for a society which was convinced it had found the key to improving the human condition through civilization and commerce.

For a start, it was *terra incognita*. So little was known about the vast, unopened land mass, that nineteenth-century maps sometimes illustrated mythical or simply nonexistent creatures dwelling in the Interior, while physical features were only guessed at. Trade along the coast, in slaves, gold and ivory, had been going on for centuries, but there it stopped. As the author Tim Jeal put it in his biography of the missionary-explorer who did so much to inspire contemporary English thinking on Africa: 'When Livingstone landed at the Cape in 1841, the geography of central Africa was still as much of a mystery to Europeans as it had been to the Greeks and Romans two thousand years before.'

Then there was the moral challenge of carrying light into darkness, of eradicating slavery and fulfilling a Christian destiny. Livingstone, in the Cambridge lectures attended by Selous's housemaster James Wilson, had summoned Englishmen with a passionate clarion call: 'I go back to Africa to try to make an open path for commerce and Christianity. Do you carry out the work which I have begun!'

Selous was not an untypical Victorian. He never doubted, for example, the superiority of the fair North European races over those of the Mediterranean, of Asia and of Africa. But it was years before he accepted that such a privilege carried with it responsibility. To another young Englishman just setting out, Cecil Rhodes, Africa meant 'philanthropy plus five per cent'. To Selous it would come in time to represent a challenge for British imperialism, but at this stage he saw it purely as a playground for sport and adventure.

31

Now suddenly, in the summer of 1871, Africa loomed large. After years of wrangling, he had finally won through. Frederick had to accept that his resolution was immovable. No evidence remains of what resolved the issue, though the Wiesbaden episode must have had some bearing. Then too, there was the fact that he was approaching his majority, when he would be able to go his own way regardless.

Perhaps his father resignedly reasoned that a year or two in Africa would be no bad thing for a young man patently not yet ready to accept conventional responsibilities. While he could never pretend to be happy with his son's choice, he would accept it. Let it be Africa; let it make him, or let it break him.

CHAPTER THREE

First Venture to the Interior

Selous's first year on the Dark Continent could hardly have been less auspicious. The eager young Nimrod spent fruitless months in an arid wilderness, where the only animals he saw were hares and the occasional antelope. His one good rifle was stolen early on, he was nastily injured, and he came within an inch of dying ignominiously. Since life had treated the young man gently so far, he was no doubt due some painful lessons during his African apprenticeship.

He was still four months short of his twentieth birthday when he landed in what is now Port Elizabeth in South Africa on 4 September 1871. Keen and resourceful he might have been, but it was as an absolute tyro that he surveyed his surroundings. He knew not a soul on the continent, and at this stage had only a vague concept of the gipsy-hunter life which he proposed to follow in the territory more than 1000 miles to the north known simply as 'the Far Interior'.

During the tedious 37-day passage Selous had met other young Englishmen seeking adventure and fortune. One of them, Arthur Laing, was fairly typical of the many ingénus who arrived in South Africa imagining that diamonds were strewn over the veld, waiting to be picked up. He would return disillusioned to England within a few months. A more determined character was George Dorehill, an eager if reckless young fellow who became a close friend of Selous's and would lead a knockabout existence in South Africa as hunter, trader and soldier.

On the voyage out Fred had again pored over the hunting memoirs of Baldwin and Gordon Cumming. Neither had much practical information on travel to the Interior, and his first problem was arranging transport north. He was voluminously equipped, his

33

300 pounds of baggage running from an array of weaponry and trading goods, to the works of Thackeray, and notes he had taken at University College Hospital in London on the treatment of syphilis. Nor was he short of money. Frederick, for all his misgivings, had sent the lad off with the considerable stake of £400.

Selous's first impressions of the continent where he hoped to make his fortune were not encouraging. Of Port Elizabeth, then known as Algoa Bay, he remarked in his first journal entry: 'Didn't like the look of it.' The little settlement was being transformed by the rush to the Diamond Fields. Horse-drawn wagons lurched north daily, carrying prospectors and traders to the new El Dorado. But when Selous made his way to the Phoenix Hotel and the offices of Cobb and Company's coaches he was told his baggage was too large, and that he would have to make his own way. Two days later he handed over £8 of his £400 to be taken to the Diamond Fields, the first stage north.

The ox-wagon journey took almost two months to cover the 440 miles, and even Selous's boundless spirits drooped. The passing country was flat and colourless, with none of the grandeur he had expected of the African bush, let alone exotic wildlife. 'One might as well look for game in Hyde Park as Griqualand,' he reflected sourly. On 15 September, nine days after setting out, he recorded in his notebook: 'Shot a hare; the first thing I shot in Africa.' By persevering, he managed to bag a few small antelope before reaching the Diamond Fields.

Southern Africa, then as now, was going through social and political upheaval stemming from cultural and racial differences. Dutch settlement of the Cape in 1652, to set up a victualling port on the voyage to the East Indies, had brought to Africa the forebears of the Boers, or Afrikaners. The original inhabitants of the Cape, the aboriginal Hottentots and Bushmen, were incapable of resisting the settlers, but as the Boers spread north-east from the Cape they came up against the great migrations of the Bantu peoples sweeping down from the north.

The Dutch East India Company was supplanted at the Cape by a British colonial presence, intended to secure the sea route to India. To the combination of Africans and Afrikaners was thus grafted on a small but administratively powerful British population. Dealings between the two white groups were always awkward, and from the beginning of the nineteenth century, Boer grievances against the Governor at the Cape multiplied. The abolition of slavery throughout the British Empire in 1833 was, for many Boers, the final affront. Two years later some 14,000 of them embarked on the remarkable exodus from the Cape known as the Great Trek. Over the next decade, approximately a sixth of the white population left the colony in covered wagons for the Interior, where they founded their own republics, the Transvaal and Orange Free State.

By the time of Selous's arrival, a new force had emerged on the South African scene and posed a potential threat to both Boer and Briton. Under the brilliant, brutal generalship of a black Napoleon named Shaka, an obscure Bantu clan was forged into the Zulu nation. Shaka had been succeeded by lesser leaders, and Zulu might had been scotched by the advancing Boers. Nevertheless, the kingdom of Zululand still loomed, powerful and ominous, to the east of the Boer republics and British colonies. Cape Colony and Natal were at the southern tip of the continent. To the north lay the Orange Free State and the Transvaal, which stretched as far as Rudyard Kipling's 'great, grey, green and greasy Limpopo' river. Beyond lay the great land mass, much of it *terra incognita*, of the Far Interior.

The Diamond Fields discovery in 1870 turned South Africa, in British terms, from a costly drain to a rewarding investment. That year of Selous's arrival, the extent of the find had been grasped and the mines were placed under Crown 'protection'. By the time his wagon deposited him at the New Rush kopje,* soon to be named Kimberley, a settlement sprawled in a profusion of tents and iron shanties over the surrounding plain.

About 10,000 prospectors were working 600 claims, and like any boomtown it was a wild and lawless place. No sooner had Selous arrived than his only good rifle was stolen. Violence, usually over claim disputes, was commonplace, but the rewards could be immense. Miners, prostitutes, traders, gamblers and conmen were earning and losing fortunes. A sickly youth of eighteen named Cecil

---

*Kopje – an Afrikaans term for a small isolated hill.

35

John Rhodes, who had come to South Africa for his health, was working a claim with dogged determination and making about £200 a week. Rhodes, who was blooming in the high, clean air of this land of opportunity, wrote to his parents at the vicarage in Bishop's Stortford, Essex: 'I should like you to have a peep at the kopje from my tent door at the present moment. It is like an immense number of antheaps covered with black ants, as thick as can be, the latter represented by human beings.'

The two teenagers, Selous and Rhodes, did not meet for another ten years, and it would be almost a quarter of a century before they joined in advancing the frontiers of empire. By then Rhodes was a millionaire from his ventures in diamonds and gold, a politician shortly to become Prime Minister of the Cape, driven by the idea of British expansion to the north. Selous, the far-travelled and hardened outdoorsman, had a smaller measure of fame but was an influential voice in regional affairs all the same, and would be wooed by Rhodes as an essential ally.

Nothing is more illustrative of the differences between Rhodes and Selous than the way each spent these early years in Africa. Rhodes stalked his goals with flexibility and judgment; he dug diamonds not for wealth but power. Selous had never been interested in wealth and did not readily grasp his dependence on even a limited amount of money. The rock-solid fixity of purpose with which he pursued objectives – which had overcome family resistance to Africa, and would bring him into confrontation with tougher obstacles – often blinded him to opportunities that were to his advantage. This would endow him in time with a simple nobility. The corollary was that the quality which he most signally lacked was imagination: there was nothing of the dreamer in Frederick Courteney Selous.

Right now, at the Diamond Fields, he was oblivious to the chance at hand. He had, of course, come to Africa to hunt. All the same, most other young adventurers faced – as he was now – with the information that it would be best to delay departure for the Interior until the start of the dry season, would have used the intervening six months to try his luck at prospecting. Fortunes were being made all around him. The idea does not seem to have crossed his mind.

Instead, he embarked on a trading excursion with young Arthur Laing, his shipboard companion, who had discovered that far from being scattered over the veld, diamonds took some finding. For the next six months, the pair journeyed around the arid Griqualand landscape, trading with local natives, selling goods like calico cloth and buying ostrich feathers for resale in Kimberley.

Among the first real Africans Selous met were the aboriginal Bushmen. His initial reaction to these primitive but remarkable people was repugnance, and he wrote in his journal that they appeared 'very few steps from the brute creation'. He later regretted this 'foolish and ignorant' judgment, and expressed admiration for the Bushmen as intelligent and good-tempered companions, as well as for a more renowned attribute, their astonishing bushcraft. After spending several months with Bushmen he declared: 'Fundamentally, there is very little difference between the natures of primitive and civilized men, so that it is quite possible for a member of one of the more cultured races to live for a time quite happily and contentedly amongst beings who are often described as degraded savages.'

The trip with Laing was a tedious and unrewarding venture. Selous quickly tired of trading, and there was no hunting to mollify him. Laing fell ill with fever. By the time they got back to Kimberley young Arthur could hardly wait to leave for England. On dividing their profits from six months of trading they were left with £50 each; diamond prospectors were averaging that in a few days.

At least the road north was now open. And it so happened that George Dorehill, Selous's other shipboard friend, had arrived in Kimberley and was keen to join him. So was T. V. Sadlier, a friend of Dorehill's. The trio agreed to make together the 700-mile journey north to Gubulawayo, capital of the Matabele king Lobengula, whose permission as undisputed ruler of the Far Interior was needed to reach the teeming hunting grounds of the Zambesi valley. In April 1872, they rode away on the so-called Missionary Road, a dusty wagon track to that ultima Thule.

Kuruman was reached after a month. Once the remotest of the London Missionary Society's outposts, it was an oasis in the surrounding scrubland, and the prettiest spot that Selous had yet seen in Africa. The Reverend Robert Moffat, its venerable founder

37

and father-in-law of David Livingstone, had departed, but the travellers got useful information on conditions in Matabeleland from an affable hunter-trader named William Williams. Selous, who was poorly armed after the theft of his rifle, paid Williams £12 for two muzzle-loading elephant guns which looked like cannon and had a similar recoil. These blunderbusses, made by Hollis of Birmingham, were his weapons for the next three years.

The road continued over baked, featureless sandveld, but by now the party was encountering chiefs of the Barolong and Bakwena people remarkable both for their civility and eccentricity. Montsua was one who – as a result of missionary influence and despite the heat at the edge of the Kalahari desert – wore full European dress, down to collar and neck-tie. Even more incongruous garb was favoured by another chief, Sechele, whose conversion to Christianity by Livingstone twenty-five years earlier had made him something of a celebrity in England. One traveller noted him wearing 'moleskin trousers, a duffel jacket, a wide-awake hat and military boots'. He had acquired other European tastes too: Selous was surprised to see a mirror, a clock and an iron bedstead in the old chief's hut, and was served with tea from a silver teapot. Sechele enquired solicitously after the health of Queen Victoria and the Prince of Wales, and Selous came away declaring his host 'the most completely civilized kaffir that I had yet seen'.

They were a congenial group of young men, just starting to enjoy themselves in these surroundings: George Dorehill had a few upper-class airs (he was inclined to go on about his father, who although he held the honorary rank of major-general had retired as an infantry captain) but was a dashing and good-humoured companion; Sadlier was another adventurous soul, who had served in the American Civil War.

A painful accident was the first interruption to their progress. One day, while Selous was removing cartridges from a powder box, Dorehill came up beside him smoking a pipe; a dropped ember caused a pound of powder to flare up furiously, burning them both badly about the face. Sadlier made up a compound of oil and salt which was rubbed into the burns. He assured them that this prevented scarring of the skin, but they suffered excruciating pain.

Selous's next mishap was due entirely to his own rashness; it was a

38

harrowing experience which almost cut short his hunting career, and left him with an abiding horror of getting lost in the bush.

They were now well beyond any sign of civilization. The dirt track wound on endlessly over the red-sand plains, the thorny scrub and sparse trees which lie to the east of the Kalahari desert. For the first time they saw large herds of antelope – mainly hartebeest and impala – and the spoor of lion. It was mid-winter and while, during the day, the sun in a cloudless blue sky warmed the golden landscape (for this is a region of summer rainfall and winter drought), the nights were bitterly cold; tea left overnight was frequently frozen.

In these surroundings Selous's spirits soared, until one afternoon his eagerness carried him too far. He was out hunting for the pot with Dorehill when they spotted a herd of giraffe, the first they had seen. A wild horseback chase over some miles ended when Selous realized that he had become separated not only from the giraffe, but from his friend. For the next four days he was alone in the wild without food, water or blanket. It was a test of constitution and determination that would have killed most men; remarkably, Selous emerged unscathed.

Having lost touch with his camp, but spotting what he believed was a landmark which would guide him back to the native town of Bamangwato, Selous set out on a nightmare trek. Cold and thirst were the worst afflictions. He was clad only in light shirt and trousers, and during the bone-chilling nights he had to stay on the move until dawn to keep from freezing. Foolishly, he had used all his powder on the first night in a vain attempt to start a fire, and was thus unable to use his rifle to hunt. Worse, on the second night, his horse wandered off and he was reduced to blundering along on foot. After two days his throat was so painfully swollen that he would have had difficulty eating even if he had found anything edible; thirst caused him agony as the temperature soared during the day. At night the dismal howl of hyena added to his misery.

One of his friends in later life, Sir Alfred Pease, once suffered a similar experience, though he was lost for just five hours. Pease knew his way about the bush, and was a brave man, but wrote: 'Any one who has been truly lost alone knows what true terror is; there is no other kind of fear like it – the horrible anxiety I have felt once or twice in the Sahara when the guide had confessed himself off the line, the close adherence to which is life or death, is nothing to being lost alone. In the course of an hour or two I confess to having been reduced to a condition when I could neither trust my eyes nor use my reason.'

Selous was still in control of his reason but on the third day, without nourishment of any kind, his strength was failing. When he reached the crest of a hill, expecting to find Bamangwato below, only to see an unending range of hills, the issue seemed settled. But even now, when he appeared 'doomed to die of starvation and thirst in the wilderness, my fate remaining a mystery to all my friends', he would not give up. And there came a feeling that, 'it was too hard to die thus like a rat in a hole . . . though things certainly looked desperate I still felt some gleam of hope that they would come right.'

Great good fortune and indomitable will saw him through. Another night in the open would have killed him, but just before sundown on the fourth day he stumbled across salvation, in the shape of two Bushmen returning from a hunt. He was so weak that he had to be helped to the shelter of their huts where, in exchange for a claspknife, he was provided with milk, a small piece of meat and a place by a fire. Thus strengthened, he was able, with a Bushman guide, to locate his friends the next day. Food, and the comfort of blankets, restored his strength and spirits.

Onward the small party forged, strengthened by the presence of a newcomer. Frank Mandy, a wandering trader from Grahamstown in the Cape, was a few years older than the others and was reputed to have served as a Papal guard. He had journeyed to Matabeleland before and his offer to take them to the royal kraal and make introductions to Lobengula was eagerly accepted. Mandy's engaging manner and worldly wisdom greatly impressed Selous.

The outlying frontier of Matabeleland was marked by a tiny, dusty settlement. It consisted of a couple of clapboard stores which catered to passing hunters and traders on the Missionary Road, and an old mineshaft where itinerant prospectors laboured with minimal success to extract gold. This drab spot was Tati, the furthest point of white settlement in Southern Africa, and a beacon to the men of the Interior. In the years ahead, Selous would spend many a night in the company of its rough, hospitable inhabitants.

Beyond Tati lay real game country, where a network of rivers –

the Ramaquabane, the Mangwe, the Shashi and the Impakwe – attracted vast herds of browsers and predators. Here, finally, at the edge of the Matabele country, was the Africa that Selous had dreamed of, and all the trials of the preceding months were forgotten. Out hunting for the pot one evening, he saw his first lions, two females and a magnificent old male with a dark mane. Hardly less impressive were sable antelope, large and statuesque creatures with horns like hussars' sabres which, he learned, could kill lion.

The surroundings, too, were becoming more interesting. From the savannah protruded grotesque baobabs, the great trees whose gnarled and twisted shape is explained by natives as an experiment of the Creator who plucked them from the ground and inverted them; beyond lay the fantastic rock formations of the Matopos Hills, where great boulders appear to defy the laws of gravity in piled combinations of impossibly precarious balance.

Through these lovely hills wound the wagon road before it emerged on the plateau of Matabeleland. When the party trundled into the royal kraal of the warrior Matabele nation, Selous had covered just over 1200 miles since landing in Africa a year before.

In 1872 the Matabele were the Spartans of the Interior, with a history which, despite its brevity, was etched in blood. Only half a century before, a Zulu general named Mzilikazi had rebelled against the authority of Shaka and fled northward. Mzilikazi took up residence across the Vaal river for several years, until being driven out by the Boers who founded Pretoria, the capital of their new republic, on the ruins of his kraal. In new territory, north of the Limpopo river, Mzilikazi set about carving out a domain, using the same methods of conquest and absorption as his Zulu mentor. The bloodthirstiness of the new nation was reflected in its nomenclature. Mzilikazi was praised in song as the 'Eater of Nations, Consumer of Men'. He drilled his warriors, the Matabele, or 'People of the Long Shields', in the fearsome disciplinary traditions of the Zulus, and exercised authority with the same ferocity as Shaka. Regular, arbitrary executions, the victim's brains being dashed out with a knobkerrie, kept subjects in the required state of terror. To sneeze in the king's presence meant instant death.

By the time Mzilikazi's son Lobengula acceded in 1870,

Matabele hegemony extended from the Limpopo river in the south to the Zambesi in the north, from the Kalahari desert in the west almost as far as the Portuguese presence in the east. It included most of present-day Zimbabwe, and parts of Botswana and Zambia. The main point about the power of the Matabele, however, was not how far it extended, but that it was absolute. Their only military superiors in the region were the Transvaal Boers.

Selous's relationship over the next twenty years with King Lobengula was one of the most important of his life. This able, shrewd and comparatively just ruler formed a special affection for Selous, as his father had for the Kuruman missionary Robert Moffat, and granted him privileges denied most whites, notably the liberty to hunt in his lands without restriction. In this odd, sad friendship, Selous was able to appreciate Lobengula as a man, without ever comprehending the challenges he faced as the ruler of a warrior people. When the tide of British expansionism swept north the friendship turned, inevitably, to enmity.

The first meeting between the slight, fair Englishman, still only twenty, and Lobengula, a man of huge girth with an astonishing appetite for beef, corn beer and champagne, was recalled later by Selous. The monarch's appearance hardly matched his fearsome reputation.

> He was dressed in a greasy shirt and a dirty pair of trousers, but I am happy to say that during the last few years that I have known him he has discarded European clothing and now always appears in his own native dress, in which he looks like what he is – the king of a savage and barbarous people. After saying a few words to Mandy, whom he knew and seemed pleased to see again, he asked who was the owner of the other wagon, and on being told that I was asked what I had come to do; I said I had come to hunt elephants, upon which he burst out laughing and said, 'Was it not steinbucks [a diminutive species of antelope] that you came to hunt? Why you're only a boy.'
>
> I replied that, although a boy, I nevertheless wished to hunt elephants, and asked his permission to do so, upon which he made some further disparaging remarks regarding my

youthful appearance, and then rose to go without giving me any answer. He was attended by about fifty natives who had all been squatting in a semi-circle during the interview, but all of whom, immediately he rose to go, cried out, 'How! How!' in a tone of intense surprise, as if some lovely apparition had burst upon their view; then as he passed, they followed, crouching down and crying out, 'Oh, thou prince of princes! Thou black one! Thou calf of the black cow! Thou black elephant!'

Another description of this extraordinary figure was left by a mineral prospector, John Cooper-Chadwick, who spent three years at Gubulawayo. 'Lobengula stands over six feet in height, but is so enormously fat that it makes him look smaller, though his proud bearing and stately walk give him all the appearance of a savage king. His features are coarse and exhibit great cunning and cruelty; but when he smiles the expression changes, and makes his face appear pleasant and good tempered.'

The brutality of the Matabele had horrified Robert Moffat, who spent much time among them and averred that they worshipped 'the god of war, rapine, beef-eating, beer-drinking and wickedness'. Mzilikazi's fondness for the missionary led him to approve the first London Missionary Society station in the Interior, at Inyati, but Moffat continued to shudder at what this 'nation of murderers' was capable of.

Lobengula – always less a soldier, more a diplomat than his father – had moderated the savage discipline with which royal authority was maintained. At first, his position on the throne was by no means secure, and he was obliged to rule by indaba, the custom of reaching consensus among indunas – the Matabele military commanders – tribal elders and clan chiefs. Unfortunately, the era of enlightenment for which the missionaries of Matabeleland had prayed after Mzilikazi's death, did not come. The Zulu tradition, of which the Matabele were heirs, was too firmly based on fear and intimidation for genuine reform. Lobengula's way with potential rivals, rather than arbitrarily ordering their execution, was to denounce them as sorcerers or witches; the outcome was the same.

There was no diminishing of dread, either, for neighbouring

tribes in the Interior, like the industrious and peaceable Shona-speakers to the east, and the Bamangwato to the south-west. Matabele raids, bringing with them slaughter, pillage and slave-taking, continued unabated under Lobengula. There has been a trend among present day historians to suggest that the extent and ferocity of these raids were later exaggerated, by Selous among others, to justify the British crushing of Matabele power. This is a subject to be more fully dealt with later; it need only be noted here that all contemporary sources were agreed on the cruelty of the Matabele towards their victims.

Towards whites, Lobengula had mixed feelings. Like his father, he was interested in their weapons and their wealth, while perceiving the danger both represented. Visitors were affably received, and once given permission to travel in Matabeleland they could be assured that the king's protection meant no man would dare raise a hand against them. There was one absolute rule, however: mineral prospecting of any kind was prohibited; even the act of picking up a stone and examining it would, if spotted, be reported to the king and lead to the offender's expulsion. Lobengula was too astute a ruler not to see the consequences once the whites to the south discovered there were riches in his domain.

Selous was now admitted to the curious white society which existed amid this bizarre combination of savagery and tolerance. Permanent white inhabitants at Lobengula's kraal included James Fairbairn, a well-born Scot who had gambled away his birthright on the Diamond Fields and had recently set up a trading store. Another flamboyant local character was George 'Elephant' Phillips, a hand-some and amiable giant of immense strength. With him, Selous formed a friendship which lasted long enough for Phillips to act as his best man when he wed the daughter of a Gloucestershire parson twenty-two years later.

Phillips earned his living by hunting and trading but did not exert himself greatly in either direction, and accomplished more by the charm which he exercised at the royal kraal. An exuberant drinker himself, Phillips had introduced Lobengula to champagne, with which the king was so taken that he declared, only half in jest, that it was meant for kings and that no one else should be allowed to drink it. Phillips's popularity at court was also helped by his flirtation with

Lobengula's favourite sister, Nini, whose grotesque fatness was matched only by her sweetness of manner, and who had a capacity for beef and beer comparable to the king's. One traveller described Nini as 'a huge fat short block of a woman, much liked by the hunters and traders', while another remarked on her 'tender passion' for Phillips.

Such frivolities were far from Selous's thoughts as he awaited another chance to ask Lobengula's permission to hunt. Phillips had acted as interpreter at their first meeting. When Selous did ask, a few days later, Lobengula was hardly less dismissive but gave assent. Elephant, he said, 'will soon drive you out of the country, but you may go and see what you can do.' Selous pressed his luck. He had heard, he said, that the king allowed hunting only in certain parts of the country. 'Oh! You may go wherever you like,' Lobengula replied carelessly. 'You are only a boy.'

It was all the 'boy' needed. He raced back excitedly to his friends. Dorehill was already committed to a trading venture, but Sadlier agreed to join him. At last, Selous was to get a taste of hunting big game.

CHAPTER FOUR

《•》

White Gold

Selous was to see the end of the elephant-hunting era in Southern Africa; even as he arrived on the scene its brief heyday had passed. For around thirty years the elephant herds had been retreating north, and within a decade would find sanctuary from the ivory hunters north of the Zambesi river.

Ivory and slaves, the white and black gold of Africa, had long been the main commodities of trade with the outside world. Even now, in 1872, Central Africa was being plundered by the Arab merchants of Zanzibar, whose impeccable courtesy towards European travellers contrasted grotesquely with their cruelty to their black victims; the leading Zanzibari trader, Tippu Tip, who acquired his nickname because of a nervous tic affecting his eyelids, held sway over a vast empire in what is now Tanzania and Uganda, and assisted Livingstone, Speke and Stanley in their explorations.

Every year, more than 400,000 pounds of ivory passed through Zanzibar *en route* to the warehouses of London, Liverpool, Hamburg and Antwerp. In Europe it might be turned into piano keys, billiard balls or a variety of Victorian knick-knacks. Or it might be shipped to the other big consumer markets of China, Japan and India.

The amount of ivory despatched from Southern Africa, where the hunting was not so systematic, was considerably less. The first white elephant hunter in Southern Africa was Sir William Cornwallis Harris, who began hunting elephant in 1837, killing for sport rather than profit. Even the next generation, which included Roualeyn Gordon Cumming and William Baldwin, whose writings had so appealed to Selous, saw ivory as a means to defray the costs of their expeditions, rather than as a source of profit. However, if the

46

hunting was not greatly organized, the effect on the elephant population by the time of Selous's arrival had nonetheless been dramatic. Cornwallis Harris had found elephants around what is now the South African capital, Pretoria, while in the western Transvaal, where not one elephant survives, he saw a herd he estimated at around 300. Later hunters, including Baldwin, had to penetrate further, beyond the Limpopo, as, taught by experience, the elephant retreated north to Matabeleland and Mashonaland. There it was that in 1859 Mzilikazi had given his blessing to a new band of white adventurers, inaugurating the age of the professional elephant hunter in Southern Africa.

It was a short-lived period; hunters mounted on horseback cleared out the healthy high ground of elephant in a few years. As the animals withdrew to the low country of the Zambesi, pursuit was discouraged, and then stemmed, by two insects. The first, *glossina morsitans*, or the tsetse fly, closely resembles the house fly. Although its bite had no intolerable effect on man, it was certain death to cattle and horses, and the Zambesi region, infested by tsetse and known as the 'fly-country', could thus not be penetrated by mounted hunters and their wagons. The second insect was the anopheline mosquito which, although none suspected it at the time, was the cause of the malaria – known simply as fever – to which the hunters were prone.

It might be regarded as quirkily fitting that two of nature's smallest creatures should have saved one of the largest from man. By some estimates, 45,000 elephants a year were killed in Africa over the last half of the nineteenth century. It was a vile and tragic business which all but wiped out the great pachyderms. All that can be said in mitigation of elephant hunting is that, like whaling, it was a product of its time. And in Southern Africa, at least, it spawned a unique folklore, along with a gallery of raffish and engaging characters.

Selous was the last of a line, a link between the old breed of hunters, whose heavy beards and weatherbeaten countenances gave them a resemblance to biblical patriarchs, and who were dead-shots with their lumbering muzzle-loaders, and a more polished generation of men who hunted with breech-loading rifles. He never met the father-figure of South African hunting, Henry 'Oubaas' Hartley, who was born amid the coalfields of Nottingham and established a dynasty in the Interior. But Selous came to know most of Hartley's contemporaries, including William Finaughty, a ramrod-straight figure whose appearance of stern rectitude – he looked like the Duke of Wellington – concealed the heart of a pirate.

First, though, he was confronted with a figure who stepped straight out of his boyhood dreams. He had read Baldwin's account of a Boer hunter named Jan Viljoen, who, even ten years earlier, had been respected as one of the ablest and most experienced men of the Interior. Now, amid the thatch huts of Lobengula's kraal, Selous suddenly came face to face with Viljoen.

Hartley and Finaughty may have been among the best known of these early frontier figures, but Viljoen and another Afrikaner, Petrus Jacobs, who was his regular companion, were, of them all, the most effective hunters. They grew up with rifles in their hands, like all the Boer hunters, and having been the first whites permitted by Mzilikazi to hunt, they knew the country as well as any of the indigenous inhabitants. The meeting was fortuitous, and offered an opportunity that Selous was unlikely to let pass. Pressed by the eager youth, Viljoen agreed to let him and Sadlier join his next hunting trip.

It was an improbable association. Viljoen, a small, wiry man in his sixties, had no reason for liking Britons, having fought in the first of the Anglo–Boer confrontations, the Battle of Boomplats in 1848. So keen was he to get away from British rule that he kept trekking almost to the Limpopo river before founding a farm he called 'Vergenoeg' (Far-enough). But, like many other Afrikaners, Viljoen was hospitable to individual Englishmen. As they rode away from Lobengula's kraal, he told Selous about what the Afrikaners saw as their history of persecution by British Governors at the Cape. Selous was impressed, and was soon condemning Britain's 'cruel, mean and unmanly' policy towards the Boers.

His willingness in later years to speak up for the Boer cause, demonstrated as it was in the teeth of public opinion, was one of Selous's most attractive qualities. The rough kindness he received as a raw youngster from men like Viljoen made no small contribution to this attitude. It took them six days to reach the Viljoen camp, where Selous was astonished to find that women and children had accompanied the men gipsy-fashion on the year's hunting foray. He marvelled at the closeness of Afrikaner family life and wrote in his journal:

> The way they live is this. In the commencement of the hunting season, which lasts from May to December, they trek with all their goods and chattels to a 'stand-place' where they build a rough-and-ready sort of hut of wattle and daub, thatched with dry grass, and here their women and children live while the men go elephant-hunting, stopping away from a week to a month at a time. During the unhealthy season they live at such places as Inyati, Gubulawayo or Tati, buying with ivory and ostrich feathers the absolute necessaries of life, such as clothing, tea, coffee and sugar, which they obtain from English traders established at those places.

With Boers as hunters he was less taken. Though they were beautiful shots and their 'bags' were certainly impressive, he was appalled at the indiscriminate way they slew game, and their ignorance of natural history. But Petrus Jacobs, Viljoen's old friend, inspired universal respect. Selous believed Jacobs's game bag was unmatched as an all-round record, estimates being that he killed 110 lions and about 750 elephants. Hartley, purely an elephant hunter, slew more than 1000. These figures come sharply into perspective when compared with Selous's career bag, which finally totalled 31 lions and 106 elephants. So it was not just modesty which caused him many years later to disparage descriptions of himself as the greatest of modern-day hunters; he was well aware that his fame was due to his ability to relate attractively his hunting adventures. Men like Jacobs and Viljoen, if they could write at all, never recorded their experiences; but they were far abler performers, though quite unheard of, than Cumming and Baldwin, who did.

A few days' travel beyond Viljoen's camp, the young Englishman had his first meeting with Jacobs, then aged almost seventy and in a precarious state of health after an encounter with a lion which had done something to even the score. Selous found the old man camped at the Sebakwe river, having dreadful wounds to his arms and thighs bathed with milk and castor oil.

Livingstone's statement that he had felt no pain while being mauled by a lion, had fascinated Selous since, as a boy, he had gazed in awe at a picture of the incident. He wasted no time in asking Jacobs if this had been his experience: 'He emphatically denied it, saying that each scrunch gave him the most acute anguish. Since then several kaffirs who have been bitten have told me the same thing, so I can but conclude that this especial mercy is one which Providence does not extend beyond ministers of the gospel.'

The young man's gaucheness appears not to have bothered the Afrikaners. He became well liked and respected around Boer campfires, for one thing because he learned their language as few Englishmen bothered to do. Among these hardy folk his stamina and toughness too were admired. Cornelius van Rooyen, another hunter and himself an anvil of a man, thought Selous had no peer for strength and resourcefulness in the wild.

There were other reasons for his popularity. Selous had, in fact, become a very likeable young man, with attributes that stood out in the rough fraternity of which he was now a part. His enthusiasm was one of these qualities; he was enjoying himself, discovering after his early mistakes that he had a natural aptitude for coping in the wild. He accepted that he had plenty to learn, and set about doing so modestly and without fuss. His honesty, and lack of either artifice or malice, were evident. Though self-contained, he clearly enjoyed company and relished telling a good story. He was always ready to bring out his zither and play one of his Strauss waltzes around the campfire.

These were simple virtues for a simple society, but there was another characteristic that distinguished him. Selous's strong personal magnetism is difficult to recapture today. It does not come across in his writing, which is meticulously detailed but lacks vivacity. It does not emerge from his letters, which were hurriedly written and repetitive. But it would be noted by almost all contemporary sources, and would inspire in time the hero-worship which cast him as an English *beau idéal*.

His hopes of hunting with Jan Viljoen were set back when he cut his foot badly the day before they were to start for elephant country. The Boers were unwilling to delay, and he watched with chagrin as Sadlier rode away with them. The accident brought unexpected benefit, however. It had been intended that he would catch up with

50

the others in a week or so, when his foot had healed. Instead, he was brought into association with one of the most extraordinary hunters in the whole colourful saga of the Interior.

Even in a region rich in exotics, Cigar stood out as an original. Ethnically he was a Hottentot, belonging to the race which inhabited the Cape before either European or migrant Bantu, and which, like the Bushmen, failed to survive the encounter. By disposition Cigar was a rogue and an alcoholic. Sober, he affected the servility required of his race in the Cape; drink released pent-up animosity. It was said of him that he tried to get rival hunters, most notably George Wood, expelled by telling Lobengula they were secretly prospecting for gold. Be that as it may, Selous knew nothing but kindness from him. A remarkable hunter, it was no elephant or lion that did for the Hottentot in the end, but grog.

Appropriately for one so slight of build, he had started his career as a jockey in Grahamstown. Then, in the 1860s, one Henry McGillewie employed him to drive a wagon to the Interior, where he learned to use a rifle. By Cigar's own account, he was terrified of elephant at first, and would only hunt from horseback. But the buccaneering William Finaughty took him on shooting 'halves', and he gradually overcame his fear. (Halves was a common form of sponsorship; a senior hunter would take on others, providing them with horse, rifle, ammunition and provisions, in return for half of the ivory, or anything else, they shot.) Cigar once killed a rhino with only one horn, albeit almost four feet long, which Finaughty kept and used to show to greenhorns as evidence that there were unicorns in the Interior. The Hottentot meanwhile had learned all a hunter's skills.

Cigar took the young Englishman in hand. Selous said later he could not have had a better, or kinder, teacher. Cigar (there is no evidence how he came by this name, though the line of speculation is obvious) is in some tracts patronized as 'the best of the non-European hunters'. Selous put him far higher. 'I have never since seen his equal as a foot hunter,' he said. The Hottentot had wonderful powers of endurance, lots of pluck and was an excellent game shot, although an indifferent marksman at a target.

Native hunters lived more frugally than even the Boers, as Selous was about to discover. Since leaving Lobengula's kraal, he had travelled about 150 miles to the north-east. Here, at the edge of 'fly-country', he and Cigar left their wagons and cattle, and went on by foot. Each man had blankets, maize-meal, a muzzle-loader, a leather bag of powder and another of four-ounce roundshot. Selous had run out of the most basic provisions of tea and sugar, while Cigar did not bother with such luxuries. Few white hunters had ever set out so sparsely equipped. Selous later reflected: 'Though this was hardly doing the thing *en grand seigneur*, I was young and enthusiastic . . . and trudged along under the intense heat with a light heart.'

They hunted in open mopane forest near the Umniati river in what is now the Midlands region of Zimbabwe. On the first day they shot a bull eland, the largest and tastiest of the African antelope. That night, as succulent steaks grilled on a wood fire, Cigar told spellbinding yarns of elephants and hunters, and when he stretched out under the stars Selous would not have changed places with anyone in the world.

The next day, walking through scattered trees and high grass, they came across elephant spoor. After years of anticipating this moment, Selous's heart beat with a fierce joy as he spotted for the first time the grey mass of a heavily-tusked bull elephant above the swaying grass. A thrill surged through him as he watched the animal feed, fanning itself with its great ears.

Killing *Loxodonta Africana* with a muzzle-loader was neither a safe nor a pretty affair. Cigar, perhaps troubled by Selous's confidence, had warned him: 'Dis oorlog, mij baas.' (This is war, master.) The muzzle-loader, which kicked brutally, rarely brought down a prey with the first shot, and an enraged bull elephant was an awesome proposition. Most showed a good deal more aggression than that demonstrated by Cumming's victim in this account which, nevertheless, gives some indication of the species' resilience:

I blazed away until I began to think that he was proof against my weapon. Having fired thirty-five rounds with my two-grooved rifle, I opened fire on him with the Dutch six pounder; and when forty bullets had perforated his hide, he began for the first time to evince signs of a dilapidated constitution.

Selous's shooting was a little more effective. He related his first elephant kill in this way:

> We advanced quietly upon our victim, who stood broadside to us, perfectly still, until we were within sixty yards of him, when he must have noticed us, for he wheeled round, spread his huge ears, and then, with raised head, advanced a few paces towards us. We stood motionless, and the suspicious brute, after staring hard for a few seconds, was just in the act of turning, when Cigar whispered to me to fire, so, aiming for his shoulder, I pressed the trigger. He gave a sort of loud roar, and rushed off, we following at our best pace, I myself with an empty gun, for I was afraid of losing sight of him if I stopped to load.
>
> Upon Cigar giving him a shot, he turned and came walking towards us, with his ears up and the end of his trunk raised. I now loaded with all expedition, and, advancing stealthily to within twenty yards of him, again fired, and striking him upon the point of the shoulder, brought him down with a crash. He tried to get up again, but could not manage it. He was now in a kneeling position, and evidently dying, and one more bullet in the back of the head from Cigar's rifle snapped the cord by which he hung to life. He was a grand old bull, that for many a decade before this, to him, fatal day, must have wandered 'monarch of all he surveyed' through these pathless forests.

If this was remorse it did not last more than a moment. The bull's tusks were long and perfect and, after the gory business of chopping them out, were found to weigh 61 pounds and 58 pounds. It was an impressive load of ivory: William Finaughty, who was never known to let truth get in the way of a good yarn, claimed to have killed one elephant with tusks which together weighed more than 250 pounds; but by this time tusks of more than 40 pounds each had become rare.

Selous was exultant. He had done it. He had overcome family resistance. He had endured boredom and discomfort since arriving in Africa more than a year earlier. Now he had ascertained that money was to be made – perhaps even a fortune – from this exhilarating way of life. He wanted no more.

That evening, around their campfire, Cigar introduced him to another pleasure – elephant's heart, roasted on a forked stick over ashes, which Selous pronounced the greatest delicacy that an African hunter could enjoy.

The wizened Hottentot and the Rugby boy spent three months along the banks of the Umniati, until the onset of the rains ended the hunting season. Chasing elephant on foot carrying a muzzle-loader was an exhausting business. Sometimes they went for days without seeing any game. Their meagre supply of maize-meal was soon finished, and on three occasions they went without any food at all for two days. Selous was often too tired to write up his journal, but the moments of triumph made up for everything else.

Early the next day we struck the spoor of a herd of elephants, and after following it for many hours under a burning sun, at last came up with them fanning themselves with their ears under a clump of trees. Cigar again gave me the first shot, and, approaching pretty close, I fired with good effect, hitting a young bull, with tusks weighing about 20 lbs apiece, right through the heart. He ran off with the herd, but fell when he had gone about a hundred yards. Loading as I ran, I got up to the elephants again, and with my second bullet brought down a fine cow that fell to the shot as if struck by lightning. Never doubting for a moment that she was dead, I ran past her, and once more getting pretty close behind the herd, I gave a young bull a shot that brought him on to his hind-quarters. He regained his legs, and walked off slowly, and I managed, though now very tired, to keep up with him until I had the satisfaction of seeing him fall to the earth with a crash. I could still hear Cigar firing, but I was so thoroughly exhausted that I did not attempt to stir from where I lay panting in the shade cast by my last elephant's carcase.

By the end of the season Selous was able to match Cigar in endurance, if not yet in accuracy of shot. He had killed twelve elephants, including another big male with tusks weighing more than fifty pounds apiece which he spent an entire day chasing on foot before running it down in a river and dropping it with one ball; to get at the tusks they had to sever the animal's head and drag it from the river.

Trekking back towards Gubulawayo they came across Dorehill and Mandy, who were on a trading trip. Selous, his apprenticeship over, was entitled to swagger a little as he showed them his tusks and relived his exploits around a fire.

His first hunting season had been an unqualified success. More than 450 pounds of ivory had fallen to his rifle, and he had bought another 1200 pounds from native hunters. The price being offered by traders at Lobengula's kraal and Tati was around 6s. a pound and additional profits were to be made from skins and hides. After his debts were paid, Selous was left with a profit of nearly £300 – this at a time when the first class fare by Royal Mail steamer from Cape Town to Southampton was £31, and coffee and sugar were regarded as being extortionately priced in the Interior at 1s. 6d. and 1s. 2d. per pound respectively. Selous could hardly wait until the next season.

But the moment of purest satisfaction came when he was ushered into the presence of Lobengula and told him that, far from having been chased out of the country by elephants, he had managed to kill a few. 'Why,' laughed the king, 'you are a man. You must take a wife.'

He was just about to turn twenty-one.

CHAPTER FIVE

In Livingstone's Footsteps

Lobengula enjoyed the company of the white hunters. As a young man he had accompanied George Phillips, and another Englishman, George Westbeech, on hunting trips. Indeed, he became a useful rifle shot himself. Above all though, Lobengula liked to hear stories of hunters' adventures, and when Selous arrived back at the kraal the king ordered one of his legendary feasts.

Diners sat in a circle around a large wooden trough of roasted beef, into which they dipped their hands. Only the king had a knife, and there were no plates. At the same time a communal calabash of corn beer was kept circulating, although Lobengula also tended to his thirst with warm champagne, drunk from a tin mug. His sister, Nini, was a considerable presence at these occasions, upbraiding visitors with timid appetites while herself putting away, according to one source, easily four pounds of beef at a sitting. The conversation, mainly about hunting, was convivial, and Selous soon noted that as well as a sharp mind, Lobengula had an excellent knowledge of wildlife.

Preparations were now under way for the harvest festival of Inxwala, an annual rite which included a show of strength by the Matabele impis.* This was a high point in the social calendar, and attracted all the whites in the Interior. While the warriors whipped themselves up during three days of drinking and dancing, before setting off on their annual raids, the whites exchanged news and indulged in a little ritual celebrating themselves. Vats of beer were prepared, and hundreds of oxen slaughtered, and one of the traders

---

*The word 'impi' – the same in the language of the Matabele and the Zulu, from whom the Matabele were descended – is used throughout this narrative in the sense of a regiment of warriors under the command of an induna, or general.

was usually able to turn up a cask of brandy hoarded for such an occasion. Even the Reverend William Sykes, the gloomy head of the London Missionary Society station, made the fifty-mile journey down from Inyati for the occasion, and there was not a trader or hunter between Tati and the Zambesi who would have missed it.

William Finaughty, in 1864, was one of the first whites to observe Inxwala, and left a colourful account in his *Recollections of an Elephant Hunter*:

> The warriors, who numbered about 25,000* were all in their war dress, wearing their plumes and carrying their assegais and shields, and they made a wonderful and impressive spectacle. To see thousands of them dancing round the camp fires at night, to listen to their singing and the dull noise of the drums, and to hear the thud of their bare feet on the earth was to get an impression of the might of the Matabele that to a youngster like myself was thrilling in the extreme. It might to some people seem dangerous for three white men to be in the midst of this huge army, worked up into a frenzy with the dancing, the beer and the general excitement; but once the chief had given us permission to enter the country there was no danger and we walked among the braves with complete confidence.

Selous was no less impressed by the display. He watched, transfixed by the transformation as Lobengula emerged from his inner kraal dressed in monkey skins and black ostrich feathers. Gone was the fat man who joked with whites and wore greasy trousers kept up by rope. In his place was a barbarously magnificent chief surrounded by thousands of warriors, beating their long ox-hide shields with assegais, and producing a noise like thunder. Tall, black and plumed, they presented to Selous 'as imposing a spectacle as any race of savages in the world'. Nini, unfortunately, cut a less imposing figure. Although splendidly arrayed in bright calico and beads, because of obesity 'her gambols were more grotesque than graceful, and she was so short-winded that she was continually obliged to stand and rest with her hands on her thighs'.

*This figure is generally considered an exaggeration. It is unlikely that the warrior strength of the Matabele ever exceeded half as many.

For visitors to Gubulawayo, there was another important social aspect to these gatherings. Apart from one or two missionary wives, and a few Boer women accompanying their husbands, there were no white women in the Interior. The Matabele kraal, however, provided a rare, and generous, display of black female flesh. After months in the bush, men were suddenly surrounded by the bronzed bodies of semi-naked young women, and amid the frenetic drinking, carousing and dancing, there was a good deal of sexual intercourse.

Miscegenation had been a fact of life since whites landed at the Cape in 1652. But the Matabele, while being among the handsomest people in Southern Africa, were also, in the early days of their contact with Europeans, among the most chaste. Finaughty said that the women 'bore a splendid reputation for virtue so far as white visitors were concerned'. Goods and trinkets wrought the inevitable change. By 1870 Thomas Baines, the artist and erstwhile member of Livingstone's Zambesi expedition, was recording that a white man had introduced to the Matabele 'a loathsome disease hitherto unknown'. (Lobengula was profoundly upset by the episode and told the Gubulawayo traders that if the man had been black, he would have been executed on the spot. As it was, the girl's life hung in the balance for a few days before being spared, while the man – whose identity is not known – was ostracized by other whites.)

When Selous reached Gubulawayo, sexual relationships between black and white were no longer rare, and would in time become commonplace. The flirtations of Nini and George Phillips, who sometimes wandered around the kraal arm in arm, may even have implied royal sanction for such liaisons. The hunters and traders were an easy-going and, by the standards of the day, egalitarian bunch, and in their sex lives took up with Matabele women both on a casual and long-term basis.

In this small white community there were few inhibitions, and indulgence was grasped when it was available. Major Henry Stabb, who had served in India during the Mutiny, kept a diary during one brief visit to the Interior which is among the most vivid records of its society. He described Phillips, his partner George Westbeech and the Gubulawayo trader James Fairbairn, as 'gentlemen by birth and education but Bohemians by nature'. Another observer wrote, 'What good-hearted, jovial fellows they all were, honourable and brave and enjoying their lives to the full.' To these men, a Matabele warrior was no less a man, and a woman was a woman, whatever her colour.

The fact that Gubulawayo became a place where hunters and travellers headed for recreation from the wilderness, added in time a commercial element to inter-racial sexual contacts. By 1890, Sam Edwards, a venerable trader, noted regretfully that the Matabele girls 'must have their beads and will risk their bodies to have them', adding, however, that it was the menfolk who sent them to the whites, 'and then collared the produce of their sin'. Not surprisingly, the missionaries were even more disapproving, and John Moffat, the son of Robert, railed in his letters against the drunkenness and debauchery of whites who kept 'native harems'.

A public school boy he may have been, but Selous was neverthe-less worldly enough to have brought with him to Africa notes on the treatment of syphilis. Years later he would mourn the passing of 'the old race of traders and hunters, with their warm hearts, but unbusinesslike habits and somewhat indifferent morals', and made little secret of the fact that he had been part of this fraternity himself.

Selous was appreciative of the charms of Matabele womanhood. In his record of the Inxwala festival he wrote that the girls wore calico skirts but were otherwise nude and, 'with their merry, pleasant faces, and upright shapely figures formed the prettiest portion of the spectacle'. He also admired their 'fine, well-devel-oped, chocolate-coloured figures, the naked beauty of which was but little hidden by their very scanty attire'.

What readers in Victorian England made of this startlingly frank appreciation when it was published eight years later is hard to know, but it is evident that Selous did not greatly care. He was candid enough about his sexual conduct to live openly for years with an African woman, and before then doubtless took his comforts as and when he could find them.

Selous did not try to conceal this, and left references in his speeches as well as his writings to let contemporaries in England know that the life of an African hunter was not all bullets and biltong. Some twenty years later, when he was inclined to be opinionated and verbose, he enlivened a long and otherwise tedious lecture at the Royal Colonial Institute with an anecdote about the Matabele view of celibacy. He was dismissive of Lord Lugard's opinion that white men 'lost caste' by forming liaisons with black women, and related to the gathering, at the Hotel Metropole in London, a dialogue he had had with a Matabele warrior confused by the celibacy of Catholic missionaries.

> He said to me: 'What sort of people are these new teachers who hate women? I don't understand them, they are uncanny. The old teachers [Protestant missionaries] bring their own women with them, and you other white men, you make love to our girls and that's alright, but a man who does not make love to any woman at all ... hauw! I don't understand it. He is not a man but a witch!'

In his candour, Selous was more honest than most of his friends, who after his death, by overlooking this earthy side to his character, so presented him as a man of unvarying high morality as to make their tributes to him sound bloodless today. The chief architect of this was Millais, who clearly believed that, in any area which might have been seen as reflecting discredit on Selous, his responsibilities to the memory of an old friend overrode his duties as a biographer.

After the apprenticeship with Cigar, Selous entered into partnership with another remarkable man. For the next two years, until Selous returned to England, they would hunt together constantly. It was the most arduous, but also the happiest, part of his life.

George Wood was one of those Englishmen who went abroad in the age of imperial expansion and who so adapted to their new environment that they never wished to leave it. Raised in the North Riding of Yorkshire, he found his true home along the banks of the Zambesi river, and died there having become a native of Africa in all but the colour of his skin. He was a cultivated and educated man who found the constraints of any settled life intolerable. Selous noticed how, when Wood left even so rudimentary a place as Gubulawayo, which was no more than a concentration of thatch huts with a population of a few thousand, his walk lightened, as if he was unshackling himself from the conventions and restraints of a city.

When they met, Wood had the reputation of being a skilful and experienced hunter. Over the next two years Selous was to find him imperturbable as well: 'one whose pulse beat as calmly when face to face with a wounded and snarling lion as it did when quietly eating his breakfast'. George Wood had another distinction. He, along with Cigar, was quite simply the best of the hardy foothunters who had emerged in recent years.

Elephant hunting had not necessarily required courage or skill in the early days, when herds on a scale which invite comparison with the American bison wandered the plains of Southern Africa. At that time a man on horseback, riding into a herd and blazing away at animals of all ages and both sexes indiscriminately, could wreak a slaughter. A good haul of ivory for a season was 3000 pounds, or around 100 elephants. It is principally this factor which accounts for the difference between Henry Hartley's lifetime bag, of between 1000 and 1200, and Selous's, which was one tenth that number.

The increasing hazards posed by tsetse fly and malaria are illustrated by the fate of a party led by Wood to the Mashona country in 1870: all eighteen members of the group were stricken, and while Wood pulled through, his wife and child, a brother, and five others died. Such difficulties persuaded the old hands to retire. Hartley and Jacobs were getting on in years anyway. Finaughty disliked the arduousness of foothunting, and was quite happy to turn to profitable rascality.* That other old hand, Jan Viljoen, kept going for a few more years, although into his sixties. So did George Wood.

After lying up for six months at Lobengula's kraal, now named Gubulawayo, Selous and Wood set forth in mid-1873. They would have left at the end of the rainy season in April, but the king had kept them waiting two months for permission to hunt. Even then he put off-limits the Mashona country, where Selous had hunted so successfully with Cigar the previous season. Instead, they headed north-west towards the Victoria Falls, through a stretch of rugged bush later to become the Wankie Game Reserve. Their wagons, drawn by a span of oxen, were loaded with supplies for a four-month

---

*He is said to have visited Australia with a counterfeiting gang; and he boasted of one enterprise which must rank among the most daring and bizarre of all South African entrepreneurial ventures. He bought three ship's cannon in Port Elizabeth and attempted to smuggle them to the Transvaal native chief Sekukuni, an enemy of the Boers. Finaughty was captured by the Boers, and only just managed to escape before they could hang him.

expedition. After two weeks of trekking they reached the Linquasi valley, about halfway to the Falls. This was the start of the 'fly-country', and as far as they could go without risking their livestock. A camp was established in the shade of a 'kameeldoring', a large umbrella-shaped acacia tree, and lion-proof enclosures built for the cattle. A couple of trusted men would be left here to watch the wagons and animals.

From camp, both hunters, accompanied by four or five bearers, launched into the fly-country on foot forays lasting from two to ten weeks. These raiding parties were pared to essentials to make them as mobile as the quarry, and able to cover thirty miles in a day. Bearers carried calabashes of water, along with rice, maize-meal and tea. Sugar, being heavy, was dispensable. Whether there was meat on the fire at the end of a day depended on the hunter. The only concession to comfort was a blanket. Selous carried one muzzle-loader, weighing twelve pounds. A bearer had another, and the ammunition. In this spartan fashion they set out on campaign.

Their hunting ground is still one of the richest game areas in Africa. In addition to elephant, species like sable and roan antelope, which were rare elsewhere, were here relatively common. Great herds of buffalo, zebra, impala and wildebeest abounded. So did rhino, including the square-lipped variety which was later slaughtered in such numbers that it came close to extinction. Lions and other predators were a hazard. Exquisites like the giraffe and the kudu moved elegantly across the veld; waterbuck and smaller antelope like bushbuck, klipspringer and steenbuck were common.

It was a naturalist's as well as a hunter's delight. In this year, 1873, Selous saw in the valley of Dett what he later described as the most varied concentration of game he ever came across:

> A herd of nine giraffes stalked slowly and majestically from the forest, and, making their way to a pool of water commenced to drink . . . one or other of them from time to time straddling out its forelegs in a most extraordinary manner in order to get its mouth down to the water . . . One after another, great herds of buffalo emerged from the forest on either side of the valley and fed slowly down to the water. One of these herds was preceded by about fifty zebras, and

another by a large herd of sable antelopes. Presently two other herds of sable antelopes appeared upon the scene, a second herd of zebras, and five magnificently horned old kudu bulls, whilst rhinoceroses both of the black and white species were scattered amongst the other game, singly or in twos or threes all down the valley.

Selous hunted elephant as Cigar had taught him, stripped down to felt hat, a thin cotton shirt and shoes. He wore no trousers, though presumably there was some kind of pouch to protect the genitals. He called it 'nice light running order'. With a tracker in front, the group would set out at daybreak in search of spoor, paying close attention to watering spots and groves of wild fruit to which elephant might be drawn. But often they trudged for a week in blazing heat, thirsty and hungry, without any sign of elephant. When spoor was found they would follow it until they came up to their quarry, generally in groups of between two and seven.

Unlike the old mounted hunters, who shot at anything which showed itself, a foothunter had to make the most of his first opportunity. Selous would pick out the animal with the heaviest tusks and get as close as possible before trying to disable it with a single ball. Usually it took more. When an elephant fell, the hunter would turn after the others, chasing the alarmed and fleeing animals, sometimes for hours, over rough ground or through thick bush to get another shot. The days of the mounted man who could bag ten elephants in a day were over. In these conditions, a single animal was a good day's work, three were bounty indeed.

What made Selous such a very good hunter were stamina and fitness. He was now in superb physical condition, his just under 12 stone on a frame of 5 feet 9 inches containing not an ounce of excess. To his ability to pursue quarry in brutally harsh conditions, was allied the gusto with which he had taken to his new life. He recorded his pleasure simply: 'I found [it] so absorbingly interesting and exciting that I never had a moment's mental weariness, and was always perfectly happy.'

So greatly did he revel in his physical prowess that as a personal challenge he once stepped out in front of a buffalo from behind a tree and, unarmed, flaunted himself like a matador. The astonished animal charged, only to have Selous dodge behind the tree at the last moment, and swing himself out of harm.

It is not easy to reconcile this cavalier of the veld with the passionate advocate of hunting controls which he became forty years later. Even then, however, he feigned no regret about the old days. Speaking to the Authors' Club in 1912 he said:

> To shoot an elephant from time to time under favourable conditions is one thing, but to hunt elephants for a living, to follow their tracks time after time without success, all day long, often in heavy sandy ground and often under a blistering sun is quite another. But if the quality of sport is to be measured by the danger and excitement it affords, then no sport on earth can equal an encounter with an elephant in one of their strongholds.

He had become a fine shot with his two Hollis muzzle-loaders, which tested strength and endurance as much as marksmanship. The impact of a handful of gunpowder behind a four-ounce lead ball inflicted severe punishment on the hunter as well as the hunted. Finaughty found his shoulder black and blue after a day's shooting; the recoil knocked him down on a number of occasions and twice threw him out of the saddle. Selous said he never found a gun which drove better, but that 'the punishment I received from these guns has affected my nerves to such an extent as to have materially influenced my shooting ever since, and I am heartily sorry that I ever had anything to do with them'.

In their first hunting season of four months, Selous killed forty-two elephants and Wood fifty, and in the course of their wanderings Selous came to have affection as well as respect for his new mentor.

No one knew Wood's age. He had come to Africa in 1865, relatively late in life, with two brothers. Since the death of his wife and child from malaria, he had acquired many African mistresses and fathered numerous children. Selous noted that, for 300 miles along the Zambesi, there were women in every village who called Wood husband. In addition to being a fine hunter, Selous found him 'a man of most lovable disposition and many fine qualities'.

When they arrived at a new village, and joined the inhabitants squatting around a fire, Wood was, Selous wrote, 'no longer a white

64

man but had become to all intents and purposes an African. As I watched the beer pot going round and listened to my friend talking to his hosts with the utmost fluency, every now and again gravely taking snuff with them, I marvelled at his dual nature.'

The success they enjoyed in the years of 1873 and 1874 is reflected in Selous's first book, *A Hunter's Wanderings in Africa*. We have already seen examples of his prose style, but the following account of an elephant hunt gives an idea of his writing at its best:

> The kaffirs here took off their raw-hide sandals, that they might walk more quietly and, following the spoor carefully, we descended cautiously into the depths of the kloof,* and came to a place from which they had evidently not long moved on, as the dung was still warm. Minyama [a tracker] suddenly came to a halt, and crouching down, with his arm pointing forwards and his head turned towards me, whispered, 'Nansia incubu!' (There are the elephants.) Ah, how those words thrill through the hunter's breast, making his heart leap again with concentrated excitement!
>
> Stooping down, I now saw them not more than 30 yards off. They were standing huddled together in a mass under the shade of a large tree, gently flapping their large ears in a sleepy, contented sort of way, all unconscious of the deadly enemy that lurked so near ... After taking a gulp of water from the calabash and giving a hitch to my belt, I beckoned to my two gun-carriers, and then taking my first gun, crept quietly to within about 20 yards of the still unconscious elephants to look for the best pair of ivories. One ... showed a fine long tusk on the right hand side, offering at the same time a good shot behind the shoulder; and so, not seeing a better chance, I fired. The elephants broke away in their panic with despatch; so calling to my second gun-carrier to keep close, I ran as hard as I could after them.
>
> At about 150 yards from the starting place, the one I had fired at fell dead, having been shot through the heart, and I dashed past him after the others. Luckily, they ran right on to the two Kafir boys that I had sent up on the hill before firing,

*An Afrikaans word. In this context it means a narrow valley between hills.

65

and on their shouting lustily immediately turned and came rushing down again, carrying trees, bushes, and everything else before them, right past me. As they went by I gave one a shot somewhere about the shoulder. However, a four-ounce round bullet is no trifle, even to such a mighty beast as an African bull elephant, and immediately on getting it he slackened his pace. I did my best to keep up with him; but I had to put my best foot foremost to maintain my position in the thick bush, as an elephant, though so large an animal, is a thing easily lost sight of.

At last, having crossed the bottom of the kloof, he either heard something or got a whiff of tainted air, and turning suddenly round, with his huge ears extended, his trunk stretched straight out, and his wicked vicious-looking eyes gazing in our direction, stood ready to charge. But small time was allowed him, for to get the gun to my shoulder and plant a bullet in his exposed chest was the work of but a few seconds. On receiving the ball he fell to his knees, but recovering, picked himself slowly up, turned, and resumed his retreat, but now only at a slow walk.

At this instant, glancing to the right, I perceived four more elephants coming down the side of a hill; so, believing that the one to which I had been paying attention was all but done for, I ran to intercept [them]. I was just in time and as they passed in front of me, at not more than 40 yards' distance, in single file, I gave the last one a shot in the middle of the shoulder. Quickly reloading, I followed, and, getting to where the bush was a little more open, shouted behind him 'Hi there! Woho, old man!' and, fatal curiosity, or perhaps a wish for vengeance, inducing him to turn, planted another four-ounce ball in his chest. He wheeled round immediately, but, his strength failing him, only walked a few yards, and stood under a tree, and, after receiving another bullet square in the shoulder, gave a fierce shake of the head and, sinking slowly down surrendered up his tough old spirit – looking, though dead, like a tame elephant when kneeling for people to ascend to the howdah . . .

Suddenly, not far to my left, the silent forest rang again

66

with short piercing trumpetings, repeated so quickly one after another, that I [was] sure one of my boys was caught – as when an elephant is either very near to his persecutor, or has actually overtaken him, he emits scream upon scream in quick succession, all the time stamping upon and ventilating his enemy with his tusks, and only ceasing to scream when he has done with him; and persons thus operated upon are seldom known to complain of their treatment after it is over.

Before I could reach the scene of action the trumpeting had ceased; so, calling to my gun-carrier by name, I listened anxiously, and in another instant was much relieved to see him, still alive, but looking very crestfallen. There he was, without gun or assegais, all scratched and bleeding from violent contact with the bushes, and his eyes almost starting out of his head with fright, which was scarcely to be wondered at, considering the trying ordeal he had just gone through . . . The elephant, having turned and waited behind a bush, let him come quite close, and then rushing out, had kept him literally under his trunk for about a hundred yards, and would no doubt have caught him if he had not been so weakened by his previous wounds. In his flight he had thrown the gun and assegais away, and he must indeed have had a miraculous escape, for his back and the calves of his legs had drops of blood upon them, that could only have come from the trunk of the elephant.

Three elephant had been accounted for, and that night, in the rough equality of the skerm, there was a celebration. At the end of each day Selous and his men would make one of these basic branch enclosures and sleep under the stars, huddled around a fire. This night they roasted tit-bits of the meat, and while the hunter reflected that, 'if I had but had a white companion with whom to talk over the day's sport and fight the battle o'er again, my happiness would have been complete', the men danced and sang his and their own praises until after midnight. (When no beer was available, the Matabele generally stimulated such celebrations with cannabis, a practice noted by Stabb: 'It does not appear to do them any harm and they seem to experience great pleasure from the use of the weed, one of

67

them every now and again being apparently seized with a fit of ecstasy, shouting out a sort of rhapsody at the top of his voice.')

By the time Selous met Wood again, two months after setting out on his own, he had bagged more ivory than a dozen bearers could carry, and had set about shifting it in stages to the original camp. The friends were delighted to see each other again, and yarned long into the night.

It was August, and the rains which would end the season were approaching, so the partners decided to stay together. One eventful day brought them a total of six elephants, but the casualties also included one of a dozen or so black hunters employed by Wood. It all happened amid the hot excitement, confusion and flying lead of weapons being discharged at random; as the man closed in on an elephant he was shot in the back by one of his fellows who was blazing away at a more discreet distance. They buried the dead man in an anthill, with a needle to remove thorns from his feet and assegais to defend him on the journey to the next world.

A few days later Selous came close to making the same journey himself. Having followed a wounded elephant into thick bush, he was ambushed by a second animal which had lain in wait.

> The trunk was whirled around, almost literally above my head, and a short, sharp scream of rage thrilled through me. The only thing I could do was run. How I got away I scarcely know. I bounded over and through thorn-bushes which, in cold blood, I should have judged impenetrable; but I was urged on by the piercing screams and by the fear of finding myself encircled by the trunk or transfixed by the tusk. It was only when the trumpeting suddenly stopped that I knew I was out of her reach. I was barelegged – as I always am when hunting on foot – and my only garment before the beast charged was a flannel shirt; but I now stood almost *in puris naturalibus*, for my hat, the leather belt that I wore round my waist, and about three parts of my shirt, had been torn off by the bushes, and I doubt if there was a square inch of skin left uninjured anywhere on the front of my body.

More perils were to come on this day of mishap, during which Selous's gun-bearers became convinced that he had been bewitched. One of his guns was mistakenly given a double charge of powder; the effect of its discharge was spectacular. Selous was blown backwards in a somersault, while the gun's stock shattered, cutting his face so badly that he was left permanently scarred. More immediately serious, his right arm was temporarily crippled and he had difficulty holding the other gun.

The bearers, by now thoroughly alarmed and sure that he was under the influence of an evil spirit, pleaded with Selous to abandon the hunt. But his blood was up, and he set off after the wounded beast – only to run into more trouble. No sooner had it spotted him than it charged.

On came the elephant, without trumpeting, and with his trunk straight down. Though very shaky, the imminence of the danger braced up my nerves, and I think I never held a gun steadier than upon this occasion. He came on at an astonishing pace, and I heard only the 'whish, whish' of the grass as his great feet swept through it. He was perhaps 20 yards off when I pulled the trigger. Directly I fired I ran out sideways as fast as I could, though I had not much running left in me. Looking over my shoulder, I saw him standing with his ears still up; the blood was pouring down his trunk from a wound exactly where I had aimed. It had saved my life, for, had he come on again, it would have been utterly impossible for me, fatigued as I was, to have avoided him. After standing still for a short time, he again turned and took across the flat.

When Selous and Wood trekked out of the fly-country at the end of November and started back to Gubulawayo, they had almost 5000 pounds of fine ivory, worth around £1700. But, profitable though the venture had been, Selous had acquired something far more precious in his first full hunting season: the unqualified respect of his partner.

George Wood's word counted for a great deal among the men of the Interior, where judgments on newcomers, reached quickly and often arbitrarily, tended to stick. When Wood pronounced Selous a brave and tenacious performer, a good fireside companion and a

69

man whose word could be trusted, it formed the basis of a lasting reputation.

In April 1874, David Livingstone's body was brought back to England from Central Africa where he had died a year before. Simultaneously, Selous was setting out on a journey to the Victoria Falls, the great cataract on the Zambesi known to Africans by its more lyrical name, Mosi-o-Tunya (Smoke that Thunders). Livingstone's journey to the Falls nineteen years earlier had inspired Selous's generation; it is unlikely that now he had even heard of his boyhood hero's death. In more than two years in the Interior, he had received not a single letter from the outside world.

Over the next decade, the journey to the Falls was to become the fashion for well-to-do young Englishmen, but at this time only a handful of whites had made the 300-mile journey north from Tati. Selous and Wood decided on it mainly because they were contemplating new hunting grounds.

They were joined by two piquant figures, Captain Francis Garden and his brother John. Forerunners of the school of wealthy English travellers in Africa, the Gardens were amateur sportsmen and travelled in impressive and luxurious style, complete with a butler named Tofts. The brothers were not twins, but each sported a red beard which made it difficult to tell which was which. In five wagons, this curious group trundled out of Tati in May 1874, following the road to Pandamatenga and Zambesia that Wood and Selous had used the previous year.

Seven weeks later they got a first, dramatic glimpse of their objective – a cloud of spray across rolling hills teeming with game. Selous was overwhelmed. The grandeur of the Falls and their setting – the great fissures and ravines of the Zambesi escarpment and the distant blue mountains to the north – left him awed.

Imagine a river more than a mile broad, suddenly tumbling over a precipice 400 feet in depth, which runs in a perfectly straight line across its entire breadth; and perhaps from these naked facts, imagination may picture in some degree how grand a sight must be that of the Victoria Falls of the Zambesi. The river tumbles into a narrow rent in the earth

70

which runs right across its course. This rent, due to some convulsion of nature, is only about 100 yards in breadth, and the outlet from it, which is near the northern bank, is still narrower.

The Zambesi itself made an even more profound impression. Like Livingstone, who described it as 'God's highway to the Interior', Selous came to love the great river. He remarked in his journal on its broad, deep-blue waters, and the feathery palm trees at its bank. 'Everything in the vicinity of this glorious river looks green and smiling.' In the years ahead he would get to know around 1000 miles of its course, either walking the bank or journeying by canoe. The cry of the fish eagle, the chorus of hippo at night, and the herds drawn to this magical waterway, cast a spell which lasted his lifetime.

After a week at the Falls, the group split up, Wood heading east downstream while the Gardens joined Selous on a sixty-mile march west to the Zambesi's confluence with another river, the Chobe. Over the next five months they hunted this stretch of territory, with profit and considerable incident. Twice Selous killed five elephant in a day, his biggest bag. Once he had the disconcerting experience of leaving an animal for dead only to find it gone when he returned the next day. He had brought it down with five bullets, and administered what he felt sure was the *coup de grâce*, two further shots in the back of the head. When he came back to chop out the tusks, all that remained was a pool of blood, and despite efforts to follow the spoor nothing more of the elephant was ever seen.

The Gardens departed before the end of the season, but Selous and Wood stayed on until the start of the rains made hunting impossible, and raised the threat of malaria. Trekking back to Gubulawayo, they met George Dorehill who, with two companions, Frank Oates and a German trader named Shinderhutte, was on his way to the Falls. Although Dorehill was as impetuous as ever, Selous managed to persuade him that it would be foolhardy to go on. But Oates, an inexperienced, obstinate young man only recently arrived from England, insisted on proceeding alone. His journal, in which he described Selous as 'a nice little fellow about 22 years old', makes melancholy reading; he reached his goal but seems to have antagonized everyone he met on the road, and finally succumbed to fever, alone and quite out of his depth in Africa.*

Selous's third season was over, and with it had come the first signs of the lean times ahead. He had magnificent specimens of sable antelope and kudu horns, and of the rare puku and lechwe which he had discovered on the Chobe. He had shot 19 buffalo, mainly to feed his men, and 9 rhino. But it was elephant which were his livelihood, and he had shot 24, compared with 42 the previous year.

On the credit side, he had in those three years travelled extensively over Southern Africa, had acquired a modest reputation and had turned his father's £400 stake into something in the order of £2000. While this did not compare with the fortunes that had been made in the heyday of the elephant hunter (Finaughty claimed to have earned £1300 in one three-month expedition) the future looked secure, and Selous was bursting with health and good spirits. He had never doubted that his destiny lay in Africa, and he could now justifiably claim to have proved a point to the sceptics at home.

He was already considering a trip to England. When he got to Tati in December 1874, and found a bundle of letters waiting at Alexander Brown's trading store – his first news from home in three years – it decided him.

There was one other significant debut that month. Three weeks before turning twenty-three, he shot his first lion on the banks of the Tati river.

---

*A worse fate awaited Shinderhutte. A heavy drinker, he had an attack of delirium tremens on his way to the Zambesi some months later, and in his madness shot dead one of his servants. Soon afterwards he disappeared, and was generally reckoned to have been murdered by the man's avenging comrades.

CHAPTER SIX

《 • 》

Years of Trial

The bundle of letters which Selous found waiting for him at Tati imparted information which was important enough to drag him away from his new life. He commented enigmatically: 'Owing to news contained in these letters, I now determined to take a run home to England.' Precisely what that news was is not known, and little detail exists of his stay in England between May 1875 and February 1876. It is clear, however, that some rebuilding of the relationship between parents and son was necessary, and took place, when he got back.

Selous himself is no help when it comes to piecing together the details of his personal life. He had an abhorrence for recording or divulging matters which might be considered intimate, and eschewed them in private correspondence almost as rigorously as he did in published work. A certain shyness and reserve had started to replace the bumptiousness of his adolescence, while a meticulous, even obsessive, attention to physical detail was to emerge as a dominant characteristic. He would spend long periods studying and recording the minutiae of natural history, the markings and coloration of animals, the lengths of horns and other dimensions. He would come to deeply regret not having trained as a zoologist in his youth. He once told an interviewer: 'I am not a hunter by nature, I am a naturalist.' There can be little doubt that in times of trial natural history study became a refuge from his troubles. It was, too, a key feature of his writing. Personalities and their interplay were of secondary importance; even references in his books to the remarkable men who were his companions are rare.

Although no letters had been exchanged between Selous and his parents for three years, there is no reason to believe that this was because of a serious rift. It was not unusual for mail to take years to

73

reach a destination in the Interior, due in no small part to the haphazard addresses kept by the residents. Letters frequently went astray.

What makes this subject of correspondence curious is that Selous, who had been a fairly conscientious letter writer from Europe, when he knew that his mother might worry about him, does not appear to have written home at all during these three years in Africa. Ann Selous kept all his letters, but there is none from 1871 to 1874. Whether he did not write because he was so happy and absorbed in his new life that he scarcely thought of his family, or whether all his letters went astray is not known.

What is certain is that as the years went by without word from Africa, the family despaired of ever seeing him again, and may even have given him up for dead. The news that he was alive caused delight, and his arrival back at Gloucester Road in May 1875 was to be the story of the Prodigal Son retold.

It may be that some of Frederick's disappointment at his son's choice of career still persisted, and while Ann Selous's affection had never wavered, she too, though for other reasons, had been distressed by his decision to earn a living as an elephant hunter. Her second son, Edmund, once remarked: 'She had a deep inborn love of the beauties of nature and great feeling for both plant and animal life. I underline that word because killing was quite another thing for her, and her whole soul shrank away from it.'

But any reservations there may have been were quickly swept away in the happiness of the reunion. And, restored to his family, Selous enjoyed basking in their attention and affection, relating his adventures and showing off his trophies to Edmund and his wide-eyed sisters.

Selous had turned into a strikingly handsome young man. His naturally fair hair had turned blond and his skin was bronzed by the years in the sun. His features were good and regular, but his eyes, which were blue – some thought violet – were the most compelling aspect of his presence. Millais wrote: 'If there was one striking feature it was his wonderful eyes, as clear and blue as a summer sea. Nearly every one who came into contact with him noticed his eyes.' He had filled out, and was now powerfully muscled in the chest, arms and legs, and had grown a beard. A touch of vanity persuaded him at this time to have a stylized, but nevertheless impressive, studio portrait done of himself in elephant hunting kit.

In addition to his physical growth he had matured emotionally as well. The brashness and conceit had been knocked out of him in Africa. He was still quick to anger though, and impatient, faults that would only be cured by the long and difficult years ahead.

These months at Gloucester Road, and at the family's second home on the Thames at Wargrave, healed the rift of the past. Fred had proved his point; he was a man and would go his own way whatever else happened. There was no gainsaying his determination – and now, while he was at home, there was every reason for all to delight in his company and charm, and for Frederick to enjoy discussing, man-to-man and as a fellow businessman, the prospects for the next hunting season. For his part, Selous realized the anguish his silence had caused his mother. Henceforth, he would be a model correspondent, writing regularly and letting her know when he would be out of touch for any length of time.

One other pleasant duty remained before he returned to Africa, a visit to James Wilson at Rugby. Selous found his old school, if not his former master, much changed. Temple's departure in 1869 had started a damaging feud over who should succeed him as head-master. Wilson was nonetheless delighted to see his old pupil, who regaled him with stories about Lobengula and other characters of the Interior. They talked about hunting, and the subject of guns came up. Selous, who thought he had successfully hoodwinked Wilson over the illicit rifle he had kept at school, was taken aback to find that the housemaster had known about it all along.

That evening there was a house supper in honour of the old boy, at which Wilson asked him to repeat the story of his meeting with the Matabele king. At first Selous demurred, but when the master started the yarn himself, he jumped to his feet crying, 'Oh! Sir, let me tell it.'

It was his first experience of public speaking, and it was a resounding success. He spoke fluently and vividly, while the boys listened in awed silence. The personal magnetism was as potent at a larger gathering as around the campfire, and Wilson described the dinner as 'a never-to-be-forgotten evening'. Selous was surprised at the impression he had created. Later he would make something of a career out of lecturing about his adventures, and while conveying the impression that he was reluctant to blow his own trumpet, in a discreet way he revelled in it.

After nine months in the family bosom, Selous started back for Africa. It was a cold winter morning in 1876 when the vessel of the Union Steamship Company sailed from Southampton. Visions of the sunset over the Zambesi shimmered pleasurably in his thoughts. The three-week voyage itself was rough and unrelievedly tedious: 'I shall not feel thoroughly happy again until I reach the Tati,' he wrote to his mother from the Atlantic island of St Helena.

His intention was to pick up where he had left off. To tackle the challenge posed by the dwindling numbers of elephant he was planning a major expedition to the Zambesi, in which he would sink most of his earlier profits, and take other hunters to shoot on 'halves' under his sponsorship. He was satisfied that he could earn enough from his gun in the next few years to return to England a prosperous man. *In extremis* there was always trade to fall back on, and he was taking out plenty of goods to barter for ivory.

Things started going wrong from the time he landed in Port Elizabeth in March. His vast baggage for the Zambesi expedition, weighing more than 6000 pounds, had to come by a second ship and he was forced to spend more than six weeks waiting helplessly around the port. In the intervening time, transport charges to the Diamond Fields went up by almost 50 per cent. The difference this made to his costs – from £51 to £74 – reduced him to fury. 'Thus it always is in this world,' he fumed, 'a man is ruined and all his plans frustrated owing to other people not keeping to their agreements.'

Two months later his wagons had covered only a couple of hundred miles, and he found himself further delayed by snow in the mountains of the Southern Cape. He was stranded with six Boers, and though he had always got on well with Afrikaners, was now in such ill-humour that he felt 'more alone with these men with whom I have not one thought, sentiment or feeling in common than with untutored savages on the banks of the Zambesi'.

Once again he was trekking north through the Cape Colony and the lands of Secheli. His mood brightened when, along the way, he met his earliest friend, George Dorehill, who was happy to accompany him. But the journey to Tati took four months in all, and by then it was too late in the season to make for elephant country. It had been a bad start to the new venture.

Tati, a focal point for much of this story, was then the most northerly white settlement in Southern Africa. It lay at the head of the Missionary Road, the barren track which was then the principal trunk road north, and whose name came from the fact that missionaries had given the northward push its impetus. By now though, the road was used more by hunters and traders. Beyond Tati lay the territory known variously as Matabeleland, Zambesia or simply the Far Interior.

There was only one reason for Tati's existence, and that was gold. Whites had been drawn by its discovery by Henry Hartley, the hunter, who in 1867 showed a few deposits to one Karl Mauch, a German geologist with a vivid imagination and a flair for publicity. Mauch promptly proclaimed that the land of Ophir mentioned in Genesis, along with its fabulous wealth, had been found. Thus a myth was created that persisted well into this century.

Lobengula, then recently and insecurely established as king, perceived from the outset the danger of the sudden European interest in his lands, but granted two mining concessions, including one on the Tati river. An all-out goldrush was averted by the discovery of the Diamond Fields, and when less gold than expected was found at Tati, interest faded. Visions of Ophir's treasure would be revived almost two decades later, but in the 1870s Tati was being worked by a mere handful of prospectors, like Hugh Dobbie, a 'digger' from the Australian outback. Other local residents included Alexander Brown, a Scot, and old van Rooyen, who ran the stores where extortionate prices were charged for, among other things, liquor. A bottle of brandy which cost 6d. in the Cape was 6s. here, and a beer 4s., but as thirsty hunters and traders streamed constantly through Tati there was never a shortage of customers.

Major Stabb's diary describes a fairly characteristic evening at the settlement:

> Having pitched our tent we played whist in the evening and then adjourned to Mrs P. Jacobs's store. [A fiddle and concertina were produced.] We set to dancing like demons in

77

a most primitive manner on the mud floor. Mrs Jacobs had two buxom daughters who immensely enjoyed the fun, which waxed faster & more furious as the brandy and water circulated more freely, till the sober portion of us thought it high time to adjourn to our own encampment, where more liquor was imbibed & the usual Kaffirland rough & tumble took place which, in the case of some of the party, finished up what the liquor had commenced, & I regret to say our two married companions were conveyed early in the morning in anything but a reputable manner to their wagons.

Selous spent most of the remaining five months of 1876 around Tati. There was no alternative but to postpone his assault on the elephants of the Zambesi until the following April, when the end of the rainy season would again reduce the danger of malaria. In the meantime, he tried to forget about elephant and, for sport, hunted the area between Tati and Gubulawayo. He and Dorehill had some exhilarating gallops after giraffe. Even more exciting was his second encounter with lion, one of those heart-stopping affairs to which – as his companions had started to remark – he was prone.

He and Dorehill had become friendly with two other English sportsmen, a stout and jovial navy lieutenant named William Grandy, a Crimean veteran, and his friend Lewis Horner. One evening an excited Selous got back to their camp on the banks of the Tati river. He had shot at and hit a big male lion, he said, and spoored it through 'wag 'n bietjie' (wait-a-bit) thornbush until dusk had fallen. They agreed on an early start the next morning.

A trail of blood guided them to the wounded beast's lair. The lion remained invisible in a cluster of thick bush but roared continually as they approached, setting up a fearsome racket. Selous, showing more bravado than sense, advanced. He was better armed than he used to be, having discarded his old muzzle-loader for a more modern ten-bore breech-loading rifle, but he was nonetheless exposed.

He heard, rather than saw, the lion's charge. Then it burst from the bush, coming at him in a rush, its body pressed against the ground, jaws agape. For so large an animal it moved at astonishing speed:

78

I was so close that I had not even time to take a sight, but, stepping a pace backwards, got the rifle to my shoulder, and, when his head was close upon the muzzle, pulled the trigger, and jumped to one side. The lion fell almost at my very feet, certainly not six feet from the muzzle of the rifle. Grandy and Horner, who had a good view of the charge, say that he just dropped in his tracks when I fired.

The pegged-out skin of this animal, a full-grown male, measured 10 feet 3 inches from nose to tail. Its teeth were long and keen. The experience helped persuade Selous that the lion, rather than the elephant or buffalo, was the most dangerous big game animal.

Life at Tati was rarely so eventful and by the end of the year Selous was bored, complaining to his mother that he had nothing interesting to tell her about. He was also starting to fret. The news from the Zambesi was that the hunting season had been disastrous. Few elephant had been seen, let alone shot. The gamble of committing all his earlier profits to the new venture had begun to look foolhardy. His fears were soon confirmed at his first meeting with George Westbeech.

It was remarkable that he had not previously encountered this redoubtable figure – a sort of Buffalo Bill in Africa – although he knew him well enough by reputation. An Englishman of uncertain age and background, Westbeech had arrived in the Interior fourteen years earlier and travelled more widely as a hunter and trader over Southern Africa than any other white man. But he was considerably more than another grizzled frontiersman. Stabb described him as a gentleman by birth and education, a *bon vivant* by nature, and a Bohemian by circumstance.

Westbeech had known and hunted with Lobengula before he became king, and built up a friendship which enabled him to establish the celebrated travellers' rendezvous and trading store at Pandamatenga, south of the Victoria Falls. Westbeech was also on good terms with Sepopa, the tyrannical ruler of the Barotse tribe, who allowed him unique access to the Upper Zambesi. The Englishman's influence with the Barotse was enormous. It was he who enabled François Coillard of the Paris Missionary Society, a French Protestant group, to get a foothold on the Upper Zambesi, which saw to it that the Jesuits were turned back.

In short, George Westbeech was the chief of the white tribe of the Interior. He was also as tough as rhino hide and reckless, with a fondness for the brandy cask. But he was a straight shooter and generous in helping those he liked. Fortunately, he took a liking to the young Selous.

From him, Selous learned that Matabeleland was almost hunted out of elephant, which had withdrawn to Barotseland. Westbeech himself was still prospering because of his friendship with Sepopa: he provided the Barotse with guns and ammunition in return for ivory traded at preferred rates. The arrangement had profited him to the tune of around 20,000 pounds of ivory each year since 1871 – though this year it was down to 12,000.

Westbeech softened the blow of his bitter news by inviting Selous, Dorehill, Grandy and Horner to accompany him to the Zambesi, possibly with the prospect of going on into Barotseland. It was an attractive offer, but Selous declined. Fearless to the point of recklessness in the hunt, he was always cautious about his health and would not risk going into malaria country before the rainy season ended. It was a sensible attitude; fever took off more men each year than elephant, lion and buffalo together. So, for that matter, did alcohol.

Fever hardly bothered Westbeech. He had survived more attacks than anyone, indeed used to joke that he never felt right without a touch of it. Dorehill, Grandy and Horner chanced their arms and joined him. It was an ill-fated decision. All three were struck down by malaria. Grandy died just when it seemed he was over the worst; Horner clung to life by a thread and eventually recovered; Dorehill survived as well, and continued to lead an enterprising and lively existence – including a spell as a volunteer in the first Boer War – although, like so many in this precarious corner of the world, he was to die before turning forty.

On his own, Selous went down to the Diamond Fields for supplies. Irritations persisted. His horse was eaten one night on the trail by a lion; then he found no letters waiting for him. Finally, however, the rains had ended and he could start. He wrote to his mother from Zeerust, a pretty little town in the western Transvaal: 'I am now going straight into the Zambesi and so shall probably not hear anything from you for a long time.'

The years of 1877, 1878 and 1879 were the most difficult, and most formative, of Selous's life. Previously his efforts had been blessed with good luck and success. Now they would end almost without exception in bitter failure. In trying to recapture the happiness and fortune he had experienced before, he would taste despair at the collapse of his livelihood, and anguish over the death of friends. Sickness affected his splendid constitution. Facing financial ruin, he suffered bouts of depression from which he escaped by a therapeutic study of natural history. Despair alternated with outbursts of rage.

From all this he emerged a sobered man, the last traces of youthful cockiness gone. He had been both steeled and calmed, but the serenity that he found was mixed with melancholy. Never would he regain the unruly exuberance of his youth.

His companions when he set forth in 1877 were Edwin Miller, a colonist with a reputation as a crack shot, and an Englishman named Kingsley, both of whom were shooting on 'halves'. Selous had also taken on a number of black hunters. It was an all-out gamble; eight or so guns represented a formidable party, but fitting it out with cattle, wagons, horses and provisions took most of his earlier profits.

As the reports from the Zambesi were so gloomy he decided to try a new hunting ground. In April, the wagons rolled northwards from Gubulawayo. At Pandamatenga, instead of continuing north, they swung westwards, travelling another 100 miles or so to the Chobe river, a tributary of the Zambesi. This swampy region was normally good game country.

In that entire season, lasting around six months, Selous and his party shot between them just three elephants. Two of these animals were barely more than calves. The total value of the ivory was less than £2, and Selous himself did not so much as see an elephant. Nor were they able to fall back on trading ivory from the Barotse; Sepopa, the Barotse chief, had been assassinated, and the region had fallen into a state of anarchy. Selous's disaster was absolute. By October he was writing to his mother in despair:

Everything looks very bad here, in fact could not be worse. Trade and elephant hunting have collapsed suddenly.

81

Unless we can get into another part of Africa we are all ruined. To stop here, south of the Zambesi is hopeless. Energy, perseverance and enterprise are thrown away here.

Nothing has gone right with me since I left England, nor do I think it ever will again. I was born under an unlucky star.

Two days later he wrote to his father: 'Last year 40,000 lbs of ivory was traded here, while this season only 2600 has been bought.'

Paradoxically, the fiasco of 1877 had one important side-effect, in that it gave Selous a new status among his fellows. The fact that he had staked everything on a major gamble, even though he had lost, was final proof of his metal. The old hands, men like Westbeech and Phillips, who had seen sportsmen come and go, now recognized him as a true kindred spirit. Although not yet twenty-six, he had become an old hand himself, an established Matabeleland figure.

This Interior fellowship, of which Selous was a part for twenty-five years, represented for him the purest friendship he ever experienced. It was a classless and broadly-based society, race being the *sine qua non* of membership. Stabb, whose two-month sojourn was during Selous's absence in England, gave a description of this 'funny mixture'. (Those who appear in the present narrative are named in brackets.)

A double-first from Oxford, now growing vegetables for the gold diggers; a high wrangler from Cambridge, now drinking himself to death; bankrupts from the Cape and others whom the judicial atmosphere of the Old Colony could not agree with [Finaughty]; discharged soldiers & deserters from the army and navy; ruined gamesters from the Diamond Fields [James Fairbairn]; gentlemen by birth and education but Bohemians by nature [Phillips, Westbeech, Brown, and one of Selous's closest friends, Robert French]; ne'er-do-wells who do no better here than anywhere else, yet always sanguine and amusing; drunkards who for months together are obliged to be sober because they are unable to indulge in their favourite vice, yet who never miss an opportunity when liquor is to be had; and an occasional odd fish known to be a scoundrel & suspected of the worst of crimes.

Despite the roughness of the mixture, Stabb found, 'yet, gentle and simple, rough & polished, blasphemer and missionary . . . all living beyond the pale of any law yet all recognizing a certain rough yet honest law to themselves. Whom in genuineness of good feeling, many of our sleekly religious and respectable good people at home might with advantage take many a wholesome lesson from.'

Selous made his friends among the gentlemen wanderers, Wood, Phillips and Westbeech, but not exclusively. There was also the ruined gambler, James Fairbairn, who ran a store at Gubulawayo; Matthew Clarkson, a stocky, popular man from the Cape who hunted with Selous in 1878 and became a firm friend, only to be killed by a bolt of lightning the following year; Alfred Cross, another Cape colonist; Henry Collison, a rustic fellow from Norfolk; and Robert French, who also suffered an untimely death, for which Selous blamed himself.

Among them, he was honoured as much for what set him apart – his quiet demeanour and ascetic tastes – as the plainer virtues of honesty and courage. In a region where men drank whatever they could lay their hands on, from Cape firewater to corn beer, Selous's gingerly sipping was an exception. Eventually he became a teetotaller, and while his friends passed an evening with a cask of brandy, he drank cup after cup of black tea. His fondness for tea became one of the stock jokes of the Interior.

Entertainment revolved around drinking and talk. Sometimes, though, Selous dusted off his zither, with sufficient effect to convince one traveller that it was 'the prettiest instrument in the world'. Once, while staying with a puritan Boer farmer who said he might play only religious music, Selous gave a rendering of the 'Blue Danube' waltz, to the pleasure of the assembled womenfolk, assuring his puzzled host that it was a French hymn.

Mainly he enjoyed conversation. When not on the subjects of hunting and wildlife, topics ranged from theology – he used to argue the Darwinian theory of evolution against the missionaries at Inyati and Hope Fountain – to the confrontation looming in the south between Britain and the Zulu nation. He eschewed gossip, the usual conversational currency of the Interior, and his stock went up even further.

This regard was noted by newcomers, including Richard Frewen, an experienced English traveller whose high-handed manner during the year he spent in the Interior won few friends and landed him in trouble with Lobengula. At their meeting Frewen wrote in his journal: 'Had a long talk with Sellew [sic] a man whom I had heard so much talk about, who is said to be the best hunter in the country.' A later arrival, a Wesleyan minister named Isaac Shimmin, noted 'a halo of peculiar distinction' when Selous's name came up in conversation.

In his attempts to find a new hunting ground, Selous had turned his attention to the region lying to the north of the Zambesi. What was to become an obsessive belief that there, in the so-called Mushuku-lumbwe country, dwelt the vanished elephant herds of the past, was to persist for years, although it brought him nothing but hardship, misfortune and peril. The Mushukulumbwe country was a blank spot on the map; even Westbeech had not ventured so far north. But Selous had heard from migrant tribesmen that elephant were to be found there. For a man desperate to recoup his losses, the challenge was irresistible.

While forming his plans, Selous met L. M. Owen, a South African who had been a soldier of fortune in the so-called Kaffir Wars against the Xhosa people in the eastern Cape Colony. It was not unusual, in the climate of informality, for travel arrangements and even partnerships to be contracted on short acquaintanceship. Selous was keen to have a companion, and he agreed that Owen should join him. Although not much was known about Owen, he rode and shot well.

It was to prove a bad decision, and one which exposed Selous's limitations as a serious African traveller. This was to be no mere hunting trip, but a plunge into unknown and almost certainly dangerous territory. It was essential that companions on such ventures should be well-suited. Selous had spent no time at all alone with Owen. The one man who had was Kingsley, and he told Selous that Owen could be moody and difficult. By then it was too late.

Immediately Selous and Owen crossed the Zambesi in October 1877, they entered a strange and hostile world. Lobengula's relatively well-ordered regime was replaced by a chaotic and brutal society in which slaves rather than ivory were the common currency, and travellers were in constant danger of extortion and violence.

Nominally the region was under control of the Portuguese, who had been lured to Africa hundreds of years before by the promise of easy wealth. In reality, the Portuguese had long since abandoned any attempt at administration in the face of disease and hostile tribes. Only along the river did they cling to any semblance of authority.

Selous and Owen encountered evidence of slave-taking almost as soon as they crossed to the north bank of the Zambesi and struck eastwards downriver. In his journal, Selous recorded the burnt-out villages and corpses, and the pathetic relief of local people on discovering that he and Owen were not raiders.

This first encounter with the Portuguese in Africa made a profound impression, convincing Selous that Portuguese colonialism was little short of barbarous, and exposing him to the concept of a British mission to civilize. Anything, it seemed, would be preferable to the anarchy here, where individual Portuguese slave-traders conducted their affairs through a network of villainous local cut-throats, either blacks or half-castes. The decay and evil which clung to the Zambesi valley grew more oppressive the further they moved on.

Near present-day Kariba, they met a slaver who belongs in the pages of Joseph Conrad's *Heart of Darkness*. A tall, spare man with black eyes, Jaoquim de Mendonça was hospitality itself to the visiting Englishmen, in chilling contrast to his treatment of slaves. He told Selous: 'Negro *diablo*, Africa *inferno*' (Blacks are devils, Africa is hell). Ten women of the Batonga tribe, some with children on their backs, were brought in with iron rings around their necks. Selous rejoiced when two young girls escaped. But soon they were recaptured, and for punishment were whipped until the blood ran down their backs. Selous wrote in his journal: 'My heart bled, and had I had the money I would have bought them.'

An even more sinister figure was Kanyemba, a chief appointed as a district official, or Capitão-mor, under the Portuguese system of exercising authority through local people. Kanyemba, a malevolently clownish figure in gold-braided uniform, cocked hat and sword, was a leading slave-trader and had been responsible for the devastation witnessed earlier by Selous and Owen. A contemporary source described him as 'one of the chronic calamities suffered by the region'.

With guides provided by Mendonça, they reached the Zambesi's confluence with the Kafue in mid-December. At this point they took a bearing north. Their initial goal was the kraal of a chief named Sitanda, some three weeks' march away, which they believed would be near the new elephant hunting ground.

However, a malign influence still dogged the party. Constant rain caused them delay, game was scarce and their provisions were running low. On Christmas Day, they breakfasted on a small piece of meat and some corn, but for dinner there was nothing. More seriously, Selous and Owen had quarrelled.

There is no evidence of what caused the trouble. Perhaps it was not due to any personality defect of Owen's, but was simply a typical rift between individuals under strain. However, it was serious enough for Selous to form a rare animosity towards his companion. Selous's remarks in *A Hunter's Wanderings in Africa* might seem mild, almost even-handed, but coming from him they were downright condemnation. He and Owen 'did not hit it off very well together', he wrote, 'as much through my fault, no doubt, as his, owing to what I may call incompatibility of temper.'

For one who rarely wrote about any kind of emotion, this was tantamount to an outburst. It was emphasized by a letter to his mother which shows the bitterness of his true feelings, while offering little more by way of explanation for them. After a hellish journey back, he wrote home: 'Curse [Owen] for spoiling my whole trip: he had the most infernal temper I have ever met with, and he gave me so much annoyance and trouble that I shall hate the name Owen as long as I live.'

Despite the problems, they pressed on well enough at this stage to Sitanda's kraal. There, however, they found the country in the grip of famine, and malaria rampant. Sitanda himself was a shrewd and wily old vulture who wished them no good. He had no objections to them shooting as many elephant as they could find. The problem was, there were no elephant: the fabled hunting grounds had turned out to be just that.

The day after reaching Sitanda's, Owen was stricken with malaria, and two days later Selous, too, fell ill. It was, he noted in his journal, a pretty predicament. They had come farther north than any whites before. But they were without provisions or quinine, the only

86

effective treatment for their fevers, and were fully 700 miles from the mission station at Inyati, the nearest outpost of civilization. Their headman, too, was sick.

There was no longer any question of hunting elephant. They were both seriously ill, and it was already obvious they would be lucky to get out of this most unhealthy spot alive, particularly as Sitanda clearly intended that they should not. Having observed their plight, he forbade any of his people to act as bearers, reasoning logically that, when the white men died, their trading goods and weapons would fall into his hands. He also refused to sell them food. By now Owen had 'lost all power in his limbs' and Selous was 'dreadfully ill'.

Two weeks after their arrival Selous wrote in his journal: 'During the last three nights I have not slept a wink. Everything looks unspeakably dismal and utterly miserable. If we only had something to eat we might stand a chance of getting well; but kaffir corn and water is all we have.' It had become essential that, sick as they were, they should get away from Sitanda's and try to return to the Zambesi. Unable to hire porters, Selous resorted to buying a slave from Kanyemba, who was passing through the kraal on a foray. The deal involved paying 320 cartridges for an eighteen-year-old youth, to whom Selous promised his freedom once they reached safety.

After almost three weeks at Sitanda's, they gathered themselves and started a slow and nightmarish retreat. Behind them they left most of their goods. Both men were so feeble that they could manage no more than five miles a day, and soon after starting the slave absconded. This was a disaster as he took all the corn and most of their cartridges. Now without any food, they were reduced to trading their meagre remaining goods to stay alive.

Fortunately, Selous found that the further they left Sitanda's behind the more his strength returned. By the middle of February they had reached the Zambesi, where even Mendonça's ghoulish hospitality was welcome. However, they were by no means out of danger yet. Gubulawayo was still hundreds of miles away, and Owen's health had deteriorated further. Completely debilitated and unable to walk, he had to be carried on a litter by eight bearers. Five weeks after setting out from Sitanda's, they crossed to the south bank of the Zambesi.

The discomfort of their plodding progress was made worse by the fact that Selous and Owen were now scarcely on speaking terms. Another problem was causing Selous a good deal of anxiety: the barter supplies of calico, on which they depended to obtain food, were getting low, and Selous estimated that at their present rate of progress they would run out well before they reached Gubulawayo. In mid-April – reduced to five bearers and two and a half pieces of calico, Owen still unable to walk, and himself suffering from fatigue and shaking with ague – Selous decided there was only one thing for it: he would leave Owen with enough calico and beads to keep him in food for six weeks, while he summoned all his strength and struck out for Inyati. If he lived, help should be back in time to save Owen.

Even in his dire condition, he was able to summon some spirit. Coming across a landmark hill near the Sengwe river in modern north Zimbabwe, he recorded grandiosely in his journal: 'This I called Mount Cromwell, in honour of him who I consider the greatest of England's rulers.' Three weeks later, and six months after first crossing the Zambesi, he arrived at the London Missionary Society station at Inyati, 'very exhausted in body but joyful in mind'. Mr Sykes, head of the Mission, despatched a party, which returned with Owen a few weeks later. Selous's constitution had saved them both.

The story of this first, disastrous, expedition to the Mushuku-lumbwe country does not quite end there. Ironically, it helped provide the inspiration for one of the most phenomenally successful literary enterprises in the English language. It was four years later that Selous published his account of the trip in *A Hunter's Wanderings in Africa* and another four years on, H. Rider Haggard's book, *King Solomon's Mines*, was released. The parallels were close enough for a rapturous public to conclude that the fictional hero Allan Quatermain was none other than Frederick Courteney Selous.

Like Selous, Quatermain is a modest, quietly-spoken elephant hunter who, when the story opens, has journeyed to a miserable spot in Africa called Sitanda's Kraal, encountering Portuguese slave-traders and falling ill with fever. Indeed, Sitanda's is the starting point of the search for Solomon's treasure. In this and other respects, Rider Haggard drew openly on Selous's book, for although he had spent some years in Natal he had no personal experience of the Interior.

It is not strictly true, however, to say that Selous 'was' Allan Quatermain. He and Rider Haggard did not meet until after *King Solomon's Mines* had been written. Haggard was in the habit of drawing on the experiences of men like Selous to add verisimilitude to his work. Insofar as Allan was anyone, he was an alter-ego. In what seems to have been an attempt to put the record straight, Haggard wrote that he found it easy to write about the hunter 'perhaps because he is only myself, set in a variety of imagined situations, thinking my thoughts and looking at life through my eyes'. The view persisted, however, that Selous was Quatermain.

It took Selous months to recover from this ordeal, and his spirits had never been lower. Four years had passed since his last successful hunting season, in which time virtually all his earlier profits had dribbled away. Money had become a source of near-neurotic anxiety – one from which he would never be entirely free again. Even when he was living, many years later, in a grand home in Surrey and with every sign of prosperity, it would take only a frisson on the Stock Market to set off his anxiety. That unhappy consequence must be dated from this period. From the depths of his gloom he wrote to his mother in July 1878:

> I am afraid that if I ever get home again you will find me much changed for the worse in temper and disposition. Continual never-ending misfortune in small matters and the failure of every speculation has changed me from a tolerably light-hearted fellow into a morose and sad-tempered man.

He was wondering where else he might try his luck, and considered North America. But Africa still held him. The life was in his blood forever now: the freedom of the plains, the sounds of the bush at night, a fire and friendship, above all the grandeur of the wildlife.

By August, he was well enough to think of hunting again, and a visit to Lobengula secured a turn of good fortune. From the start of his rule, the king had perceived that keeping good relations with the whites was in his interests, and he cultivated the leaders of their community by the exercise of patronage, and a subtle gradation of rewards and favours. The status that Selous had acquired among the other hunters and traders was not lost on Lobengula, and he was a welcome visitor to the royal kraal. For his part, Selous enjoyed their conversations in which the king demonstrated his knowledge of animals and their habits.

This year, for the first time since 1872, Lobengula gave him permission to hunt in Mashonaland. This concession, to what was then the last area where elephant were found in any numbers, had also been granted to George Wood, Matthew Clarkson and Alfred Cross. Delighted, Selous started after his friends and in September caught up with them near the Umfuli river. In this rarely-hunted country, where it was still possible to hunt from horseback, they had found elephant in some numbers, and around the campfire Selous heard of their adventures.

The hunters had been reminded of the dangers of their trade two weeks earlier when Wood's foreman, a Zulu named Quabeet, had been chased and caught by an elephant which held him down with a foot and, using its trunk, wrenched him into three pieces. The head, chest and arms were tossed on one side. Then a leg and thigh were torn off, and the elephant, having wreaked its fury, departed.

On this trip, Selous was to come within an inch of a similarly terrible death – 'one of the narrowest escapes of his whole adventurous life', Millais said. It happened on the most successful day of the season, when a total of twenty-two elephants fell to the four guns. Selous, Wood, Clarkson and Cross had come across a herd of between sixty and seventy and had galloped alongside, shouting and picking off the biggest first, until both elephants and horses were out of wind. Selous chose a big cow as his fifth victim, but two shots failed to bring her down. Suddenly, she came at him.

He dug in his spurs, but his horse was so tired that it could manage no more than a trot. Then the elephant was on them. Selous heard two screams from the enraged creature immediately above his head, and only had time to reflect that it was all up with him before he and his horse were dashed to the ground.

> For a few seconds I was half stunned by the violence of the shock, and the first thing I became aware of, was a very strong smell of elephant. At the same instant I felt that I was unhurt and that, though in an unpleasant predicament, I still had a chance for life.

He was, in fact, right underneath the creature, which in its rage to kill, had charged over him and come down on its forelegs, trapping him under its chest. While the elephant was still immobilized, he managed to pull himself free and beat a retreat into the bush. He was bruised and smeared all over with elephant blood, which made him a terrifying sight, but otherwise unhurt. It had been a desperately near thing, though. Well might his companions have shaken their heads admiringly at yet another of Selous's hairbreadth escapes.

The following year, 1879, saw the crowning bitterness of this desolate period in his life. The accumulation of tragedies and misfortunes that surrounded him in that final year of the decade convinced him that a dark star was following him.

Selous had no conventional Christian faith. Indeed, he was noted by one contemporary source for his 'irreligious ways' (which were not specified) and frequently teased the Matabeleland missionaries about their failure to have made a single convert in more than forty-five years. But the maturing he underwent during this time, the meditations of many a long evening alone, produced in him the seeds of doubt in his creed of materialism. A convinced Darwinian, he would nevertheless come to be troubled by intimations of spiritual existence. When finally he left Africa, a magazine profile would note his profound conviction 'that the rule of life which Plato, Confucius and Jesus formulated centuries ago, Do unto others what you would others should do unto you, sums up best the whole duty of man. Thus would Mr Selous sum up all the law and the prophets. But sometimes when inclined to say that man is the beast that perishes, and that at death there is an end of personality, there comes a doubt born of many strange phenomena.'

One of Selous's closest friends, Heatley Noble, remarked that he had held 'strong views about what he called Psychic Force'. The incident that most shaped these views occurred, as we shall see, some years in the future. But events now, in 1879, may have contributed to them.

Once again that year Selous had taken a gamble, fitting out a big expedition to the Chobe and Botlete rivers. He had gone ahead and was awaiting the arrival of his friends, French, Clarkson and Collison, from the Transvaal. Clarkson never got there, being struck soon after leaving Klerksdorp by a bolt of lightning which bored a hole clean through his hat as it killed him.

A few months later, Selous and his other two friends were hunting along the Chobe when French marched off into the bush after a wounded animal. It was the last they ever saw of him. When French failed to return that night, Selous went out with a search party and fired several shots to signal their whereabouts to his missing friend. Some time later there was an answering shot, and Selous saw a fire burning some distance off. He followed these signals but failed to locate French. The search was restarted the next day, but no sign of spoor could be found. As the days went by, hopes for French's return died. He had, in fact, succumbed as early as the second day. A week later, his bearers got back to camp exhausted, carrying his rifle with a message scratched on the stock: 'I cannot go any further, when I die peace with all.'

French's fate had been sealed by his own obstinacy; the bearers had told him of a way which, by following a river, was certain to lead him back to the camp, but he had cursed them and blundered on by compass. With remarkable loyalty, they stayed at his side until he died, then found their own way back.

Although no blame could be attached to him, Selous, as the most experienced member of the group, felt personally responsible. He recalled his own experience of nearly dying lost in the bush, and he was tormented by visions of his friend's death. He determined that there should be a proper burial and offered a large reward for the discovery of French's remains, but no trace was ever found. Years later the incident still gnawed at him, and he would become visibly distressed at the mention of French's name.

The trauma aggravated a severe attack of fever, and for a few days Selous hovered near death himself. By the time the worst had passed, he and Collison, the only other survivor of the original four-man group, had no heart to continue hunting. They trekked to the Transvaal, where Selous spent months recuperating with friends. Another season had ended in disaster.

His days as an elephant hunter were over. He had persisted because no ready alternative presented itself, and in the hope that those idyllic early years might be recaptured. The fact was now inescapable, however: ivory was finished in Southern Africa. If he was to stay – and he could not bear to turn his back on the Interior – a fundamental change would have to be made.

The outlook was not promising. The principal alternatives for an outdoorsman were farming and prospecting, neither of which interested him. All Selous had to show for a decade of hunting were guns, wagons, horses and cattle. And hard-won experience. Somehow, with these resources, he had to fashion a new life.

CHAPTER SEVEN

A Change of Direction

In the first month of the new decade Selous wrote to his mother: 'I shall now give up hunting elephants, as it is impossible to make it pay.' His plan was simple. He would make a journey of real exploration through the *terra incognita* beyond Sitanda's country, penetrating as far as Lake Tanganyika. Then he would go home and write a book about his adventures. The Victorian public was ever-receptive to books on Africa, although Selous may have been over-optimistic in thinking that it could earn him a lot of money. With a touch of pomposity he told his mother: 'I know that people have got good sums for writing bad books on Africa, full of lies, though I don't know if a true book will sell well. My book at any rate will command a large sale out here, as I am so well known, and have a reputation for speaking nothing but the truth.'

This was to be the start of a period of forced improvisation in his life. To the English public, he was always simply the Great Hunter. In reality, like other hunters and traders who stayed on after the end of the ivory era, he had now to turn his hand to whatever he could to earn a living. In the years ahead he would shoot specimens for museums, and act as one of the first paid hunter-guides to wealthy sportsmen. He would dabble at exploration, and would, indeed, write a best-selling book, only to discover indignantly how little it paid. He even thought about giving up life in the Interior altogether, and settling down as a farmer in the eastern Cape.

On 25 January 1880, he wrote to his mother in a tone simultaneously self-pitying and self-dramatizing:

> During the last four years, though I have led a life of great hardship and privation, yet I have lost much money and

94

almost ruined a good constitution; to throw away a little more money and health after what has already gone, will not much matter. My plans are liable to modification owing to fever, tsetse flies and other circumstances.

He intended his journey to take about two years, and, as well as entitling him to claim credibility as a genuine explorer, felt that it would make an admirable centrepiece for his book. His plans were well advanced when he applied to Sir Owen Lanyon, the Administrator of the Transvaal, for an ammunition licence. On this apparently straightforward request, the entire venture foundered.

Selous had, somewhat optimistically, applied for almost five times the powder allocation he had been permitted the previous year, based on the time he expected to be away. Lanyon was initially inclined to let him have half what he requested, but abruptly and without explanation, changed his mind. On 12 February he wrote to his secretary: 'Reply that I have received instructions not to allow munitions of war to be taken out of the country.'

Lanyon was probably influenced by the political temperature, as Southern Africa was in one of its most turbulent cycles. The previous year, Britain had provoked a final, decisive confrontation with the Zulu nation. It also appeared to Whitehall that a conflict was becoming inevitable with the Transvaal Boers. This new expansionist mood in Britain had been felt even in Matabeleland, where a British emissary named Captain R. Patterson took an injudiciously provocative attitude at Lobengula's court and disappeared forever. He had set off for the Victoria Falls against the king's wishes, and although the first report was that he and his companions died after drinking bad water, it was widely believed that Lobengula had had them murdered.

Selous had been left surprisingly untouched by these events, although, as we shall see, he had pronounced views on them. The Administrator's decision, which seems to have been based on an unduly sensitive concern about having ammunition in circulation, was another bitter blow. Selous was forced to abandon his Lake Tanganyika expedition, and conceived a lasting grudge against Lanyon.

He had not planned to go back to England for at least another two years, but he now decided on a visit home to write his book, after making one more hunting trip. In the event, the hunt was one of the happiest of his life, and did much to erase unhappy memories. His companion was James Jameson, a wealthy scion of the Irish whisky family, with whom he formed a solid friendship – and a happy accommodation too, as Jameson shouldered the cost of fitting out and maintaining their party, while Selous acted as guide and mentor. In later years, other affluent sportsmen would come to similar arrangements with Selous who, in this way, became the first well-known professional hunter-guide. It is unlikely that any money actually changed hands as a result of these partnerships, Selous and others of his kind being content enough to enjoy their sport 'all-found' while tutoring a wealthy or famous novice – provided, always, that he was a congenial companion too.

There were no problems on that score with Jameson. 'We have contracted a great friendship,' Selous wrote, 'our tastes are very similar.' It was an abiding regard, as he would show years later when, in coming to the defence of his old friend, Selous confronted the formidable Henry Stanley.

He and Jameson enjoyed plenty of action that season, and at the end of it Selous was able to write home with a touch of his old *joie de vivre*: 'I have been leading an active life in a fine climate, and am now as well both in look and in feeling as it is possible to be.'

Only one unpleasant incident interrupted their five months of wandering over the high plateau of the Mashona country. During a chaotic incursion by a lion into their camp one night, Jameson's valet, a man named Ruthven, had half his head shot away accidentally by a frenzied bearer. Lions were never far off, and the hunters had a number of nerve-tingling encounters with them. In one day Selous shot three of the great cats with four bullets, including one enormous creature, more than eleven feet long and weighing well over 400 pounds, the biggest he had so far killed.

A discovery during this journey brought his name to the attention of the Royal Geographical Society, the headquarters of world exploration. In the far north of Mashonaland (as the region was just starting to be called), amid the purple and russet-coloured leaves of the msasa trees in spring, he and Jameson came to the kraal of Lomagondi, a wizened petty chief. Selous conceived a real affection for this perky character, and his murder years later by one of Lobengula's raiding parties would contribute to Selous's eventual detestation of the Matabele. Lomagondi now told him and Jameson that the Umfuli river ran into the Sanyati and not the Zambesi, as was shown on all previous maps of Southern Africa. A few days' march brought them to the rivers' confluence, which confirmed Lomagondi's information.

It was not a discovery of the first importance, but it helped establish Selous as an expert on the geography of Mashonaland. By now Selous had virtual *carte blanche* from Lobengula to travel, and, increasingly, he chose to roam the Mashona plateau. The knowledge he gained of this relatively unknown territory would form the basis of his reputation as an explorer and geographer, a qualification which not only brought him the Royal Geographical Society's Gold Medal in 1890, but made him indispensable to the designs of Cecil Rhodes.

Something else that Selous learned on this trip led to his first meeting with Rhodes. Cecil's favourite elder brother, Herbert, had himself been a wanderer, who had died in a fire the previous year in the area to the north of the Mashona country. Selous was the first white man to hear of Herbert Rhodes's death, and on his way home to England, he called on Cecil in Port Elizabeth to tell him the news. Selous was aged twenty-eight. Rhodes, a year younger, had just returned to South Africa from studying at Oxford, and although he had recently announced the formation of the De Beers Mining Company with capital of £200,000, had given little indication of the colossal achievements that lay ahead.

By the time he got back to England, Selous had a new plan. It was time, he told his delighted parents, to 'bid adieu to savage beasts and barbarous men, and settle down and become a respectable citizen'. He was finished with hunting, he said, and would stay in England long enough to write his book, then sail back to the Cape and become a farmer.

The idea had come from Frank Mandy, one of Selous's oldest friends and a figure who drifted in and out of his life in Africa. Mandy had given up hunting himself and told Selous he was making a fortune at ostrich farming near Port Elizabeth. Mandy introduced

97

him to a speculator named Bennett, who said he would be delighted to set up such a likely young fellow in the same business. Selous may have been further encouraged by the Mandy family, and the fact that Frank had two pretty sisters.

First, however, there was the book. Selous had previously written articles on giraffe and elephant hunting for the *Field*, the magazine of the sporting gentry. But he had never attempted anything of book length before. Now he set to work, using as his basis the journals in which he had recorded the minutiae of his daily life. Within a few months he produced one of the classics of hunting literature.

A Hunter's Wanderings in Africa, published that same year, 1881, was the first book of its kind since Baldwin's *African Hunting and Adventure* almost twenty years earlier. Bearing a dedication to the Interior fraternity of hunters, traders and missionaries, 'from whom I have ever met with the truest kindness and the most generous hospitality', it was partly intended as a guide for the prospective sportsman; there were drawings identifying species of antelope, notes on the distribution of animals, and useful tips.

But the book made its real mark, as Selous had hoped, as an adventure story. The clarity of his observation was served by simple but telling prose, while close shaves with charging lion and elephant were given immediacy by illustrations. Remembering how, as a boy, he had been transfixed by the drawings in Baldwin's and Cumming's books, he had insisted on having illustrations, although he had to bear the cost himself. *A Hunter's Wanderings in Africa* was an immediate success, and the first edition of 1000 copies was sold out within a year.

It reads less well today. The protracted succession of hunting accounts becomes at times monotonous, while Selous is infuriatingly miserly with details on the life and characters of the Interior. It remains, however, one of the great works of Africana, and an incomparably evocative record of what it was like to hunt elephant on foot with a muzzle-loader.

Among those who admired it was a rising American politician named Theodore Roosevelt. Long before they met, Roosevelt, who was a keen sportsman himself, wrote: 'You have the most extraordinary power of seeing things with minute accuracy of detail, and then the equally necessary power to describe vividly and accurately what you have seen. After reading your articles I can see the actual struggle as the lion kills a big buffalo.'

Less welcome to Selous was the attention the book attracted from animal welfare campaigners. He had appended a list of the 548 animals he had killed in the previous four years – mainly antelope, but also including 20 elephant, 12 rhinoceros, 100 buffalo and 13 lions. It was not, in fact, a particularly big bag by the standards of the day. Certainly, there was plenty of casual shooting, and the fact that more than half the buffalo had been accounted for in a season when there were no elephant to be found seems to suggest that shooting sometimes provided an outlet for any and every frustration. On the whole, however, Selous was a careful shot, choosing his targets either because they presented an appearance of some distinction as specimens, or for food.

This second point provided the most ready defence against a general criticism by one reviewer that he was responsible for 'wholesale, senseless slaughter'. Selous replied that he had been followed constantly by blacks who were eager for meat, and that no animal he killed, from an elephant to a steenbuck, had ever gone to waste. His defence had a certain logic. He noted tartly after once killing three hippopotamuses for a village in Mashonaland: 'We had the satisfaction of knowing that the slaughter would bring more joy to the hearts of these poor but voracious heathen, than all the tracts and Bibles ever published for their benefit.'

A Hunter's Wanderings sold briskly, and another three editions followed the first. But Selous's expectation that this would bring him prosperity showed the kind of naivety in financial matters to which he was only too prone. A year after publication he had received only £61 in royalties, this after putting £73 of his own money towards the cost of illustrations. Small wonder that he should suspect the publishers, Richard Bentley & Son, of doing considerably better out of the book than him, or that he should subsequently change to Rowland Ward & Co., who specialized in hunting publications, and with whom he formed a lasting contact.

Fred's six-month stay in the grandeur of Gloucester Road and at Barrymore House in Wargrave, must have brought home to him his recent failure. His working capital had been reduced to a mere £400, the amount with which Frederick had sent him off ten years earlier, while all he had to show for his time in Africa were a large number of trophies and a rather modest reputation as an explorer. At the home of some relatives who lived in Harley Street, he met a diminutive, puckish-looking young man named Harry Johnston, who although little more than twenty-one, had already made a bigger impact in London circles as an explorer. Johnston, self-conscious about his own rather odd appearance, was more impressed by his new acquaintance's physical presence than anything else: '[Selous] was exceedingly good looking [with] blond hair and violet-grey eyes,' he wrote later. Another person was taken with his handsomeness, too. There is evidence that at this time Selous had a short-lived love affair.

There were obvious problems. For all his dash and good looks, he had spent little of his adult life in 'civilized' company. He was undoubtedly sexually experienced, and had probably known the charms of many Matabele girls, but he had never formed a relationship with a white woman before.

The affair seems to have foundered on the state of his finances. This is attested to by a descendant who remembers seeing a letter in which Selous wrote that he was in love, but could not marry because he was all but penniless. Nothing further came of it, and it is not even certain who had been the object of his affections. But probably she was Fanny Maxwell, the daughter of a romantic novelist who wrote under the pen-name M. E. Braddon. A few years later Fanny married Selous's younger brother Edmund, who had grown up a shy, preoccupied young man. Many years later, after both brothers were dead, Fanny told her grandson she had found Fred 'witty and handsome' and wished that she had married him instead of Edmund.

Another important meeting occurred during this brief but eventful trip home. Albert Gunther, keeper of the zoological department at the British Museum, was, above all, the man to whom London owes the building of the Natural History Museum in South Kensington. That was still some years ahead, but Gunther had lobbied successfully for the zoological section to be separated from the main museum collection at Bloomsbury. He was expanding his own department, and what he needed were specimens of African mammals.

Selous's meeting with Gunther was the start of a long and fruitful association. Gunther listed species – rhinoceros, zebra and numerous antelope – which Selous provided in a steady supply over the next few years. In his letters to Gunther, he carped constantly about payments, but crates of bones and skins continued to arrive in London and the African mammal display grew impressively. Selous came to have a personal, even proprietorial, interest in the Natural History Museum. His own collection of specimens, then the biggest in private hands in Britain, was bequeathed to the museum, which set aside a Selous Room for their display. It was fitting that, of all the bodies with which he was associated, it should be the museum that honoured him after his death. The bronze bust in the main hall, raised by public subscription, is the only official monument to his memory.

Selous arrived back in South Africa to encounter yet another blow to his plans. Bennett, his prospective benefactor as a farmer, had ruined himself and committed suicide. Ostrich farming was in a slump. Selous did not immediately abandon the idea of farming, but the response to his enquiries about other opportunities tended to be sceptical; it was not believed that he was capable of settling to a quiet life on a farm.

It was probably true, and one suspects that he did not protest too much. Hunting, adventure and the camaraderie of the Interior were as close as Selous had yet come to finding a purpose in life. This is not to say that years in the bush had left him a shallow man, for now, perhaps more than ever before, he felt deep emotion, and began to develop strong convictions. But the life of 'a wandering Englishman with a taste for natural history and sport' – which was how he saw himself – had become balm to his restless soul. Inactivity he found physical torture, as if he had a personal demon which could only be appeased through constant activity.

As he rode north at the beginning of 1882 he might have been thought a forlorn figure. He had passed the age of thirty, yet on the face of it was worse off than when he arrived in Africa, aged nineteen. He was pinning his hopes on the uncertain proposition that he could earn a living by hunting for specimens, but had only managed to raise an expedition at all by putting himself in debt to the tune of almost £500 with Thomas Leask, a prominent Klerksdorp trader. Nothing in past events or in his plans for the future, such as they were, could have encouraged him to believe that the most dramatic and rewarding period of his life lay ahead.

CHAPTER EIGHT

An Imperial Dream

For some years, Southern Africa had been passing through a convulsive phase in its evolution, and although Selous had not been directly involved in the events, he was well aware of them. The opinions he formed in this time ensured that when eventually the tide of British expansionism swept north he would be in the vanguard, not just as the strong right arm of Cecil Rhodes, but as an ardent imperial propagandist in his own right.

British foreign policy, in Southern Africa as elsewhere, alternated throughout the nineteenth century between isolationism and expansionism. In the late 1870s, Whitehall embarked on a 'forward' policy which had as its objective the incorporation of the Boer republics, the Transvaal and the Orange Free State, and additionally the Zulu kingdom, in a federation of British South Africa. The principal agent of this policy was Sir Bartle Frere, Governor of the Cape, who enjoyed the full support of Disraeli's Colonial Secretary, Lord Carnarvon. In 1877 the annexation of an effectively bankrupt Transvaal was accomplished bloodlessly.

Once again, the Boers had come under the British control which they had sought to escape by the Great Trek. This time they could not escape or, it seemed, offer resistance. The Zulus, on the other hand, under their king, Cetshwayo, retained a standing army of 40,000 warriors convinced of their invincibility. Frere set about engineering the sort of showdown in which Britain could portray itself as a victim of aggression. A classic formula unfolded: rising tension and frontier 'incidents' gave rise to an ultimatum with conditions patently unacceptable to the Zulus.

The question of how a colonizing white power could effect the downfall of a black rival with the fewest casualties on either side

103

would occupy Selous a decade later, when he was in a position to influence policy towards the Matabele. Fortunately, he had by then gained in both wisdom and compassion, qualities which were signally absent when he wrote to his mother shortly before the Zulu War. This jingoistic outburst, against the sympathy which the Zulus enjoyed in some quarters in England, is perhaps the ugliest prose ever to come from his pen:

> It is to be hoped that the Exeter Hall clique and Aborigines Protection Society will not be able to prevent Sir Theophilius Shepstone [Administrator of the Transvaal] from checking the insolence of the Zulus. If he and sensible men are only able to have their own way there will soon be an end to these kaffir outbreaks, and the brutal savages will find out that there are more things in Woolwich Arsenal – in the shape of Gatling guns etc. – than ever dreamt of in their philosophy. If they will only come out into the open they will be slaughtered by the thousand, and their carcasses given to the hyenas and vultures, the only thing they are good for.

The Zulus did indeed come out into the open, with a vengeance. In the attack by Cetshwayo's impis on a camp at Isandhlwana, Britain suffered one of its most humiliating military catastrophes. About 900 of a white force of 950 were massacred. The British public was stunned that such a reversal could be inflicted by an enemy without firearms, and shudders went through the white communities of Southern Africa. Still, it was to be the Zulus' last triumph. They had suffered severely at Isandhlwana too, and their loss of thousands more men, at the Battle of Ulundi five months later, where only ten British soldiers died, broke Cetshwayo's power.

One of the most interested observers of the Zulu War was Lobengula. Ever since the flight of his father, Mzilikazi, from Shaka's wrath, the Matabele had kept a wary eye on the Zulus, whose capability for reprisal they regarded with a healthy fear. Lobengula's relief at the annihilation of that avenging angel must have been tempered by the apprehension that a new military paramountcy had been established in its place. Just then, however, he gained a respite. In the watershed British election of 1880,

Disraeli's 'forward' policy was thrown into reverse by the return of the Liberals under Gladstone.

Selous, a liberal by upbringing and inclination, but now an imperialist by persuasion, was mortified by the Liberal victory. He felt that so drastic a change of policy would be interpreted as yet another backdown in a history of British weakness and vacillation in Southern Africa. The point was underlined when the Transvaal, under Paul Kruger, rebelled in the first Anglo–Boer War of 1880. The might of British arms was again humiliated, at the Battle of Majuba, a setback compounded in imperialist eyes by Gladstone's prompt settlement restoring self-government to the Boers. The blow to the self-esteem of the jingoes was immense.

Selous had the man of action's liking for straight answers and simple solutions. Complex issues he reduced to black and white in a way that could make him inconsistent. He sympathized with the Afrikaners' history and traditions, and would later take up their cause with passion. However, the challenges being posed at this time to Britain's regional role aroused him. Having savoured the extinction of Zulu power, he now poured scorn on the Boers, writing that they were inferior to Englishmen in intelligence and to the Zulus in courage. Furthermore, he added, the war with the Transvaal had added 'a more disgraceful page to the history of England than any yet written'.

If in these tirades his heart ruled his head, Selous was right enough about one thing. The first Anglo–Boer War would leave a legacy of hatred lasting generations. The seeds of a second, infinitely more damaging, conflict had been sown. Already the call had been heard in England to 'Avenge Majuba'.

Selous was made especially welcome by Lobengula when he arrived back at Gubulawayo at the beginning of 1882. The Matabele king had always cultivated whites, and may even have genuinely liked some of them, Selous included. Now, however, Lobengula was feeling vulnerable. Not only the British were looking northwards. The Transvaal Boers, having tweaked the tail of the British lion, were in expansionist mood as well. So were European powers, notably the Germans and the Portuguese. The Scramble for Africa was looming, and Lobengula was too astute a politician not to have foreseen his peril.

The weak power base which he inherited, had made of the king a consummate manipulator, rather than a military commander in the mould of Mzilikazi or Shaka. For the next decade, he would be at the centre of the turbulence gathering over the Interior, threatening a cataclysmic clash between black and white militarism. It is a testament to his shrewdness, and persuasiveness, that he restrained the impetuous spirits as long as he did. Only in 1893 did he finally, and fatally, lose that control.

Already there were those among the indunas, the king's generals, who were restive about the white traders and hangers-on at Gubulawayo, who were said by some to be spies. Rumours of an invasion from the south by a white impi were rife. Under Mzilikazi, the Matabele had been driven from the Transvaal by the Boers; now the call was heard at indabas, the tribal councils, for whites to be driven from Matabeleland.

One casualty of the ferment in Gubulawayo was Lobengula's favourite sister, Nini, who had wielded an influence at court proportionate to her immense size. She was jolly with it, and her grotesque flirtations with George Phillips had made her well-liked by the traders. What decided Lobengula to have her put to death, supposedly for witchcraft, was never established. The theories included luridly Freudian concepts, though it was also whispered that Nini's popularity with whites had prompted a conspiracy against her by the soothsayers. The details of her execution are unclear, but she was probably clubbed to death with knobkerries, the Matabele war-clubs.

Another factor unsettling the king was the new mood of opportunism that had seized previously trusted white confidants, who were suddenly petitioning him for mining concessions. Phillips, who had known him for as long as Westbeech, and had often given good counsel on dealing with whites, had joined a consortium with two other old advisers, James Fairbairn and Thomas Leask, to try to obtain from Lobengula a permit to dig for minerals in Mashonaland.

It was at this stage that Selous presented himself at Bulawayo after an absence of about a year. Artless and patently uninterested in minerals, he was one of the few men Lobengula would have trusted at a time when he needed a new white confidant.

The king had already considered that he might have to treat with Boer or Briton. He now entrusted to Selous an extraordinary document which he had just received, a letter in Afrikaans from the Transvaal Commandant-General, Piet Joubert, and asked him for a translation. Selous read with astonishment; it was an invitation from the Boers to join an anti-British alliance:

> You must have heard that the English took away our country, the Transvaal, or as they say, annexed it.
>
> We then talked nicely for four years, and begged for our country, but no, when an Englishman once has your property in his hand then he is like an ape that has its hand full of pumpkin seeds. If you don't beat him to death he will never let go.
>
> Then the English commenced to arrest us because we were dissatisfied, and that caused the shooting and fighting. Then the English found it would be better to give us back our country. Now they are gone and our country is free, and we will once more live in friendship with Lobengula.

A copy of his translation was later found in Selous's papers. There is no indication of what he did with it, although it is a fairly safe assumption that he would have passed a copy to the British authorities at the Cape. Selous never doubted that Lobengula preferred to deal with Englishmen, and would rebuff Boer overtures – as, indeed, he did. Selous's own status with the Matabele king was at its highest point; he enjoyed special trust and privilege, being in that year of 1882 the only white given leave to hunt in Mashonaland. Lobengula sent him on his way with the gift of a fine shooting horse. But, although Selous lacked the sensitivity to realize it at the time, the strained circumstances had introduced a tension within the friendship which would eventually destroy it.

Selous's dealings with blacks were guided by the simple conviction that 'kaffirs' benefited from contact with Englishmen. There was, of course, nothing unusual in that idea, but nor was there, as might be suggested, anything racially hostile in it. There was not then in Southern Africa the ugly, pejorative character to the word kaffir that there is today. As in America, whites who felt racial hatred, as distinct from racial superiority, used the term 'nigger'.

Selous had none of the spiritual egalitarianism that he had once so admired in Livingstone; as we have seen, his view of Christian proselytizing was jaundiced. But he should be seen, according to that well-worn but apt phrase, in the context of his time, one in which radical liberalism was not uncommon in London drawing rooms, but was rarely expressed around the campfires of the Interior. Even the devout missionary Robert Moffat once said that 'in the natives of South Africa there is nothing naturally engaging; their extreme selfishness, filthiness, obstinate stupidity and want of sensibility have a tendency to disgust.'

Selous's own views were often contradictory. He could speak of 'filthy, soulless, sordid, mean and vermin-swarming savages' in virtually the same breath as 'a good, brave, honest, heathen gentle-man'. Overall, he thought 'certain kaffirs are better men than certain white men [although] the fact remains that as a whole the kaffirs are an inferior people.' All men, however, he thought were entitled to fair treatment and consideration. Africans were 'responsive to kindness and of cheerful disposition'.

Benevolent paternalism this might have been, but in the region, and at that time, such opinions were relatively advanced. Towards the end of his life he remarked: 'Whenever I was told, as I often was in South Africa, that all natives were black brutes who could not understand kindness and were incapable of gratitude, I always knew the masterful gentleman or fair lady who was speaking to me had no kindness in their own natures, and that never in all their lives had they given any native the slightest reason to be grateful to them.'

It is also worth noting that Selous was among the few early visitors to the Interior who correctly attributed the ancient ruins of Great Zimbabwe in Mashonaland to the indigenous people. The view was widespread that such fine stonework could not possibly have been executed by 'savages', and the claim in 1895 by one early scholar, J. Theodore Bent in his book *The Ruined Cities of Mashonaland*, that Zimbabwe was built by settlers from Arabia, was accepted by those with a prejudiced axe to grind until the 1970s, long after it had been disproved by scientific evidence. Selous thought Bent's thesis absurd and maintained, rightly, that Zimbabwe had been built by the Mashona, a people for whom he came to have an abiding affection.

Individual Africans whom he held in high esteem included the pro-British chief Khama, to whom he ascribed personal nobility as well as greatness as a ruler, and whose assistance to Rhodes during the settlement of Mashonaland he felt was shamefully overlooked.

At the same time, he was ever mistrustful of what he termed 'kaffir information'. He cited a case of being assured by a Mashona chief that there were no tsetse fly in his country, only to immediately find fly on his livestock: 'That is the character of the untutored savage. Without malice prepense, but just through carelessness, ignorance or cussedness, he will do you an irreparable injury, or, at any rate, allow you to do yourself one, and remain all the time perfectly unconcerned either at his fault or your misfortune.'

There is no record of what blacks thought of him, but according to contemporary sources, he was seen as a kindly, fair employer, and was at least as highly regarded for his generosity as a food-giver. It has already been recorded that, when hunting, he kept the people in the area supplied with meat, and his camp functioned as a soup-kitchen, with a large cauldron permanently on the fire, available to all.

Sexual relations with black women had helped encourage egalitarianism among the old hunters, and by now Selous had almost certainly embarked on the first of the two long-term relationships that he formed with women. The second was with Gladys Maddy, who he married in 1894. The first was with an unknown African woman, probably from Khama's court, who lived with Selous for some years and bore him at least two children.

This relationship was clearly important to Selous. The woman accompanied him on most of his travels in the years ahead, and was a companion at the fireside as well as a bed partner. Furthermore, Selous was fond enough of the children to hope that they might stay with him when the relationship ended.

It needs to be admitted, however, that little is known about the most fundamental aspects of the affair. Who was the woman, for a start? What became of her when Selous cast her off, as he did six years later? What happened to their children? There is simply no information to answer these questions.

This shortage of evidence is not entirely accidental. Although Selous made no secret of the relationship, and it was well known in the Interior, documents referring to it were tampered with or destroyed for the purpose of concealment. One such was a letter, intended by Selous as a last will, which he sent to the Klerksdorp trader, Thomas Leask, in 1890. The letter starts out by requesting that in the event of his death in a possible conflict with the Matabele, Leask should act as his executor. He then instructs that his cash assets should be divided between his sisters. However, at the point in the document where he starts to deal with disposing of the rest of his estate, the letter is torn. It is reasonable to suggest that in the lost section, Selous made provision for his other dependants, his children, and that the letter was mutilated, perhaps by Leask, to conceal their existence.

For years Selous had been travelling over a natural geographic region bound in the south by the Limpopo river, in the north by the Zambesi, in the west by the Kalahari desert and in the east by the highlands of Mozambique. These very frontiers would define the new colony of Rhodesia, but the imperial dream which now started to take shape in his mind concerned only a portion of that territory.

An indigenous civilization, the kingdom of Monomatapa, had flourished from the fifteenth century on the high plateau which rose in the centre of the Interior. The inhabitants spoke a common language, mined gold which they traded with Arab and Portuguese travellers, and produced one major cultural landmark, the ruins of Great Zimbabwe. By the time Englishmen arrived on the scene, however, these people, the so-called Mashona tribes, were in a pitiful state.

It was not just the normal process of degeneration that had reduced them to the 'abject, broken people' found by Livingstone and others, but the arrival of the Matabele from the south in about 1840. Having established themselves to the west of the plateau, the Matabele sallied out with their short assegais and long shields in raiding parties that were as avid in the pursuit of slaughter as of plunder. The peaceful Mashona were convenient and vulnerable prey. Matabele hegemony was extended eastwards over the plateau, and tribute exacted from those Mashona vassals fortunate enough to escape with their lives. Just how far east this control extended would become a thorny geopolitical issue during the colonial 'scramble'. So far as Lobengula was concerned, the entire plateau was within his domain. His impis could range over the Mashona country unopposed.

It was on the Mashonaland plateau that Selous was now spending most of his time, and the observations he made here were no longer those of a mere sportsman. In 1882 and 1883, he travelled into the unmapped territory beyond the Hunyani river, noting the balmy climate and plentiful supply of water, the fertile soil and the gentle nature of the people. He found that they were unburdened by guilt, or fear of malicious spirits, and decided that he liked them 'better than any other African tribe with which I have come in contact':

> They seem to have but little of the ferocity which usually forms so marked a feature in the character of uncivilized races, and in their inter-tribal quarrels blood is seldom shed ... Even in cases where a man is believed to be guilty of witchcraft he is not killed but merely banished from his tribe, his property of course being confiscated.

Travel in Mashonaland also brought him face to face with the consequences of Matabele raiding. The prosperous settlements through which he passed one season might by the next have been razed, their inhabitants slaughtered and scattered. Mashona chiefs whom he came to know and like, such as Chameluga, the wizard king of Situngweesa, and Lomagondi, were being killed by the marauding hordes. The brutality and militarism of the Matabele had always repelled him, but his antipathy was turning to something harder.

Somewhere in the course of these journeys, the simple adventurer, content to wander the bush on horseback with a gun, became something more – if not an architect, then certainly a promoter of British expansionism. The early advocacy by Selous of the occupation of Mashonaland is often overlooked by Rhodesian historians in favour of his role as the man of action in carrying it out. It was, however, a positive factor in opening up the Interior.

Selous it was who, early in the 1880s, took down to Kimberley a few quills of gold obtained in Mashonaland, and showed them to Cecil Rhodes, recently elected an MP in the Cape parliament, stimulating his interest in northern expansion. At the same time, Selous was lifting the veil over Mashonaland to his fellow countrymen. By 1880 the Royal Geographical Society had started publishing his despatches and maps in its proceedings. In that year he had sent a sketch map of Mashonaland to the RGS, naming one landmark Mount Hampden after John Hampden, 'who gave his life in defence of the liberties of his countrymen in those evil days when the second prince of the House of Stewart reigned'. Selous's explorations beyond the Hunyani river in 1882 enabled him to fill in blanks on his earlier map of Mashonaland, and it was in recognition of this work, and his map-making north of the Zambesi and around the Chobe, that the RGS made him the recipient of the Cuthbert Peek Award in 1883. Encouraged to continue his travels in Mashonaland, Selous wrote to the RGS in 1884 describing a tract of high country between the Hunyani and Mazoe rivers as the best-suited to European occupation in the whole of Southern Africa: 'The very best parts of the Transvaal are not to be compared to it; it is splendidly watered, droughts and famines are unknown, and nowhere do the natives get such abundant and diversified crops as here.'

A few years later he would guide a column of pioneer settlers to this same area, where the British flag was raised at Fort Salisbury.

Exploration may have been satisfying but it did not pay the interest on his debt to Leask. Throughout this time, Selous was under pressure to secure wildlife specimens for Gunther and the South African Museum in Cape Town, which had also given him commissions. It was, if his letters to Gunther are to be believed, a constant strain to meet his obligations, and he was becoming obsessed with his financial situation. 'My outfit came to about 900 pounds of which I paid about 400 pounds down, getting the rest on credit,' he wrote to Gunther from Mashonaland in August 1882. He had not seen so much as the spoor of an elephant for two months, while paying 9 per cent on his loan, and had just lost livestock worth £100. The following February he sent Gunther an account for £165 for ten skulls and skins, while emphasizing the difficulties that had been involved in obtaining them – 'I have brought them 1000 miles in an ox wagon and they must go another 250 miles to the Natal coast' – and again fretting about his debt. Matters would get worse still.

He had become isolated from his own kind. Travelling in remote country meant he spent long stretches on end with no more than a small following of Africans. Sometimes he went six months without seeing a white man or speaking English. Occasionally there were chance meetings, like the one with a trader named Frank Watson who was taking supplies up to George Westbeech on the Zambesi. Selous's description is an engaging picture of an encounter between Englishmen abroad.

How inexpressibly delightful are such meetings in the wilderness, and how different the conduct of two English-men to one another on such occasions from the Continental idea, as expressed in caricatures! Watson offered to broach a case of brandy, in the old interior style, and the orthodox thing to have done would have been for us to have remained until the case was finished – and a day or two longer to recover from the effects of it. However, as I am practically a total abstainer, and knew too that poor George Westbeech wanted all the brandy he could get to help him withstand the deadly climate of the Zambesi, I would not consent to my friend's proposition; so we only had a friendly chat over numerous cups of tea, and exchanged news.

By now most of his closest friends had gone. Clarkson and French, of course, were dead. George Wood, the Yorkshireman who had been his first partner, had also taken one risk too many. With his new wife and their baby, he had ventured into the fever-ridden Barotse valley in 1882; one by one the Woods were stricken by malaria, and a retreat to higher ground was made too late. They were wiped out. Another old comrade, George Dorehill, was also to die soon of malaria.

One of the few new friends Selous made was an Afrikaner. Cornelius van Rooyen, the son of a Tati trader, was actually held by some contemporaries to have been the better hunter. Certainly,

Selous held him in the highest regard, both for his hunting prowess and as a companion. The esteem was reciprocated. Another hunting friend, H. A. Bryden, relates that the Afrikaner, himself as tough as biltong, once shook his head in wonderment at some feat of endurance and said, 'Ag, Selous! That is a man. He has a heart of iron.' This friendship helped break down the last of Selous's anti-Boer prejudices.

Despite his admitted loneliness, he was now quite content among Africans. He would never 'go native' to the same extent that George Wood had, but he had his woman and a companionable party of six or seven men. When they sheltered in a skerm at night there were no racial barriers. He was not troubled by solitude, being self-sufficient with his specimens and continuing studies of natural history. On days when he longed for the company of a fellow Englishman, he would stretch out under a msasa tree with his favourite Thackeray and be transported to the world of *Vanity Fair*.

His entourage was small, consisting of three Mashonas, two Bakwena and two Matabele, and a youngster named Laer – a half Griqua, half Bushman with an astonishing talent for tracking, who, although only a teenager, soon became Selous's closest companion. In addition to an animal-like instinct for tracking, which came from his Bushman heritage, Laer had a happy knack for turning up lions.

The animals for which Selous had museum commissions were mainly antelope – Lichtenstein's hartebeest, tsessebe and eland – but once again it was the lion which added incident, and the occasional heart-stopping moment, to life. On one occasion, Selous and Laer brought a lion to bay. Despite being wounded, the animal came at them at the charge. Both wheeled their horses to escape, but Laer's mount shied, throwing him into the lion's path. He stood, frozen with fear, and unable to flee because a thong from his waist tied him to the horse. It was not resolved whether the lion would have taken the man or the horse, as Selous, who had seen Laer's fall and reined in, put a bullet clean through its right eye at forty yards.

Another time, his aim at a big male lion was less sure. Having snapped off a shot which missed altogether, he found the brute charging him with open mouth and flaming eyes, growling savagely.

There was no time to reload or escape. He held his ground with the vague idea of trying to force his rifle into the lion's mouth. It came to him then that he would at last be able to test for himself the assertion by Livingstone that had always fascinated him – that a lion's victim feels no pain. When the beast was only six yards off, it veered away.

Hunting of a different sort ruptured the amity and trust of Selous's dealings with Lobengula in December 1883. What was ever known in the Interior as the 'Sea-Cow Row' contained elements of high farce; but the affair was symbolic of the rising Matabele antagonism in Bulawayo towards outsiders, and the friendship between king and hunter would never be the same again.

Signs of frustration were already evident when Selous got back to Gubulawayo at the end of the hunting season. The Matabele were in ugly mood after an ill-conceived raid against the Batauwani people of Lake Ngami, in which the spoils failed to match the effort of an 800-mile round trip.

Lobengula's humour had been further soured by flagrant violation of a royal edict forbidding indiscriminate killing of hippopotamuses. The Matabele believed that a slaughter of the great sea-cows would provoke a drought, and hunters and traders had to give an undertaking not to kill these animals without the king's permission. By and large the order was obeyed, but that year a trader named McMenemy unleashed carnage on the hippopotamus population by undertaking to buy as much of the supple hide of these creatures as he could obtain. It is unlikely that Selous was involved in this enterprise, but one of his wagon-drivers, a Griqua named John Slaipstein, did shoot one hippo for meat.

At first there was no hint of trouble. The royal welcome was warm, and news was ritually exchanged before Lobengula even touched on his anger at the hippopotamus slaughter. Selous sympathized, and, in order to leave no room for misunderstanding, mentioned that one of his party had killed a hippo for the pot. 'That's nothing,' the king assured him. 'There's no case against you.'

A few days later, however, Selous was summoned back to the royal kraal. The indunas, who for some time had been agitating against whites, had persuaded or coerced Lobengula to charge Selous, along with two other hunters named Oosthuizen and Grant, and McMenemy. They were to be tried for killing the king's sea-cows.

It was a scene which belongs more in the pages of a boy's adventure yarn than real life: the black potentate, able to order a man's death with a click of his fingers, looking down on the hapless white hunters who had incurred his wrath.

But their plight was real enough. The mood of the indunas was aggressive and volatile, and for three days the accused were hectored constantly. One witness was Ralph Williams, an adventurous young Englishman, who had been drawn to Matabeleland by Selous's book, *A Hunter's Wanderings*, and brought with him his wife and seven-year-old son. He was alarmed by the atmosphere in Gubulawayo and, unable to leave, passed Christmas in a fever of anxiety.

Ominously, allegations of witchcraft were made against Selous. An induna named Makwaykwi, who had been friendly in the past, now denounced him, demanding that he bring back to life the elephant and buffalo he had killed. When Selous, himself roused to fury, glowered at his accusers one induna jumped up, shouting: 'I will tear those eyes out of your head, and throw them on the ground and stamp on them.'

There was no defence. For all his indignation, Selous was compelled to admit that his man had killed a hippopotamus. Finally, Lobengula gave his judgment. Selous would pay compensation of ten cattle, worth £60, while McMenemy, the worst offender, was ordered to pay fifty cattle.

In retrospect, the Sea-Cow Row benefited rather than damaged the cause of the hunters and traders, by purging for a while the anti-white sentiment among the indunas. Antagonism had been rising and needed an outlet if it was not to boil over with potentially catastrophic consequences. Lobengula, although he may not have engineered the affair, had been quick to see and exploit the possibilities. Giving the indunas their scapegoats once more postponed the evil day when he would not be able to stop a dam-burst of violence against the whites.

The pity is that Selous himself did not read the situation better. Imagination had never been his strong suit, and he was quite unable to comprehend the pressures on Lobengula, or to appreciate the subtlety with which the king kept these forces in check. All he saw was the wrong done him, the affront to his dignity. The friendship he regarded as irreparably ruptured. His own account of the affair is more concerned with showing that he comported himself with the disdain demanded of an Englishman at the mercy of capricious savages, than in considering the substance of the case.

A year later he still nursed a grievance, and told the king so. Lobengula merely shrugged. 'Hauw! That case is finished, dead. What is the use of thinking about it? Go and hunt nicely until your heart is white.'

It was good advice, but Selous failed to heed it. A poisonous seed had been planted.

CHAPTER NINE

Enemy of the Matabele

Gold fever, triggered by fanciful talk that 'Ophir's treasure' was to be found within his dominions, had been a perennial source of irritation to Lobengula. However, a firm hand with would-be prospectors, and the failure of the one established digging in the Interior, at Tati, kept external pressure under control until the middle of the 1880s. At that point, two forces, each vital in its own way, combined to start the rumblings of an avalanche that would eventually sweep Lobengula away.

The first was the climax to the Scramble for Africa, in which the greed of European powers for colonies was stoked by their rivalries. For most of the era it appeared that Britain had been left a free hand in Southern Africa, as, with Portuguese ambition moribund, no other European power seemed in a position to mount a challenge. Then suddenly, in 1883, in an initiative that took all Europe aback, the German flag was raised on the Atlantic coast at the edge of the South-West African desert.

The second development was less overtly dramatic but, in the end, even more significant, and it ensured that the stakes in Southern Africa would be high indeed. In the Transvaal in 1886, at first gradually, but then spectacularly, the Reefs of the White Waters, the Witwatersrand, gave up their secret. Real gold fever, compelling and consuming, broke out. Nothing in Southern Africa would ever be the same again.

Concern in Whitehall about Bismarck's flanking movement in South-West Africa was not based on the intrinsic worth of the territory itself, but in the potential it presented for an anti-British alliance. A linking of hands between the Germans in the west and the Boers in the Transvaal, would sever the Missionary Road from the Cape to the Interior, and strangle any possibility of British expansion. Rhodes – by now enunciating his vision of a map of Africa painted pink from the Cape to Cairo – declaimed vehemently on the need to protect the Missionary Road, 'the Suez Canal to the Interior'. The point was taken in Westminster. A military force under Sir Charles Warren was despatched to annex the southern part of Bechuanaland. Rhodes relaxed briefly. The road to the Interior was secure.

Meanwhile, Selous was continuing to suffer from financial troubles which were becoming chronic. The rewards of specimen hunting often did not cover outgoings, and his debt to Leask was increasing. In 1884 he was out of action for two months of the season after breaking his collar-bone in a riding accident. The following year he was complaining to Gunther that the struggle for existence did not permit him to neglect any chance to earn an honest penny. Later he apologized for harping on about money, but added: 'I am now getting so deeply into debt that I do not know how I am going to extricate myself. During the last four years I have led a very hard life and certainly a very frugal one, yet instead of making anything by my collecting I have lost the 400 pounds I brought with me.'

Another letter, to Leask, discloses that his original debt of £500 had mounted to almost £750, while his earnings for a year were around £300. Money worries were driving him to do things in which he could have taken no pride – such as hunting the sad, clumsy rhinoceros. Demand in the Far East for rhino horn, because of its supposed aphrodisiacal properties, had boosted the price to four shillings a pound. In later life Selous became a vigorous supporter of the embryonic conservation movement, and argued eloquently for legislation to protect such species as rhinoceros and elephant. He may then have reflected guiltily that in the year 1885 he had sold 570 pounds of rhinoceros horn to Leask. Much of this he had obtained from African hunters, but it was an unworthy trade and shows how desperate he was.

Melancholia surfaced again. A letter to his mother shows the spiritual confusion that lay near the uncomplicated exterior of his personality:

At present I believe nothing, but am inclined towards

119

materialism, but at the same time I do not believe everything, and am in a state of doubt. If I felt sure – quite sure – that I was merely material, I think I should before long take a good dose of laudanum and stop the working of my inward mechanism, for life, on the whole, is a failure – to me, at any rate – who, I think, am naturally of a rather sad turn of mind, though I can quite understand it being very different to sanguine hopeful people. However, as I feel doubtful on the subject, I certainly shall not have recourse to violent measures but shall protect my vital spark as long as I can.

Family troubles may have contributed to his gloom. He had just been visited by his younger brother Edmund, and it had not been a success. Family history suggests that during his stay the brothers had a serious quarrel, although the cause is not known. It may be that Edmund objected to his brother living with, and having children by, a black woman; or that the source of tension was Edmund's impending marriage to Fred's former flame, Fanny Maxwell. Whatever the reason, or combination of reasons, it is clear that the brothers were not afterwards close. They corresponded hardly at all, and had little contact in later life, even though the study of nature was a driving force in both.

Edmund was, in fact, the superior naturalist. Although he never approached his brother's fame, and is now almost forgotten, Edmund Selous was the most influential writer on birdlife of his generation. Schoolboys were given his books to encourage interest in the wild creatures of the English countryside and his observations on birds' sexual habits broke new ground. Julian Huxley was an early admirer, while H. J. Massingham, another expert, described him as 'the greatest field-detective in the habits of wild birds who has ever lived'.

Gold fever brought newcomers rushing to the Interior, like boys to a playground brawl. They came to Gubulawayo clamouring for concessions, but while Lobengula presented a genial countenance – and contentedly pocketed the payments and gifts pressed on him by petitioners – they came away empty-handed.

The changing times brought a new breed of whites. Brash and

ruthless, they had, in many cases, as little respect for the old timers, with their generosity and easy-going, if dissolute, ways, as they had for blacks. They had no interest in the land, its people or their traditions. They were gamblers, scenting the big break. Characteristic of the type were four young fellows who arrived in Gubulawayo in May 1887. Frank Johnson, Maurice Heany, Henry Borrow and Ted Burnett had all been members of General Warren's force in Bechuanaland. Each of these men has a place in Rhodesian history, and for years their fortunes would be interwoven with those of Selous.

They were an eclectic band. Unquestionably the leader, Frank Johnson was aged only twenty-one, a squat, dark man with an ugly temper and enormous vigour, who had grown up in King's Lynn, home town of a great African explorer and artist, Thomas Baines. Maurice Heany, an American who had deserted from the military academy at West Point, was, at thirty or so, the oldest of the group, with a shock of red hair and a lean figure which gave him the appearance of a man of action. He was also probably the shrewdest. Borrow was a good-looking English public schoolboy of twenty-two and, until he was possessed by avarice, a charming and eager cavalier. Burnett lived in Johnson's shadow, a willing and obedient lieutenant; like Borrow, he would be killed in the first of the Matabele wars.

Borrow wrote home about his first view of Lobengula:

> The king is a gross fat man of about 50 with a remarkably stern face, though when he smiles he is rather pleasant looking. Whenever he gets up to go anywhere all the people around crouch and get out of his way saying 'Heugh! Oh you black elephant! Son of a black bull!' and other pleasing idioms.
>
> On visiting the king meat and beer are set before you, and you eat until you feel like a well-blown football, but must keep on until all that has been set before you is finished, or it is considered bad form. It is then particularly good etiquette to belch for five minutes or so to show you have fed well off the king's country.

Soon after the arrival of Johnson, Heany, Borrow and Burnett, a welcoming party was thrown by the gregarious George Phillips, whom Borrow described as 'a great big burly man, a sort of court attache'. All the Gubulawayo whites attended. Great joints of meat and wildfowl were washed down by gallons of native beer and topped off with a lethal mixture which Phillips called 'snake punch'. This was made from a spirit which Selous had brought for pickling snakes, but which, after the addition of a few local ingredients, Henry Collison pronounced perfectly potable. The fact that Collison was known as one who would drink anything dissuaded few from tackling the brew with relish, and it disappeared rapidly. A grand bash ended when a German trader took exception to Phillips singing 'Rule Britannia'. The guests lurched off to their tents and wagons, leaving Phillips on his knees, kissing the Union Jack.

Johnson and his friends had a letter showing them to be agents of the Great Northern Gold Fields Exploration Company, and arrived at Gubulawayo assuming, like others before them, that obtaining permission to prospect would be little more than a formality. Over the copious royal feasts, Johnson noted the gifts made to Lobengula by previous supplicants – crates of champagne, a barrel organ, binoculars and rifles. Johnson was willing to make his contribution too, and promised to bring a balloon and a toy boat on his next visit.

But at any mention of concessions, Lobengula prevaricated. He pointed to the one concession he had ever granted in Mashonaland – that to Thomas Baines almost twenty years ago. Look, Lobengula said, there was evidence that there was no gold in his country. Johnson retorted that all he wanted was permission to see for himself. Ah, replied Lobengula, but what if he and his friends became sick and died? Surely Johnson could see that this might bring trouble to the Matabele from other white men.

Summoned to put his case to the indunas, Johnson was asked how he knew about the gold. Through Baines, he said. Why then had Johnson not brought Baines with him, they wanted to know. Because Baines was dead. Indeed? And how long had he been dead? For eighteen years, Johnson replied. So why, if there was gold in the ground had he waited eighteen years to come? Well, because he had only just heard Baines's word. But how was it possible to hear the word of a man who had been dead for eighteen years? And so it went on. Like many Asian peoples, the Matabele had evolved a way of refusing, not by saying no but by avoiding an answer, which many Europeans mistook for evidence of obtuseness.

It was testimony to Johnson's determination that he did not, like most others, depart in defeated exasperation. After almost two months, even Logenbula's resistance was buckling, and finally he gave in. Precisely what terms he granted it is not possible to say, for there was no written agreement. But it does seem that he 'gave the road' to Johnson in circumstances in which some form of prospecting was implicit.

Visions of wealth swam in Johnson's head. Only one other white had been allowed into Mashonaland that year, and that was Selous. Although Johnson had only heard of the hunter, it was known that he had no interest in gold, and was acting as guide to a trio of sportsmen. Johnson and Burnett would follow them, heading for the Mazoe river. In July 1887 they set out with an escort of twenty-one warriors, whose orders from Lobengula may have had less to do with protecting the white men than keeping a sharp eye on them.

The commission Selous received that year must have seemed a windfall at first. Three wealthy Englishmen wanted a guide for a hunting trip in Mashonaland. They were J. A. Jameson, brother of Selous's old friend, James, and also a whisky heir, Captain A. C. Fountaine, master of the Prince of Wales's foxhounds, and Frank Cooper, a landowner. Selous would be all-found for the year, at the least.

The evident importance of these visitors impressed Lobengula, but he may have been suspicious of their intentions from the outset. Obviously wealthy, and bringing a retinue of servants, they were very different to most of the white visitors who came to Gubulawayo. Selous's good offices were sufficient to obtain hunting permission for Mashonaland, but when the party left it was with an even larger escort than Johnson's – about 150 warriors.

The events of the next few months brought the Selous and Johnson groups together, and came to a bloody climax on the Mashonaland plateau. This episode has been smothered in secrecy ever since, and some speculation has been necessary in the following account. There can be no doubt, however, of the events themselves, or that they caused Selous's final breach with Lobengula.

Once on his way, Johnson's patience with African ways was quickly exhausted. He decided that the headman of his escort, an elderly warrior named Machesa, had 'a big idea of his own importance and a determination to be awkward'. Johnson had little subtlety in dealing with dark races. He was, in fact, rather proud in later life of a bit of doggerel relating to his part in suppressing a Punjab uprising in 1919. It went in part:

> You do not say, 'Oh, dearie dear,'
> When handing out a big thick ear.
> Or, 'Oh, babu! How you vex us,'
> When striking at the solar plexus.
> Nor do you bale out reams of law
> When plugging someone on the jaw.

Manners like these were bound to provoke the Matabele, and Johnson's escort soon became ugly-tempered and rebellious. Matters came to a head when, according to Johnson, a number of men 'cocked their muskets at us, flourished their assegais and did a wild war-dance, calling us slaves and swearing that we would all be killed before sundown'.

Johnson was enraged, but a diary entry discloses his impotence to deal with the warriors as he would have wished: 'Oh ye spirits of departed negrophilists and follows of Exeter Hall if only you could feel what is felt by us today, at the knowledge that we white men and Englishmen too, are under the thumb and utterly in the power of a lot of black scoundrels there is little doubt that your brotherly love for niggars [sic] would receive a serious check!! Brothers indeed! Damned scoundrels!!'

It so happened that Selous and his party were in the same area, near the Umfule river. When Jameson, Fountaine and Cooper heard that an Englishman was being subjected to humiliating treatment by natives, they were all for charging down on the Matabele, killing them and then making for the Zambesi. Selous, horrified by the suggestion, was in a very uncomfortable position and managed to restrain them only with the greatest difficulty; so he later told Johnson's partner, Henry Borrow.

The next day he rode over to Johnson's camp, and heard his account of events. No doubt Selous felt constrained, amid demands from his impetuous clients to put the savages in their place, to take Johnson's part and assert his influence with the king. But the way in which he did so was ill-considered.

He wrote a letter which started 'To Lo Beng-oola, Chief of the thrice accursed tribe of the Amandebele', and went on:

> I ask you to remember that [Johnson and Burnett] are men of consideration in their own country and not dogs to be barked at and annoyed by any maholie [slave] who chooses to tell you lies about them. You are ready to believe any lies your accursed God forgotten Hell begotten slaves choose to tell you. The hearts of my friends are very black and they are very sorry they came to your country.

The letter was sent to Gubulawayo by messenger.

Although still furious, Johnson's escort offered no further danger, and the two parties went their own ways. The parting may not have been on the happiest terms, however. Johnson was inordinately sensitive to any slight. He had bitterly resented not only his humiliation at black hands, but having been rescued by Selous. He later told his friends a fanciful story that he had starved the mutinous escort into submission. Far from expressing any gratitude towards Selous, he seems to have conceived an early animosity for the older man. Notwithstanding a brief and ill-conceived partnership a year later, this would fester over the years until it became something akin to hatred. As we shall see, if ever Selous had an enemy it was Sir Frank Johnson.

Hardly had the trouble with his escort been resolved than Johnson received a message from Lobengula abrogating permission to prospect. But Johnson felt himself too close to Ophir's treasure to turn back, and in defiance of the king's orders he crossed the Umfule river and started to pan for gold along the Mazoe.

Selous, meanwhile, forged on with his companions. Having put out of their minds the recent unpleasantness, they were delighted with African sport. A dozen lions fell to their rifles. And, on a gallop with which Fountaine must have regaled his friends on the Prince of Wales's hunt for years afterwards, they brought to bay a cheetah, the fastest of all land animals.

The tragedy was that Johnson's gold fever had proved infectious.

At some point Selous's caravan left the usual hunting grounds and went beyond the Umfule, to Baines's old gold working around Hartley. Here, two of the party, Fountaine and Cooper, collected some mineral samples. Probably it was only idle curiosity that prompted them, but Selous knew how imprudent was any dabbling with minerals, and should have stopped it immediately.

What followed is described in a report in the *Transvaal Advertiser* of 22 November 1887. Under the headline 'The slaughter in Matabeleland' it reads:

> The Bamangwato correspondent of the Standard gives the following particulars of the slaughter of 150 Matabele sent as an escort to a hunting party. It was stated in the telegram that 900 men had been slain by order of Lo Bengulo, but it appears from the following statement that the report was exaggerated. The case, as it stands, is bad enough, and the attention of the British Government should be called to it, inasmuch as British subjects were apparently the primary cause of the terrible catastrophe.

What had happened, according to the correspondent, was that the king had been told by an emissary about the prospecting activities of Fountaine and Cooper, and promptly despatched one of his regiments to exact retribution – not from the offending whites, but from the accompanying escort which had failed to stop them. The reporter had a big story, and he told it vividly:

> In due time the regiment overtook the hunting party. Without more ado, the fearful slaughter commenced, close to Selous's wagons. Not a single man of the transgressing party uttered a cry, but accepted his fate unmurmuringly, with Stoic calmness. Two spear thrusts in the body and the blow on the head from a kerrie, and all was over. In this manner 150 Matabele subjects, of splendid physique, received their quietus, and crossed the Stygian ferry to that happy hunting ground.
>
> It can be imagined that the white hunters were, as far as they knew to the contrary, in a nice quandary, although assured by Selous that no harm would come to them per-

126

sonally. They had, however, to witness the cold-blooded butchery of their late dark-skinned hunting companions – a sickening sight which they were only too glad to trek away from, leaving the bodies to be devoured by the wild beasts and carrion.

The publication of this report caused a minor sensation in the Interior, and Maurice Heany, the West Point deserter now established at Bamangwato, wrote: 'Everyone here much excited . . . Whoever the writer is he knows much of our business and is very mischief making and I should dearly like the job of kicking him.'

Clearly, Lobengula had intended making a point. Yet the cynicism with which he was able to weigh the balance of black and white lives became apparent soon afterwards, when Johnson returned to Gubulawayo. If anyone had invited retribution it was he, who had openly defied the king's order to stop prospecting. But after the furore of a show trial by the indunas which lasted for two days, he was fined £300, later reduced to £100, and ordered to leave the country. He did so, nurturing designs for revenge.

Perhaps, in the circumstances, it was not surprising that whites also held black lives cheaply. There was no wider reaction to the atrocity, even though, as the newspaper pointed out, British subjects were partly responsible. The affair seems to have been quickly forgotten, and is not mentioned in any of the standard works of the period. The British authorities seem to have taken no interest in it. In any event, there was no inquiry.

On the surface, the episode had served as a barbarous reminder of Lobengula's authority. The real significance, however, was in the effect it had on the Matabele themselves. The sudden outside interest in what they regarded as their territory, brought home to the indunas the peril which lay to the south. More and more, their fears concerned an invasion by a white impi. The upshot was that Lobengula closed Mashonaland to whites, once and for all. Henceforth, until the occupation took place three years later, in 1890, the only way they could reach Mashonaland was from the Portuguese-controlled east coast. That did nothing to discourage concession-seekers, however, who continued to wend their way up the Missionary Road to importune Lobengula with ever more extravagant offers.

The experience had been a watershed for Selous too. What passed between him and the king when he got back to Gubulawayo can only be guessed at. From this point, however, they were on opposing sides, and Matabele power was synonymous in the Englishman's mind with a diabolical force which, sooner or later, would have to be confronted. If it should be by his fellow countrymen, so much the better. Borrow, who met Selous soon afterwards, remarked: 'He hates this nation most cordially.'

It is not possible to say whether he felt any guilt, or whether he should have. In retrospect it is easy to blame such an incident on the blundering and greed of the invaders, and to forget the cruelty of the perpetrators. Nevertheless, Selous's judgment had been poor throughout the affair, and he knew it reflected no credit on him. He never mentioned it, and in his subsequent writings almost entirely glossed over the hunting trip of 1887.

After this trauma, Selous planned a new trip as far away as possible from Lobengula's lands. However, peril and misfortune were to follow him north of the Zambesi, where he now turned.

There was something ill-fated about Selous's journeys to the Mushukulumbwe country, where, for him, adversity recurred as surely as the rainy season. Each time he ventured there he only just emerged with his life, and, with it all, poorer than before. It had happened on his expedition with Owen, and it would happen again now. A critical analysis might even conclude that these journeys exposed Selous's limitations as an African traveller, that he was undermined by his own haphazard planning and an over-sanguine attitude to wandering in *terra incognita*. But the 1888 journey to the Mushukulumbwe country was, by any measure, bizarre. The dark star which Selous had come to suspect influenced his affairs was never more evident than in this journey into what is now Zambia.

Early that year of 1888, Selous was in the western Transvaal, probably in the town of Zeerust, among the family of the Reverend Thomas Morgan Thomas, who had been a missionary at the London Missionary Society station at Inyati. Thomas had died four years earlier. He had not been long survived by his son, David, a friend of Selous's, who, aged only twenty-six, had been killed in 1886 by a hostile tribe on the Zambesi. It seems that now, when

Selous announced he was about to start for the same region, a sister of David Thomas suggested that they try to receive a message from him from 'the other side'. What followed, Selous later described to a journalist who repeated the story:

> He [Selous] took a pencil in his hand and took up a position to write. [Miss Thomas] then placed her hand lightly upon the back of his fingers. Almost immediately the pencil began to write. Mr Selous is quite convinced that he had no idea what letters were being formed but purposely turned away his head. The message ran as follows: 'David Thomas. Selous, go out of the country.' After reading this Mr Selous asked 'Why?' His hand wrote: 'Because you will be murdered.' Then it stopped. Presently it began again and wrote, 'Because you will be murdered by the natives.'

This statement was apparently repeated twice more. But the materialist Selous was at this stage still not much susceptible to demonstrations of psychic phenomena, and ignored the warnings. He proceeded from the Transvaal to Bamangwato. Here it was that the break occurred with the woman who had shared his life for some years.

It appears that she was reluctant to accompany him on this new journey, although for what reason is not clear. Selous, anyway, seems to have been tiring of her and used this as an excuse to dismiss her in accordance with African custom. The end of the relationship was signalled in a letter from Heany to James Dawson, a trader at Gubulawayo, in March:

> Selous got into Shoshong [Bamangwato] on the 27th inst. He brought his woman down with him and means to get rid of her. She did not care to go into Zambesi and he did not press her. He keeps the children. While at Shoshong he messed with Borrow and I, and we saw much of him. He is a grand fellow in every respect.

Once again it is necessary to acknowledge how little is known about Selous's lost family. It would seem that the children, presumably two boys, may have stayed in his care for the time being. There is a reference by a contemporary source, Adrian Darter, to 'Jan

Selous, a Mangwato boy, who had been with the hunter for many years and could not be induced to leave his master'. Was he more? Selous himself refers in one of his books to one of the constant members of his party as 'my boy John'. All we can say with certainty is that no children accompanied Selous when he eventually returned to Britain. In all probability his offspring joined the quite substantial mixed-race community, the so-called Coloureds, formed by liaisons across the colour line in the pioneering days and shunned as a guilty legacy by the white society of Rhodesia.*

Selous left Bamangwato in April with a mixed bag of companions, including two Mashonas, a Zulu and a Hottentot. Porters would be hired along the way, but the principal burden for a round trip of more than 1500 miles was to be borne by donkeys, the pack animal best suited to survive in tsetse-fly country. In addition to his guns and volumes by Thackeray, Byron, Dickens and Hardy, he took a small net which greatly puzzled his men. At the age of thirty-six, Selous had started collecting butterflies again.

The first of his objectives that year was the new mission station established by Frederick Arnot of the Plymouth Brethren in Garanganze, west of Lake Bengweolo, an area better known today as Katanga. It was more than 700 miles away, but Arnot, with whom Selous had previously struck up a warm friendship, had sent word that elephant were still common in Garanganze, and invited him to make a visit. This message was relayed by George Westbeech at Pandamatenga in May. It was Selous's last meeting with the old Zambesi trader. Already a sick man, he had overcome another bout of malaria, but his liver had taken severe punishment from the brandy cask over the years, and in a couple of months this engagingly raffish figure was dead. Ralph Williams, another traveller, wrote an epitaph which might serve for many of what had become a dying

*There is a family living in Harare today who believe they are related to Selous. Mrs Lydia Selous told me in 1984 that her late husband, James John Selous, had been one of the missing children. Mr Selous attended mission schools and became a policeman, then a government storeman, before buying a farm at Ruwa, east of Salisbury. In the capital, he owned a house which he called 'Hunter's Lodge'. But Mr Selous's claim to have ridden as a child with Frederick Courteney Selous on his wanderings cannot be correct. Mr Selous was born in 1900, fully ten years after the end of the relationship between Selous and his African mistress, and four years after he left the country for the last time. It is possible, however, that Mr Selous was a grandson of the hunter.

breed. Westbeech, he said, was 'a man of excellent manners, well educated, and of many cultured qualities. Why or how he came to be there I do not know, remaining thus far away, living the oddest sort of life.'

Selous's party crossed the Zambesi at Wankie in June. Despite his first inclination to shrug off the warning of the psychic handwriting, he now felt oppressed by a sense of foreboding. He later confessed he had never been aware of such a sense before, but so strong was it that for the first time in his life he made a will and sent it to the trader, Leask. Within two days of arriving at the Zambesi, Selous had lost his Hottentot wagon driver, who died of fever, and all the porters, who deserted. Then the party started to encounter large and aggressive Batonga war parties. David Livingstone had despised this river tribe, finding them lacking in 'all self-respect, savage and cruel under success, but easily cowed and devoid of all moral courage'. In a few days Selous lost a substantial portion of his barter goods to extortion. One thing he had learned, however, and that was 'to preserve an outward appearance of equanimity, talk, argue and pay calmly'.

The expedition made its way north over parched and hilly terrain towards the Kafue river. Having veered away from Batonga country, they encountered a party of fifteen hostile Barotse, all armed with guns. These odds were more even, however, and Selous felt able to defy another attempted hold-up. The Barotse retreated threatening to return with reinforcements, saying: 'You will live two days more but on the third day your head will lie in a different place.' The Barotse threat proved to be empty, but at the edge of the Kafue, among the warlike Mushukulumbwe people, Selous met real trouble.

They had arrived at the kraal of a chief named Minenga. The Mushukulumbwe warriors were exotic as well as warlike, being completely naked and with a unique head-dress which involved the wearer's hair being gathered in a conical pile around a long, thin strip of antelope horn. These head-dresses were estimated by Selous to be five feet high in some cases, but despite their fearsome aspect, the warriors showed no initial hostility. Minenga received them quite hospitably, and seemed pleased by a gift of a blanket and calico, and by Selous shooting a zebra for him. Camped near the village, Selous felt that the Mushukulumbwe, 'though wild and savage . . . were easy to deal with if properly treated'.

It was on the second night that he was disabused. He and most of the group were in the rough shelter of a skerm made of branches when one of his men arrived to say all the women had left the village and he feared something was amiss. At this news Selous ordered the fire extinguished. Almost immediately the skerm was surrounded. Attackers sent a volley of shots into the shelter, and assegais rained down. All was chaos and shouting. Selous was unhurt and managed to grab a rifle before retreating through a confused crowd in which it was impossible to distinguish foes from the twenty-five members of his own band. His two headmen, Paul, a Zulu, and Charley, also managed separately to escape to the long grass behind the camp. But of Selous's party, twelve had died in the attack, and six more were wounded.

Hiding in the bush, separated from his companions, the earlier warning came back to Selous. At the same time the horror of his position was brought home to him. He was: 'A solitary Englishman, in the middle of a hostile country, without blankets or anything else but what he stood up in, and a rifle with four cartridges.' There was nothing for it but to turn back for the Zambesi, but he could expect no help before Pandamatenga, more than 300 miles away. Unable even to speak the local tongues, he started to make his way south, guided by the Southern Cross.

The journey was the most perilous of Selous's life. Hunted by the Mushukulumbwe, he swam a crocodile-infested river before coming to a village on the second night of his journey, where he made the mistake of seeking shelter. While he was dozing by a fire, his rifle was stolen from his side. Then he awoke to see a man ten yards away taking aim at him. Selous sprang into the darkness before the shot came, resuming his hike south without his gun, and having only the last of some meat he had shot on the first day.

From village to village, he made his way, never far from enemies, assisted by the goodwill of a few individuals. A week's hard walking brought him back to the relative safety of the Zambesi. Here he met Paul and Charley, and the rest of the survivors, who were delighted to see him, having long since given him up for dead. They too had had their narrow escapes in the pursuit by the Mushukulumbwe.

Three weeks after the attack on the camp, they arrived back at Pandamatenga. It had been another catastrophic venture. Half the party had been wiped out. Selous had lost his entire caravan of donkeys and trading goods, along with four rifles, and all his personal possessions, maps, books and medicines. He had, in the past weeks, suffered fatigue and privation, having slept on the bare ground without blanket or shelter, and gone for days without food. Remarkably, however, he felt in excellent health. His physique was now honed to a spare hardness which could stand up to the severest test.

No less remarkably, his spirit remained undaunted as well. Within a month he had gathered the resources for another trip to the Zambesi. The spur this time was an opportunity to trade with Lewanika, the Barotse king. Since Westbeech's death, no white trader had been willing to brave the turbulent Barotse valley. Westbeech had profited greatly through his dealings with Lewanika, and Selous might have felt there was an opportunity to fill the trader's shoes on the Upper Zambesi.

Over the next three months, he travelled up the river to Lealui and back, a round trip of more than 600 miles. At Sefula, he met the redoubtable François and Christina Coillard of the Paris Missionary Society. It was a remote and desolate spot, and the missionaries had not seen a white man for a year. We can but speculate what passed between these strangers at their sole meeting, but it evidently made a deep impression. Coillard, who spent almost fifty years in Southern Africa, in Basotoland and Barotseland, remaining on the Zambesi through innumerable trials until his death in 1904, was fascinated to hear of the trials that had befallen Selous, and remarked on the magnetism of his personality: 'As he related his adventures, I felt singularly drawn to him. He is a noble character.'

Selous's meeting with Lewanika went well too, and a trade of horses for ivory was accomplished. It seemed inevitable, however, that something would go wrong, and it did. On the way back down the river, a hippopotamus attacked and sank the canoe carrying the ivory, his cartridges and a collection of butterflies. Everything was lost.

The wonder is that by the end of 1888 he did not take his mother's advice, and pack up and try Australia. Heany put it succinctly in a

133

letter to a mutual friend: 'He had a couple of very narrow squeaks of it this year.'

The experiences of 1888 came at the climax of this painful period in Selous's life. It would be a mistake to over-emphasize the reappraisal of his views that had been taking place in this time, though some kind of reappraisal had indeed been stimulated, both by his all-too-frequent brushes with death, and by the encounter with the Thomas family. We know that together these factors afforded a basis for reflection and meditation, for Selous had undoubtedly matured. And just as once he had had no interest in designs other than those of his own making, now he was ready to participate in corporate enterprise on a grand scale. It was almost as if all his years in Africa had been in preparation for just such a role.

PART TWO

1888–1917

CHAPTER TEN

Mr Rhodes

At a luncheon of his British South Africa Company in 1896, Cecil John Rhodes ushered forward a guest. Both men were in their mid-forties, and both had piercing blue eyes. But there similarities ended. Rhodes was almost six feet tall and burly. Although he had no interest in creature comforts and was careless of dress, his heavy jowls and florid complexion marked him out as a heavy eater and drinker. His guest, almost three inches shorter but powerfully built, was a picture of abstemious good health. He had fair hair, starting to recede, and a neatly-trimmed beard of a kind popularized by Queen Victoria's eldest son, Bertie. The guest's manner was shy, even diffident, but his gaze was startlingly direct.

'Let me introduce you to Mr Selous, the man above all others to whom we owe Rhodesia to the British Crown,' Rhodes said.

It was an apt postscript to the era. Over the previous six years, Rhodes and Selous had seen their ambitions for imperial expansion in Southern Africa realized. The designs of Portugal, Germany and the Transvaal had been thwarted. The impis had been crushed in battle, and the tribes of the Interior pacified. British colonists were tilling and mining the territories of Matabeleland and Mashonaland.

Rhodes's tribute to Selous was typical – bold, sweeping and generous. These same characteristics of his had helped advance the frontiers of Empire. Rhodes's magnetism made allies in every quarter: among establishment aristocrats and impoverished wanderers, donnish intellectuals and men of action. His power to inspire others with the scale of his ideas was compelling, but he could work on a small canvas too, conveying not just vision, but intimacy and warmth. Selous was far from being the only sceptic,

137

critic or opponent to have been won over by the sheer force of Cecil Rhodes's personality.

Though both had arrived in Africa as teenagers, Rhodes had left England for reasons quite different from Selous's: he had a cardiac weakness, and doctors believed that even in the clean, high air of one of the colonies he would not survive beyond the age of thirty. In the Diamond Fields, the young Rhodes did a good deal better than that, fossicking profitably while dreaming on an epic scale. While still in his early twenties, Rhodes resolved to devote himself to spreading British civilization. For the rest of his life, he pursued his mission with a fervour which only Livingstone of Englishmen in Southern Africa could be said to have equalled. By the age of twenty-six he had formed De Beers, destined to be the world's greatest diamond company. On this platform of wealth, Rhodes entered the Cape parliament. He would become Prime Minister of the colony at thirty-six, but by then he had already established himself as one of the most influential men in the British colonies, and not long afterwards was sworn in as a member of the Privy Council.

If he was inspired by idealism and moved by nobility, Rhodes nevertheless frequently revealed himself as unscrupulous and cynical, both in business and politics. He was feared as much as he was admired, and mistrusted by almost everyone who knew him by reputation only. Perhaps that had something to do with his awkwardly incongruous personality. The son of a prosperous vicar in Bishop's Stortford, Cecil was more at home in the rough, quirky society of Kimberley than anywhere else. He had considered taking holy orders himself, but relished, to the point of exaggeration, stories of his own ruthlessness in business. He was, as Robert Blake has pointed out, no parvenu. But he was certainly no gentleman either. While he was passionately attached to the idea of Englishness, he resented the time he spent in the mother country. Even in his role as a statesman, there was something seemingly perverse about Rhodes, as he delivered his appeals to the highest spiritual instincts in a squeaky voice and with excited, flapping motions of his hands.

Judged by his record, however, there is no question about Rhodes's stature. In the words of Frank Clements: 'Cecil John Rhodes was an Elizabethan – the endless rolling plains of Africa his sea.'

The decade of British expansion in Central Africa was a cataclysmic era in which much blood, including some of Selous's, was spilt. The Matabele tried to resist, twice. The Mashona tribes too, although initially welcoming white settlers, rebelled. Both were subdued in conflicts which, in terms of the pitiless savagery of black towards white, and white towards black – if not the scale of the actual carnage – bear comparison with the Indian Mutiny. At the end, British dominion had been established over the whole of Zambesia, a region now defined by the frontiers of Zambia, Zimbabwe and Malawi.

The course of these events was dictated essentially by two men. One was Rhodes. The other was Lobengula, whose impis blocked the path of expansion. In between stood Selous.

There are two versions of Selous's part in this story. The original one, bequeathed by Rhodesian folklore and Selous's biographer John Millais, represents him as an outdoorsman of transparent integrity and unique ability who emerged from the wilderness at precisely the right time to join forces with Rhodes; who, in an enterprise for which he alone was qualified, guided English settlers safely through peril to found a new country; who, when obliged to take up arms, did so with compassion and chivalry; and who finally, duty done, retired to the quiet of the English countryside without even the knighthood he had so richly deserved.

The second version goes somewhat differently and constitutes, at least partly, a reaction to the uncritical adulation accorded Selous by his contemporaries. The basis for it was advanced by a Rhodesian historian, Professor Terence Ranger, in a paper presented to the Rhodes-Livingstone Institute in Lusaka in 1963. It proposes that Selous's much-vaunted honesty was compromised during the Scramble for Africa. Specifically, Professor Ranger has suggested that Selous became a paid propagandist for the British South Africa Company, the chartered company created by the Crown empowering Rhodes to settle Zambesia. It is also suggested that Selous so fell under Rhodes's spell that he was prepared to join in deception – even that he was 'squared' by Rhodes to distort the situation in Zambesia to the English public.

Both portraits are simplistic. The first inevitably tends towards hagiography, although, in overlooking Selous's contributions towards preserving peace, it does him less than justice in an important respect. As for the second, Professor Ranger's paper was a necessary counter-balance to the conventional image of Selous, and raises valid questions about the way he lent himself to the chartered company. But it has an air of contrived debunking, and is demonstrably mistaken in some respects.

These are the elements which will be examined in the following chapters, covering the period from 1889, the year in which Selous and Rhodes became allies, to 1896 when, the Matabele and Mashona uprisings having been put down, he quit Africa once and for all. During these years he had a hand, often a crucial one, in all the major historical events which took place. More than any other man, he plotted the geographical course of British occupation. His influence on policy was considerable, and generally for the good, especially in the way he sought to prevent confrontation between black and white. Crucially, he stopped Rhodes from launching a pre-emptive strike against Lobengula. When the conduct of many other white men became marked by rapacity and unscrupulousness, Selous stood out for fair play. He had no part in the reckless corruption which spread through the chartered company, and which found its ultimate expression in the Jameson Raid. In the end, he fell out completely with 'the chartered crowd'.

Nevertheless, he did – after initial resistance – throw himself wholeheartedly behind Rhodes's endeavours. In so doing, he allowed himself to be used in a way which compromised both his integrity and his simple ideals. Always an imperialist, he neverthe-less had little understanding of the connections between politics and commerce, or stomach for the naked exercise of power. The artless society in which he had passed his adult life had left him ill-equipped for dealing with men like Rutherfoord Harris, the Com-pany's secretary, or Leander Starr Jameson, Rhodes's right-hand man. In the arcane, labyrinthine ways of the Company, Selous was out of his depth.

When he realized that he had been used, it rankled. Millais was no ordinary biographer, but a close friend, and it may be thought that he spoke for Selous when he wrote:

Cecil Rhodes was a big man – big in almost every way except

140

in the matter of gratitude. When he found that Selous was – to use an Americanism – such an 'easy mark', he exploited him to the limit of his capacity. Rhodes knew that without Selous's immense local knowledge and tact with the native Mashuna chiefs his best-laid schemes might go astray, so he played on his patriotism, and promised him many things, not one of which he ever performed.

Selous did feel that he was not adequately paid for his services to Rhodes. His chronic financial problems had left him inordinately sensitive about money and, although he earned in his three years with the Company enough to retire in some comfort to England, he was never entirely without worry. At times of new austerity he would brood and make unfavourable comparisons with the far larger sums which Rhodes had laid out during the Mashonaland enterprise, particularly when he was 'squaring' rivals or opponents.

Millais also hints that Selous might have expected an honour for his work for Queen and Empire. Here we are on uncertain ground. There were indeed those, Millais among them, who thought it shameful that he did not receive a knighthood, but it is unlikely that Selous was among them. He never demonstrated any regard for the trappings of fame. Few other celebrities invited by royalty to visit Balmoral Castle would have refused on the grounds that they 'couldn't stand all that fuss'.

If in the end Selous received less recognition than was his due, it was because he did not have the assertiveness that commands reward and acclaim as a right. Without detracting from his contribution, it can be fairly said that it was Selous's fortune to fall in with another, and greater, man's destiny. Rhodes would have succeeded in painting Central Africa red without Selous. Without Rhodes, Selous's mark on history would have been slight.

It is also fair to say he recognized this. In an interview with the historian, Basil Williams, he mixed criticism of Rhodes over his treatment of Lobengula with praise for Rhodes's far-sightedness in negotiations with the Matabele once they had been defeated and his patience in dealing with Boer politicians. Selous's main tribute to Rhodes, however, was in his book, *Travel and Adventure in South-East Africa*:

He alone of all Englishmen possessed at the same time the prescience and breadth of mind to appreciate the ultimate value [of Mashonaland] combined with the strong will which in spite of all obstacles compelled the means and the power successfully to carry out the scheme for its immediate occupation.

Whatever his differences with Rhodes, Selous never wavered from the objective they shared, the British occupation of Mashonaland. He joined hands with the extraordinary mob of idealists, adventurers, buccaneers, opportunists and outright confidence tricksters who attached themselves to Rhodes's star. Indeed, with the candour which was his best safeguard against pomposity, Selous recognized himself as one of the adventurers, and was not bothered by the description. After all, he maintained, the British Empire had been founded by adventurers, 'and were not Drake and Raleigh, Clive and Warren Hastings, adventurers too?'

In order to see the region as Selous found it when he emerged from the wilderness at the beginning of 1889, it is necessary to trace the events that had occurred in his absence, and to focus on the incongruous pair of figures occupying the centre stage.

Lobengula and Rhodes never met. It is tempting to speculate how these two men whose talent was essentially for manipulating others would have reacted to one another. At a time when confrontation was looming, Selous tried to bring about a meeting at Lobengula's request, but Rhodes evaded it. Even if Selous had been successful, a test of strength between Matabele and Briton could only have been delayed.

The die had been cast as far back as 1887, and Lobengula was far too shrewd to have misread the signs. Behind the growing number of whites making their way to Gubulawayo, he perceived the stirring of forces beyond his control. He related an allegory to the missionary Charles Helm about the chameleon which advances slowly and gently on a fly, before darting out its tongue to swallow it. 'England is the chameleon, and I am the fly,' the king said.

For all this wry fatalism, Lobengula never displayed to more telling effect his qualities as a ruler than in these final years of his reign. Hot-headed warriors and gold-hungry settlers made a highly combustible blend, and the wonder is that a showdown was so long averted. As the pressure developed, Lobengula's position was imperilled by rebellious indunas, so that to keep his throne, as well as the peace, he had to resort to every trick known to diplomacy. His own people he cajoled and threatened, playing factions off against one another and creating scapegoats to ease tension. The whites he stalled with a combination of affability and prevarication. Playing for time with mounting desperation, he dissembled and evaded. Somehow, he maintained his dignity. His eventual downfall, in the war of 1893, was a tragedy from which he alone emerged with honour.

It was Lobengula's misfortune that Cecil Rhodes, after some years on the Diamond Fields, had returned to England while still in his twenties to study at Oxford. There he came under the influence of John Ruskin, the writer, artist and philosopher. Ruskin's inaugural lecture as Slade professor of art in 1870 ignited Rhodes, and part of it is worth repeating, not only for the beauty of its language, but as it exemplifies the gospel of imperialism as it was understood by Selous's generation:

> There is a destiny now possible to us, the highest ever set before a nation to be accepted or refused. Will you youths of England make your country again a royal throne of kings; a sceptered isle, for all the world a source of light, a centre of peace? . . . This is what England must do or perish: she must found colonies as fast and as far as she is able, formed of her most energetic and worthiest men; seizing every piece of fruitful waste ground she can set her foot on . . . If we can get men, for little pay, to cast themselves against cannon-mouths for love of England, we may find men also who will plough and sow for her, who will behave kindly and righteously for her, and who will bring up their children to love her.

When Rhodes returned to Africa it was with a fully-formed and compelling vision of his destiny. In the words of his biographers, J. G. Lockhart and C. M. Woodhouse: 'In the background was that grand design to paint large portions of the map red, to settle the earth with Anglo-Saxons, and to federate the British Empire. In the foreground were his plans for South Africa – the union of the Cape

Colony and Natal with the two Dutch republics, and the opening up of a road to the north.'

There have been numerous portraits of the only Englishman to have a country named after him. But the historian Robert Blake is especially persuasive:

> He lived simply and had no expensive tastes. Anyone who interprets his political aims in terms of his economic interests puts the cart before the horse. His wealth was useful to him as a means of power and he employed it as ruthlessly as he had gained it. Yet his huge fortune was not enough to give him his extraordinary position. He might half in jest talk about 'squaring' the Mahdi, the Pope, the Kaiser. But he possessed another gift no less valuable than gold and diamonds. He could, as was said of Lloyd George, 'charm a bird out of a bush'. . . .
>
> Rhodes could be arrogant, autocratic and rude when he saw no reason to be charming. He talked endlessly himself and disliked listening to others. He could fly into a temper and use brutally scathing language. He could also be generous, kind and considerate – especially to young men of no importance. He was intensely loyal to his friends, some of whom scarcely deserved his trust, but he never forgave an enemy or forgot an injury. If on the debit side he was unscrupulous in his dealings, harsh to his opponents, reckless in taking the short cut to his objective, much can be forgiven to a man conscious that his time was running out and obsessed by the goal he had set himself.

As the 1880s drew to a close, the Scramble for Africa was in full swing. Rivalry for influence in the southern part of the continent pitted Britain against its oldest ally, Portugal, as well as against Germany and the Boer government of the Transvaal. Rhodes's vision was fixed on the great lakes of Central Africa, which had been fully explored a decade earlier by Henry Stanley, but beyond lay the Sudan and Egypt, and he could imagine a spinal cord of British enterprise running the length of Africa, a railway from the Cape to Cairo.

The young Selous: 'a veritable Tom Brown'.

Selous aged twenty-three, pictured
(with one of his muzzle-loaders) on
a visit home in 1875 after his first
venture to Africa.

F.C. SELOUS

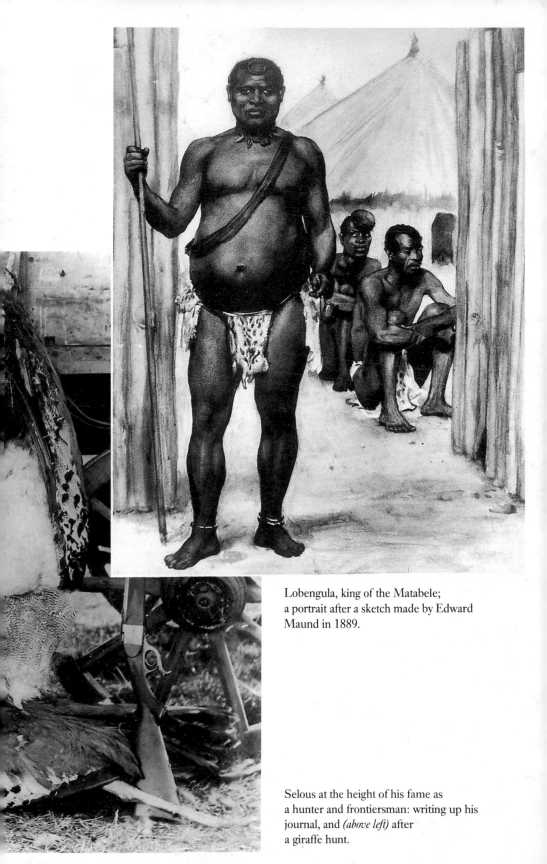

Lobengula, king of the Matabele;
a portrait after a sketch made by Edward
Maund in 1889.

Selous at the height of his fame as
a hunter and frontiersman: writing up his
journal, and *(above left)* after
a giraffe hunt.

Some of Selous's many hair's-breadth escapes from big game. These illustrations were by E. Whymper for Selous's first book.

The Maddy family at the Rectory at Down Hatherley, soon after Gladys's engagement to Selous in 1893. Her hand, resting on Canon Maddy's shoulder, clearly displays her engagement ring.

Cecil Rhodes and Leander Starr Jameson at Groote Schuur, Rhodes's residence *(left)* and *(above)* Selous and Roosevelt on the voyage from Naples to Mombasa, 1909.

Selous as he appeared shortly before the outbreak of the First World War; *(below left)* Gladys in her later years, and *(right)* Freddy Selous as a young officer in the Royal Flying Corps not long before his death.

The key that would unlock the continent was the region we have defined here as Zambesia. With a typical touch of the dramatic Rhodes told Sir Sidney Shippard, the Administrator of British Bechuanaland: 'If we get Mashonaland we shall get the balance of Africa.'

It is as well to remember today, when Rhodes's impact on Southern Africa is a matter of history, that the omens at the time were bleak. In 1888, the Government of Lord Salisbury – preoccupied with the issues of Ireland, Egypt and Russia – was unenthusiastic about embarking on new adventures in barbaric and strange-sounding parts of Africa. Treasury purse-holders were particularly resistant. Furthermore, although Rhodes was the Cape Colony's leading citizen, he was virtually unknown in Britain.

What he had come to possess, however, were riches on a scale which made even governments take notice. The creation of De Beers Consolidated Mines in 1888 gave Rhodes control of the entire Diamond Fields and a nominal fortune of more than £2 million. (His final estate was valued at £4.1 million.) And if his name did not yet reverberate around Westminster, a growing number of influential Englishmen, including the main colonial officials, had started attaching themselves to his coat-tails. Shippard was one important ally. Another was Sir Hercules Robinson, the High Commissioner for South Africa.

Through these men, Rhodes took his first step on the road north. At Rhodes's behest, Shippard sent his deputy, John Moffat, to Gubulawayo with orders to secure if possible a treaty of friendship with Lobengula on Britain's behalf. The choice of Moffat was a shrewd one. A son of the missionary Robert Moffat, who had been a close friend of Lobengula's father Mzilikazi, he was known and liked by Lobengula. Moffat reciprocated this regard, but held no brief for the Matabele nation and thought the curbing of their power would be a blessing. 'The Matabele are a miserable people and have made myriads of other people miserable too,' he wrote.

Moffat's arrival at Gubulawayo reassured Lobengula, who had been feeling pressure from a new quarter. On top of the concession seekers, and his young warriors, the amatjaha – who now wanted nothing more than to deal with the intruders by slaughtering the lot – he had been discomfited by overtures from the Transvaal Boers.

Paul Kruger's government also had an expansionist eye on Mashonaland, and an emissary, Piet Grobler, had been sent to Gubulawayo. Lobengula, with memories of how the Boers had driven the Matabele from the Transvaal a half-century earlier, regarded them with sufficient anxiety and suspicion to agree to sign a friendship treaty with Pretoria.

This made Moffat's task easier, as Lobengula was keen to maintain a balance in his dealings with Boer and Briton. Already, however, Moffat noted that the king was 'far from being a free agent':

> He has in fact behind him forces which he can ill control, and, if a combination of circumstances were to occur, and the jealous and suspicious nature of his fighting men [were] aroused, any agreement . . . with white men would be of little account.

It was in these circumstances that Lobengula signed the first of the two documents which opened the door to Rhodes. The so-called Moffat Treaty of February 1888 contained no concessions on land or minerals, although under it, Lobengula relinquished the right to dispose of territory without first obtaining British approval. However, as he had no intention of giving up any land, it must have seemed a proposition without risk, and the king believed that, in return, he was being given a guarantee of protection against possible aggression by the Boers to the south, and the Portuguese in the east.

One aspect of the Moffat Treaty attracted little attention at the time, but needs to be emphasized, as it was later to give an arbitrary definition to the boundary of British expansion. The document made it a matter of record that Lobengula's domain consisted not only of Matabeleland, but of the territory known as Mashonaland, too. (At the time perhaps a handful of Whitehall officials could have said on which continent the Mashona lived, let alone whose tributaries they were.) As for giving a definition of 'Mashonaland', Selous was one of the few men who could have attempted it. He maintained that the territory was ill-defined in its eastern extremities, and furthermore that although the chiefs in the west paid tribute to Lobengula, some of those in the east had maintained their independence from the Matabele, and also from the Portuguese. In short, although part of Mashonaland was within Lobengula's gift, a large sector was not.

The Moffat Treaty provoked immediate objections from the Transvaal and Portugal, which claimed, with little justification, to have exercised *de facto* control over Mashonaland for centuries. The Colonial Secretary, Lord Knutsford, was undeterred, and within a few months Matabeleland and Mashonaland were declared 'exclusively within the British Sphere of Interest'. Important a step though this was, Rhodes knew it committed Britain to nothing. The situation called for a body modelled on the East India Company. To create it he needed a mineral concession from Lobengula on which he could base an application for a royal charter.

The task of obtaining such a document was entrusted to Charles Rudd, who had been Rhodes's first partner and in whom he reposed absolute trust. Rudd was to lead a party consisting of Rochfort Maguire, an Oxford lawyer with colonial experience, and an out-doorsman, Francis 'Matabele' Thompson, who would be their guide and translator. In August they started for Gubulawayo, with something in the order of 500 gold sovereigns and ample champagne to ease Lobengula's thirst.

Rhodes was not to know it at the time, but the king's defences had already started to slip. A month earlier, he had finally given in to the most experienced of the concession seekers. The consortium con-sisting of Thomas Leask, George Phillips and James Fairbairn was granted, on 14 July, 'the sole right to dig for Gold & other minerals in my country'. (As the document was being signed, the fourth member of the consortium, George Westbeech, lay ill in the Transvaal, and would die three days later.) The members of this group were among the few supplicants well known to Lobengula, and under their agreement he was to get half of any proceeds. In the end, the so-called Leask Concession would amount to little, as the concessionaires could never rival Rhodes's resources and, when offered the opportunity to sell their interest to him, they quickly took it. But the episode was important in creating a precedent for Lobengula to sign a gold-mining agreement.

On arriving at Gubulawayo, Rudd and his group waited their turn to parley in the dusty heat of the royal kraal, anticipating the usual interminable delays of negotiating with the Matabele. Again, however, Rhodes's allies in the British Colonial Service came to his assistance. After weeks of fruitless effort, the situation was transformed by the arrival of Shippard. The Administrator of Bechuanaland, representing the Great White Queen, cut an impressive figure in the midday sun, dressed in a black frock coat encrusted with decorations, white pith helmet and a silver-topped malacca cane.

Shippard found Lobengula 'completely naked except for a very long piece of dark blue cloth rolled very small and wound round his body, which it in nowise concealed, and a monkey-skin worn as a small apron and about the size of a Highland sporran'. Shippard was nonetheless impressed. 'Altogether he is a very fine looking man, and in spite of his obesity, he has a most majestic carriage.' The Matabele warriors, however, made the Administrator shudder: 'Never, till I saw these wretches, did I understand the true mercy and love of humanity contained in the injunction given to the Israelites to destroy the Canaanites.'

There can be little doubt that Shippard made it known that the English queen would look upon a concession granted to Rudd as a favour. Negotiations continued for a few days, but in the end were concluded more easily than might have been expected. On 30 October, Lobengula's elephant seal was applied to a concession granting Rudd and his co-signatories 'complete and exclusive charge over all metals and minerals contained in my kingdom, principalities and dominions'. In return the king was to receive 1000 Martini-Henry rifles with ammunition, and a stipend of £100 a month.

According to the missionary Helm, Rudd had given a verbal assurance that no more than ten white men would be involved in digging for gold at any time, and that they would submit to the king's authority, as whites always had. Lobengula may have hoped that the Great White Queen's men would see off the other concession seekers who beset him, and that once the gold was dug up they would leave. In fact, he had handed Rhodes the wedge with which to prise him from his throne.

Throughout these events Selous had been cut off north of the Zambesi, suffering disaster among the Mushukulumbwe, and in Barotseland. He arrived back at Bamangwato in January 1889, knowing nothing of the advantages that had fallen to Britain in Zambesia.

It had never been much of a place, Bamangwato: a cluster of thatch huts on a dry, spare plain surrounded by low hills. Certainly it was not likely to buck Selous up at the end of a disastrous season. His losses had by now technically ruined him, and it was uncertain whether Leask, to whom he was already deeply in debt, would be prepared to back him for yet another expedition. Selous was finding, as well, that Africa had lost some of its magic for him. The great animal herds had migrated north of the Zambesi, and the wonder he felt on the rolling plains on a golden afternoon was fading. Even the aroma of a wood fire under a glittering night sky no longer evoked the same pleasure. Many of the old hands 'with their warm hearts, unbusinesslike habits and somewhat indifferent morals', were dead or gone, and he mourned to see their places taken by 'men of a more advanced type, who keep books and seek to grow rich'. In moments of depression he was tempted to throw in his hand, return to England and write another book.

The first people Selous met at Bamangwato were Johnson, Heany and Borrow. The welcome extended by Johnson was tepid. There had been from the outset an instinctive dislike on both sides, and Johnson – ambitious young hustler that he was – found Selous's occasionally patrician air, with its tone of moral reproof, aggravating. Heany and Borrow, on the other hand, were delighted to see the hunter again. Indeed, there was a strong element of public school hero-worship in Henry Borrow's attitude. 'It is a great pleasure to Heany and I to have him with us,' he wrote home. Selous was simply 'the finest and pluckiest man I have ever met', he declared. From this ill-matched quartet a partnership was born which launched Selous headlong into the Scramble for Africa.

Of all the men who sought to grow rich in Southern Africa, few pursued their goal so avidly as Frank Johnson. Since his brush with the Matabele a couple of years before, he had devised two plans to make himself and his partners wealthy. The first was through the Bechuanaland Exploration Company, a gold enterprise headed by two prominent London financiers, George Cawston and Lord Gifford. The BEC was a rival to Rhodes's hopes for a royal charter, and kept an emissary in Gubulawayo, a plausible rogue named

Lieutenant Edward Maund, who claimed, falsely, to have obtained yet another mineral concession from Lobengula. In attempting to undermine Rhodes, Maund had, however, managed to plant doubt at Gubulawayo about the existence of the Great White Queen, sufficient for the king to despatch two indunas to London to make sure for themselves. Maund was to accompany them.

The second of Johnson's projects was to involve Selous more immediately. On a visit to Portugal, Johnson had obtained a concession to prospect along the Mazoe river in east Mashonaland, which the Portuguese continued to insist lay within their sovereignty. He had done nothing to exploit this concession but as he talked to Selous an idea came to him. Here, he saw, was the ideal man to lead an expedition to the distant river valley. The idea took shape as Johnson recognized that Selous's reputation could attract financial support in London. It became irresistible when he learned that Selous, as the son of a former Stock Exchange chairman, had useful connections.

It is a mark of Selous's desperation that he agreed to the proposals that were now put to him. He disliked Johnson, and opposed Portuguese territorial claims in Mashonaland, yet he accepted the proposal that he guide a prospecting party to the Mazoe from the east coast. A rough contract of partnership was drawn up under which Selous was to get a half share in any profits.

The expedition would have to await the end of the rainy season two or three months later, and it may be that Selous was considering taking a quick trip home anyway. If so, Johnson would have been happy to encourage him. It was agreed that Selous would go to London, and while there would call on the directors of the Bechuanaland Exploration Company. Johnson gave him a letter of introduction to Lord Gifford, in which it was proposed that the Mazoe concession, Selous's name and Gifford's influence in the City could be profitably combined in a mineral enterprise. Borrow, at least, was ebullient about the prospects. 'We could not possibly have got a better man, and his name should go a long way to floating the thing into a company,' he wrote to his father.

It so happened that when Selous sailed from Cape Town in February 1889, he was not the only one on board with a keen interest in Mashonaland. Among the passengers were Maund and his two charges, the indunas Babyan and Mshete. Selous thought Maund 'an awful windbag', but he got along well with a fellow hunter, Johan Colenbrander, who, as translator for the indunas, was another of the leathery frontiersmen who had become part of the financial designs being woven over Zambesia.

It was a chill and foggy dawn in late winter when the 'Mighty Nimrod', as Selous had been dubbed by the popular press – to his acute embarrassment – stepped from the ship *Moor* on to English soil. Three years had passed since his last visit to the Gloucester Road household. His father, Frederick, was eighty-seven, while Ann, with whom Selous kept up an affectionate correspondence, was sixty-four. Brother Edmund had married Fanny Maxwell. One sister, Florence, had married, but the others, Ann and Sybil ('Tottie' and 'Dei'), were still living at home. Selous's mother worried about her daughters, but within the next two years they married well, to brothers, Richard and Charles Jones, sons of a former mayor of Gloucester. When Fred was into his forties and apparently settled in confirmed bachelorhood, he would meet and woo the Jones's strikingly handsome niece, Gladys Maddy.

Fred was now aged thirty-eight, and his parents were increasingly keen that he should come home and take charge of a prosperous estate. There were no recriminations over the failure of his African enterprises. Frederick, who, despite his age, continued to dabble shrewdly in the stock market, offered to take over his son's debt to Thomas Leask and repay it at £50 a quarter.

Selous had other ideas, but his entry into the world of high finance and politics was not immediate. When he called on Lord Gifford, chairman of the Bechuanaland Exploration Company, to invite investment in the Mazoe venture, he was rudely fobbed off. Gifford, an impeccably-connected aristocrat, was preoccupied with thoughts about Lobengula; he may have considered he knew a thing or two about dealing with recalcitrant African potentates, having won a VC in the first Ashanti War against King Coffee Kalkali of the Gold Coast. In any event, Gifford passed Selous to another BEC director, George Cawston, who was compiling a map of the British Sphere of Influence in Southern Africa, and who recognized Selous as a valuable source of data.

The arrival of the indunas had, quite naturally, created a public stir, which increased as they were escorted to Aldershot for a military demonstration, to a function hosted by the Aborigines Protection Society, and to an audience with the Great White Queen herself. Meanwhile, Rhodes had also arrived in London, bearing the Rudd concession, to apply in person to Lord Knutsford at the Colonial Office for a royal charter.

It was a confusing picture, but Zambesia was suddenly on everyone's lips. Whitehall and the City were floundering in their ignorance of a part of the world which seemed destined to be the next acquisition in the expanding Empire. At this stage Selous emerged on the scene, to find himself in great demand. The officials and financiers were delighted to find someone who could not only point out Mashonaland on a map but who could actually speak about it with expert knowledge. He also seemed reassuringly trustworthy. As 'the man over from Mashonaland' Selous's own brand of magnetism soon communicated itself. A reporter for the weekly journal *South Africa* wrote: 'You cannot be in his company a minute before you feel that Diogenes would have stopped his search and said: "Here, at last, is an honest man." '

For his part, Selous, long an advocate of British settlement in Mashonaland, was thrilled to find a wind of change blowing through Whitehall policy. Lord Knutsford had him round to the Colonial Office, and confided that Portugal had been persuaded to give up its claims to Zambesia. That could only mean that, one way or another, Britain would exercise an imperial role.

Selous's confidence that the tide had turned is shown in a letter of 19 March 1889 to the Anti-Slavery Society, in reply to an invitation to a breakfast 'in honour of the two Matabele envoys'. After apologizing for declining as 'I might have been led to say something very uncomplimentary,' Selous went on:

> It does strike me as incomprehensible that your society above all others should have chosen to do honour to the envoys of such a tribe as the Matabele . . . a people who, year after year, send out their armies of pitiless, bloodthirsty savages and slaughter men, women and children indiscriminately – except for those just the ages to be taken for slaves . . . They

are no more aborigines of the country they now occupy than the Romans were aborigines of Britain. They are invaders and have almost utterly exterminated the aboriginal population. However, they are bound to go; neither your society nor the British Government can save them. They have lived by the sword; by the sword they will die.

Please excuse me for inflicting this letter upon you but I have lived sixteen years in the countries 'within the sphere of Matabele influence' and I know what I am talking about.

Men of influence other than Knutsford sought Selous out. He met Frank Harris, whose libidinous memoirs have overshadowed his editorship of the respected *Fortnightly Review*, and his assistant John Verschoyle, who, under the *nom de plume* 'Vindex', would become one of Rhodes's most ardent acolytes. Selous renewed his acquaintanceship with Harry Johnston, fresh from diplomatic achievements in Niger, and about to be sent to Portugal for new negotiations on respective spheres of influence in Southern Africa. Cawston offered Selous a job with the BEC. Most crucially, he met Cecil Rhodes again.

Rhodes had arrived in London a few weeks after Selous, a fabulously wealthy but little-known colonial MP. In pursuing his application for a royal charter, he had cultivated London society relentlessly, making some notable allies and a few implacable opponents. Among the former were W. T. Stead, editor of the *Pall Mall Gazette*, and Flora Shaw, who, in the pre-suffragette age, was colonial correspondent of *The Times*; grandees like the Duke of Abercorn and the Duke of Fife had been won over by Rhodes's charm; Lord Knutsford, initially hostile, was brought round. The enemy camp included the Aborigines Protection Society, and the radical MP, Henry Labouchère, but Rhodes had made an astonishingly positive impact on London in a short time.

The meeting between Selous and Rhodes seems to have been relatively brief, but both men were already aware that for the realization of their ambitions they were dependent on one another. Selous, who some years earlier had given Rhodes a few quills of Mashonaland gold, now urged him not to be content just with prospecting. Selous repeated what had become an article of faith –

that the plateau of Mashonaland was the most suitable place for new settlement by Britons in Southern Africa. Especially, he said, it would reward pioneers who were prepared to settle and cultivate the land. Rhodes was not yet ready to talk about detail, being preoccupied with the grand design, forging alliances and squaring rivals. But he said: 'Well I can't tell you much, but I shall soon have a job for you.' When Selous said he was contracted to take an expedition to the Mazoe, Rhodes told him to go ahead and to report to Kimberley when he got back.

Selous's tribute to Rhodes at the completion of the charter venture was, by his own standards, fulsome. 'It is due to Mr Cecil Rhodes alone, I cannot too often repeat, that today our country's flag flies over Mashunaland,' he wrote. This remark has tended to reinforce the historical view of the man of action and the visionary working hand-in-glove from the outset for the sake of Empire. The truth is otherwise: initially, Selous and Rhodes found a great deal to disagree about.

Rhodes at this point had only the vaguest concept of Zambesia, which he saw as an area on a map, a stage on the road north. His friend, (Sir) Ralph Williams, the British agent at Pretoria, wrote:

> The fact is that Rhodes knew very little about the actual countries between the Cape and 'the object of all my endeavours' – i.e. the African Lakes. He knew there was a high watershed more or less healthy through Lobengula's country and he knew that he had determined if possible to build a railway on it and to get it within the sphere of British influence . . . but I am sure in my own mind that he had no real sketch of 'Rhodesia' in his head.

Selous, on the other hand, had by now spent almost twenty years in the region. He knew it better than any white man, and had strong views on how it should be developed. Crucially, he believed that both the Moffat Treaty and the Rudd concession were worthless in establishing any claim to much of Mashonaland. Certainly Matabeleland and, and to some extent western and central Mashonaland, were within Lobengula's gift. But the eastern extremity of the British Sphere of Influence, based on the Moffat Treaty, was supposedly defined by the range of Matabele raids.

Selous held that the limit of these raids was the Umfule river. Mount Hampden, the place he would propose to Rhodes as the best spot for establishing a European settlement, was well beyond the Umfule – beyond even the Hunyani.

Selous was in favour of establishing title to the Mashonaland plateau by securing treaties directly with local chiefs. His paternal liking for the Mashona, and detestation of the Matabele, were reflected in the conviction that the former would welcome white settlers as protectors against the latter. The Rudd concession he saw as a red herring, and, moreover, as containing the seeds of a confrontation with Lobengula, who, he was certain, would never willingly allow the settlement of Mashonaland on the strength of it. Avoid the Matabele entirely, he argued, and treat purely with the Mashona.

It is not clear whether Selous put forward this argument immediately he saw Rhodes, but even if he did not, this fundamental difference between them was not long in emerging. Soon after arriving in London, Rhodes had concluded a deal to amalgamate his concession interests with those of the directors of the Bechuanaland Exploration Company, Lord Gifford and George Cawston, turning these formidable rivals into allies in the campaign for a royal charter. Cawston, it appears, was involved in inviting Selous to write an article for the *Fortnightly Review* about the territory in which they now all shared a common interest. An article by the acknowledged expert on the subject would, it was reasoned, give a timely boost to the application for a charter.

Selous's original manuscript for the article 'Mashunaland and the Mashunas' has been lost, but that it caused immense consternation is attested to by correspondence which indicates that Cawston and Verschoyle, deputy editor at the *Fortnightly*, conspired to see that Selous's anti-concession views were toned down. After a gruelling session with the hunter, Verschoyle wrote to Cawston: 'I have, not without difficulty, got rid of the pages of dangerous matter in S's article, but please not to allude to these omissions on any account to anyone but Seaver not even to Selous himself. He is still sore about the omissions I have insisted on making.'

'Mashunaland and the Mashunas' appeared in a May issue. The charter application had been submitted only a few days earlier, in the names of Rhodes, Cawston and Rudd. Up to a point the article was helpful: Selous had given vent to his anti-Matabele prejudices, portraying them as a cruel and barbarous people who had inflicted misery on the peaceable and industrious Mashona. More, he indicated that Britons had a mission as saviours. Only settlement of the depopulated countryside – 'a country that is now lying idle, and that may be repeopled by Europeans without wronging any human being' – could save the Mashona from annihilation, he maintained.

However, Verschoyle had been unable to curb Selous altogether. Another passage pointed explicitly to the flaws in the Rudd concession:

> Since my return to England I have gathered that it is believed by the few men who have any idea on the subject that the Mashunas are a people conquered by the Matabele . . . and now paying tribute to their king, Lobengula. There are several communities of Mashunas who are subject to Lobengula . . . But besides these, there are numerous tribes of Mashunas who are in no wise subject to Lobengula.

Frank Johnson wrote that when Rhodes saw this article he became so livid he could scarcely speak, and stamped around shouting that Selous had to be stopped or the charter would be lost. As he did frequently in his specious memoir, *Great Days*, Johnson was exaggerating or fabricating an incident in an attempt to blacken Selous's name. It was common wisdom, however, that Rhodes was greatly alarmed that 'Mashunaland and the Mashunas' might be used by lobbies opposed to the charter, such as the Aborigines Protection Society, or the radicals. In the event, there were no repercussions, perhaps because of Selous's dubious assertion that British settlement would save the Mashona. But Rhodes noted for future reference that Selous's pen could be dangerous as well as helpful.

CHAPTER ELEVEN

The Syndicate

Well before he was due to return to South Africa, Selous was deeply regretting his commitment to go prospecting up the Zambesi. The venture became even less attractive when Johnson's Mazoe concession was rescinded by the Lisbon authorities. Selous wrote with obvious annoyance to Johnson:

I shall leave England by the Union boat that steams on May 3. However as I suppose you know, since I last saw you circumstances have entirely changed the aspect of affairs in Mashonaland . . . As matters now stand I am very sorry that I agreed to take your party up the Zambesi as it would be very much more in my own interests to remain in England at present. However as I have signed an agreement I will come out and see you in Cape Town, though under the altered conditions I do not think I am bound to carry out the stipulations of that agreement.

The interests he regretted leaving were the offers of employment made by Rhodes and Cawston. In addition he had had approaches from a few London publishers interested in a second volume of hunting and adventure tales to follow *A Hunter's Wanderings in Africa*.

The prospect of the three-week voyage did not improve Selous's humour as the ship *Spartan* steamed out of Southampton. The female company on board he described dismissively to his mother as consisting of 'two much-bejewelled and vulgar Jewesses, and three very uninteresting Christian women'. But there were some hearty male companions, and soon he was joining in tennis and cricket on

157

deck, and neglecting the book with the tentative title *Travel and Adventure in South-East Africa*, which he had just started.

Another passenger was Sir Frederick Young, a vice-president of the Royal Colonial Institute, who persuaded him to relieve the monotony of the voyage by giving a talk in the second-class lounge. Selous's air of diffidence somehow disappeared before an audience, and an extemporization on the warlike Matabele and his hunting adventures was so enthusiastically received by about 200 passengers and crew that he had to repeat it a few days later. Young wrote of the 'attractive simplicity of his style . . . charm and modesty', and Selous too was pleased. 'I really think that I interested everybody,' he wrote home.

On 25 May, the *Spartan* berthed in the shadow of Table Mountain. Selous took a room at the City Club, and went straight round to see Frank Johnson. It is unlikely that Johnson was then aware of the disaster that the BEC merger with Rhodes meant for his fortunes – that he, Borrow and Heany would be summarily jettisoned. But matters were serious enough as a result of the cancellation of his Mazoe valley concession.

Whatever his defects, Johnson was not one to lie down and accept defeat. Since his visit to Mashonaland in 1887, when he had prospected in defiance of Lobengula's orders, Johnson had been convinced that the Mazoe river was the true source of Ophir's treasure. There emerged from his talks with Selous a new plan of action, which combined this theory with Selous's belief in the 'independence' of the eastern Mashona chiefs. The idea was that Selous would proceed, from Mozambique, on the prospecting expedition as planned. But once he had reached the Mazoe he would try to obtain a mineral concession from the Makorikori, one of the numerous sub-groups which made up the so-called Mashona people. Johnson, meanwhile, would use his influence in financial circles in Cape Town to raise capital for a company. Heany and Borrow would join the venture too, but Selous's name would be the lure for investors.

Borrow explained the idea to his father: 'Selous says there are several Mashona chiefs who have always successfully defended themselves against Loben's marauders, and to them he intends to apply for rights to dig for gold, and he adds that we can with equity and justice support them in their claims.' Borrow was equally confident about what would follow. If Rhodes was granted a charter, the syndicate would have a concession for an area with potential for settlement, and be in a strong position to negotiate an amalgamation. Alternatively, any concession obtained by Selous could be exploited directly. Either way, the outcome would be profitable.

The Selous Exploration Syndicate was floated in June 1889, with capital of £10,000 raised from a group of Cape Town businessmen headed by Tom Anderson, a friend of Johnson's. Selous was allotted £1000 worth of shares while Johnson, Heany and Borrow got £800 worth each. The issue was an immediate success. Gold fever had been endemic in Southern Africa since the Witwatersrand discovery, and the likelihood of a 'second Rand' beyond the Limpopo, combined with the glamour of Selous's name, caused the value of shares in the syndicate to double in a matter of days. 'How easy it does seem to make money up here,' Borrow wrote.

Selous was astonished by the windfall. Never had he imagined money could be so easily made. He told Borrow with an air of bewilderment that he had been almost bankrupted by hunting, and that the best he could expect to make from his second book was £400. Now, without stirring from the City Club, he had made almost five times that amount.

Borrow chuckled at his hero's innocence in a letter: 'Selous altho a pretty smart fellow is entirely new to the mysteries of company mongering, and is not in the know. Clearly he does not yet understand the beauties of S African "golds".'

A few days later Selous was on his way, steaming up the east coast towards the Portuguese ports of Delagoa Bay, Beira and Quelimane. His companions were a tough, profane old prospector named Stephen Thomas, and Ted Burnett, a useful companion who knew the bush and was a crack shot. Johnson, whom he served faithfully, said there was no one he would rather have had in a tight corner.

They landed on 15 July at Quelimane, the picturesque port founded by the Portuguese on the Zambesi delta three centuries earlier. Dhows reached the port from the Gulf and Zanzibar to trade in ivory, but there was not much to the town, a single street with red-roofed dwellings set among palm trees.

What Selous saw here confirmed the antipathy he had felt for the

159

Portuguese in Africa since his first trip to the Zambesi. Decay and torpor were everywhere. After 'three hellish days', unloading and checking baggage, he wrote the first of a series of ill-tempered despatches to Johnson: 'I would sooner walk 500 miles round than go through another Portuguese customs house. You and Heany are so fond of the Portuguese because you know damned little about them ... They are simply obstructionist and hinderers of all enterprise here.'

Lobengula's closure of the road to Mashonaland had made this journey necessary. But Selous had seen in it, too, the opportunity to examine whether settlement of Mashonaland might not be launched up the Zambesi from the east coast. The idea that the river could be an artery for British influence and commerce had been around since Livingstone declared it 'God's highway to the Interior'. For Selous the concept had two principal attractions. Firstly, it avoided the Matabele. Secondly, the Mazoe valley was only a third as far from Quelimane as from Cape Town; if the Zambesi could be navigated, at least as far as the garrison town of Tete, the journey to Mashonaland would be much shortened. The drawback was that it would be contingent upon Portuguese cooperation.

Selous's observations would demonstrate that hopes in these directions were futile. The Zambesi, although well over a mile wide in some places, was reduced in others to barely a foot in depth. Other difficulties, with rapids and unreliable porterage, posed daunting obstacles to a large-scale expedition. Furthermore, it became clear during the journey that the Portuguese were not about to provide help to British enterprise. Roused from complacency, the House of Braganza was making a belated effort to re-establish its position in Southern Africa.

Early that year a force of annexation had been despatched under Major Alexandre de Serpa Pinto towards the Shire highlands, about 300 miles north-east of Mashonaland, in present-day Malawi. This manoeuvre was to end in debacle: when Serpa Pinto crossed the boundary separating the British and Portuguese spheres of influence, Westminster issued an ultimatum, and the subsequent Portuguese collapse caused the Lisbon government to fall. Meanwhile, however, the Portuguese had been active in Mashonaland as well. Colonel Joaquim Paiva de Andrada, one of the few men of vigour and enterprise in the colonial administration, had set off to get Mashona chiefs to fly the Portuguese flag.

This Portuguese connection with his enterprise made Selous uneasy. To some extent he was travelling under the Portuguese flag himself, as he was carrying a letter of introduction from Lisbon's consul at the Cape. This had been decided by the syndicate on the urging of Johnson and Heany, who still saw possible benefits from the sources through whom Johnson had obtained his now-defunct concession. Selous later acknowledged that without the letter he might not have been allowed to pass to Mashonaland. Nevertheless, he bridled at the connection, and his determination to belittle Portuguese influence on the Zambesi is a recurrent theme of the peppery notes he sent back to Johnson. A week after leaving Quelimane he wrote from Vincenti on the Lower Zambesi:

> They [the Portuguese] are intensely jealous of all foreigners ... and are doing all they can to thwart British enterprise ... The fact is that after what I have seen and heard since landing at Quelimane I have become very anti-Portuguese in my feelings and very much dislike the idea of supporting their claim to any part of the Mashuna country. However the first thing is to find payable gold. It will then be time enough to devise the ways and means of working it.

Between July and December, when they returned to Cape Town, the party travelled by canoe and on foot, down the Zambesi as far as Tete, thence to the source of the Mazoe, and back – a round trip of almost 1000 miles over brutally punishing terrain. Despite his initial misgivings, it is clear from Selous's correspondence with his mother that he enjoyed himself immensely. He was confident that the disasters and misfortunes were behind him, and strode along cheerfully. Ted Burnett, a fit young man, wrote to Johnson: 'Man, Selous does travel. I kept up with him, but had to do a little run now and again.'

They took just over three weeks to reach Tete, an ugly trading station established in 1632 on a rocky and barren plain, which swelters all year round in scorching heat. Most other travellers would agree with Selous's description of it as 'a damned hole'. Here they met a Jesuit priest named Father Courtois who told the travellers that in his six years at Tete, nine fellow missionaries had died, and several more been invalided home. Burnett came down with a severe malaria attack, but was well enough to travel within a week.

From Tete, they struck south from the Zambesi to higher ground. Two weeks later their porters deserted, stranding them with their baggage. The local chief, Maziwa, demanded huge payment for providing replacements, declaring with satisfaction that they were an elephant which had died in his country and he intended to get fat off the carcass. Selous, rather than submit 'to the extortions of a miserable savage', made a bonfire of their excess baggage, before marching on, leaving Maziwa furiously threatening retribution.

Back in north-east Mashonaland, they were on familiar ground, among the msasa trees, which in spring turn the hills shades of purple, plum and russet with their new leaves. Selous picked out two of the highest points, and recorded names with the Royal Geographical Society. Portuguese maps, he said, showed total ignorance of the country, and he wanted to demonstrate that an Englishman had been there. Mount Darwin (named for 'an illustrious man whose far-reaching theories have revolutionized modern thought, and destroyed many beliefs which have held men's minds in thrall for centuries') and Mount Thackeray (for 'the immortal novelist whose genius has so often enabled me to escape, for the time being, from my surroundings') survive on maps to this day.

The main business at hand was accomplished with ease. In September, two months after landing at Quelimane, the expedition reached the valley of the Mazoe. The local Makorikori people told Selous that Colonel Paiva de Andrada had recently been in a neighbouring district, handing out Portuguese flags. However, they remembered Selous as a generous provider of food from earlier sojourns in the district and this stood him in good stead now, in meetings with the headmen, Mapondera and Temaringa. Within a day, he had been given a mineral concession in return for a few blankets, some calico and ten guns with ammunition. He also obtained a statement that the chiefs had never seen a white Portuguese, or paid tribute of any kind; nor were they vassals of the Matabele, who had made only three minor incursions into the area.

The validity of this concession has been questioned by some scholars, including Professor Ranger, as it was obtained from headmen rather than Nigomo, paramount chief of the Makorikori. The point is well made, although the territory concerned – a large tract of the Mazoe valley – was still within the gift of the chiefs.

What is more striking is Selous's preparedness, now that riches were in sight, to resort to the well-tried techniques used to obtain advantage from less sophisticated people. The chiefs who so readily put their marks to the papers of white men had, in most cases, no inkling of their significance, and Mapondera and Temaringa were no exceptions. Here, to the Mazoe valley, white men would come flocking within the next few years to build a town and seize African land for farms and mines. Selous justified this to himself by arguing that the arrival of Europeans would protect the Makorikori from the Matabele, but that sat ill with his protestations that the Mashona in these parts were independent of Lobengula.

He was, in fact, showing symptoms of the greed which became a conspicuous feature of the era. Others were, it is fair to say, more affected. Some, including the tragic Borrow, would be consumed by it. Still, it is evident that after all his failures, Selous had scented riches, and his interest in settling Mashonaland was no longer altruistic. The report he sent now to the Selous Exploration Syndicate is an unedifying blend of pomposity and self-satisfaction:

> This concession is perfectly square, fair and genuine, and nothing can upset it. The Matabele claim to the country is utterly preposterous. Should the matter at some future time be enquired into by a commission, I can and shall be prepared with evidence – and my evidence must be taken, for no one knows as much about the subject as I do – in the face of which the Matabele claim could never be allowed. It is the same with the Portuguese pretensions. They are equally absurd.
>
> At any rate, here you have a concession embracing probably the richest little piece of country in all Africa.

Before starting back for the coast, Selous spent a few days on geographical observations, among them locating the Mazoe's source. But his main concern now was the Portuguese. In particular, he feared that de Andrada's military force might be successful in persuading the eastern Mashona chiefs to swear allegiance to Lisbon. The idea that, at this late stage in the game, Portugal might yet gain control of the region was intolerable. But it was still a possibility, he feared, if Rhodes focused his efforts on Lobengula's country rather than Mashonaland.

From Tete he sent back an impassioned address to the syndicate:

> Should Mr Cecil Rhodes have got the charter then this is his true policy: to open up a southern route from the British Protectorate [Bechuanaland] to Mashunaland . . . and not only exploit and work the gold there, but send in emigrants and settle up and occupy the country.
>
> It is folly to promulgate wild schemes for the colonization of Central Africa [Selous is referring to Lobengula's territory] and to leave a country with the glorious climate and great natural resources of Mashunaland out in the cold. In Mashunaland Europeans can live and thrive and rear strong healthy children. In Central Africa they cannot. Once get a footing in Eastern Mashunaland, and the country will quickly be settled up westwards, and before very long the Matabili question will settle itself. Now or never is the time to act . . . If Mashunaland is not worth this experiment, then there is no country in the interior of Africa that it will pay any company to spend money upon.

Selous's adventures in Mozambique ended with a flourish – and a touch of cloak-and-dagger farce. In Tete, he was summoned to the residence of the Governor, Senhor Alfredo Alpuina, where a furious exchange followed. The Governor enquired icily how Selous had dared to seek territorial advantage in Portuguese territory, and accused him of being a British spy.

'I can lay no claim to that honour,' he retorted.

Senhor Alpuina then demanded that he hand over the concession. Selous refused, insisting it had been obtained outside Portuguese jurisdiction. He was threatened with arrest. After a great deal of haggling, the Governor agreed to settle for a copy.

Two weeks later, Selous and his party emerged from the grassland along the Zambesi into the lush swampland of the delta, just fifty miles from Quelimane, where the liner, SS *Courland*, awaited them. In sweltering heat, Selous mounted the gangplank and marched boldly past a Portuguese guard, clutching the concession, his journals and maps.

Early in December 1889, he arrived back in Cape Town to find a letter from Rhodes, summoning him to Kimberley. The charter had been given royal assent two months earlier. The next day he caught the train north.

CHAPTER TWELVE

Destiny in Kimberley

The consequences of Selous's meeting with Rhodes at the Kimberley Club were profound. Over 6 and 7 December 1889, the principal features of the occupation of Mashonaland were resolved, these being the route of the pioneer force and the sites where settlements would be made. Selous's relief at finding that Rhodes now had his eye on Mashonaland, rather than Matabeleland, was tempered by the discovery that Rhodes was preparing to launch a pre-emptive attack on Gubulawayo. By dissuading him from this cynical filibuster, Selous rendered as valuable a service to the land he loved, and to the Crown, as anything else he did in his lifetime. At the least, it preserved an uneasy peace in Zambesia for another four years.

One of the most remarkable aspects of this period in the 'scramble' is the speed of developments. Rhodes had dreamed of the North for years without making any perceptible progress. Now, within a year, he had acquired the concession and been granted a royal charter of formidable scope. The British South Africa Company was licensed to engage in mining, commerce and trade. It was also empowered to make and enforce laws, build roads, railways and other public works. The area of its operations was bound in the south by Bechuanaland and the Transvaal, and in the east by undefined 'Portuguese possessions'. No limit was imposed on its northern operations. Barotseland and Nyasaland were within grasp, and the lakes of Central Africa beckoned. The game was half won, or so it must have seemed to Rhodes.

The charter deserves some re-examination here. Even at a time when the exercise of power was frequently cloaked in a spurious propriety, the Chartered Company was a flimsy basis for territorial

166

acquisition. All Lobengula had agreed to in the Rudd concession was that whites could prospect for gold in his lands. Furthermore, there was Rudd's verbal assurance that no more than ten men would come 'to dig a hole', and that they would subject themselves to the king's authority. This was the basis on which Rhodes had been given *carte blanche* in Zambesia.

In the normal course of events, the Matabele themselves had no use for legal niceties. But, cornered and vulnerable, Lobengula was trying to play the game by European rules. Having realized his mistake in signing the concession, he had tried to repudiate it. A notice declaring the suspension of the agreement had appeared above the king's name in the *Bechuanaland News and Malmani Chronicle* earlier that year. He did not deny granting the concession, but said he was reconsidering it. To signal his demur, he declined to take delivery of the rifles stipulated by the concession, although he did accept the monthly payment of £100.

The king's resistance had been stiffened by two forces. The first was Rhodes's rival concessionaires, including Fairbairn and Phillips, who remained influential at court. The second was the indunas and the amatjaha, who were demanding with increasing vociferousness for the whites to be swept from the country. In using all his diplomatic wiles to avoid Matabele self-immolation, Lobengula was being exposed to risk. Some outsiders thought there was a real danger of a coup. The king told the militant indunas at one meeting: 'You told me you were afraid of guns – the white men will bring guns and horses. If you go against me I will have to call the white men – they are my friends, and if I must put kraal against kraal I must.'

At this juncture, another character appears on the scene. In all his dealings with Lobengula – as in much else that required dealings 'on the quiet' – Rhodes turned to his closest companion, a man impetuous and unscrupulous, charming and daring, a doctor and a gambler, Leander Starr Jameson.

The sheer dash of the name is suggestive of recklessness, but nothing in Jameson's appearance suggested the filibustering freebooter whose invasion of the Transvaal in 1896 ruined his mentor. 'The Doctor' was slight and balding, and something of a dandy. His most remarkable feature was his dark, restless eyes, which belied a languidly convivial manner. Jameson was a Scot, the same age as Rhodes and a year or so younger than Selous. He shared with Rhodes a poor constitution, and had come to South Africa in his mid-twenties to set up a practice in Kimberley. There his quick-witted charm and gambling exploits had established him as a leading citizen and confidant of Rhodes. Gradually his practice was allowed to fall into decline as he was drawn into Rhodes's affairs.

On his first visit to Gubulawayo, Jameson had won Lobengula's gratitude by easing the royal gout with morphine. In September 1889 Rhodes asked him to return, to see if he could persuade the king to accept the charter, and to 'give the road' to a Mashonaland expedition. Jameson was still at the royal kraal when Selous arrived in Kimberley in December.

Rhodes's headquarters was the Kimberley Club, the centre of Diamond Fields society, with a broad, shady verandah and reputedly the only tended lawn in Kimberley. Its codes were somewhat quirky; wealth or social distinction were prerequisites, but dress standards were slapdash, even shabby, and wayfarers like Selous had traditionally been welcome. Archibald Colquhoun, a colonial bureaucrat who had come to work for Rhodes, said it had 'more millionaires to the square foot than any other place in the world'. Drinking and gambling were on a heroic scale. The food was appalling.

Colquhoun found the atmosphere at Kimberley 'electric . . . Anyone might be a millionaire the next day . . . Big things were in the air. "Northern expansion" was on everyone's lips.' Rhodes was living in a tin-roofed shanty, owned by Jameson, opposite the club, where he took meals at his own table. He was also inclined to hold court on the verandah, gesticulating wildly to 'the North', often with a better sense of drama than direction. Eventually, to still argument, an arrow was put up, to point clearly whither the north actually lay.

Selous found Rhodes discussing routes north with Frank Johnson and Maurice Heany. His fellow members of the Selous Exploration Syndicate had come to Kimberley after being thrown out of work by Rhodes's amalgamation with the Bechuanaland Exploration Company. Initially, Johnson had tried to convince Rhodes that they were due compensation. When that failed, he set about making himself indispensable to the Colossus. Now he was talking about leading an invasion of Matabeleland.

168

Rhodes was frustrated and impatient. Despite the best efforts of Jameson and his morphine, Lobengula continued to bar the way to Mashonaland. 'Nature abhors a vacuum', was Rhodes's maxim, and a vacuum undoubtedly existed. Two possibilities existed in his mind: Mashonaland would have to be occupied from the east coast via the Zambesi; or the Matabele would have to be confronted directly by a superior military force.

As they would show again, neither Rhodes nor Jameson had any qualms about filibustering. In Gubulawayo, Jameson had taken soundings among the whites on the likely reaction to a confrontation with the Matabele, and was encouraged. In November he wrote to Rutherfoord Harris, the Company's secretary in Kimberley: 'I have spoken freely [to the missionaries Helm and Moffat] and they are convinced that Rhodes is right that he will never be able to work peaceably alongside the [Matabele], and that the sooner the brush is over the better.'

Frank Johnson had scented the mood in Kimberley, and was only too keen to work off his grudge against Lobengula. Soon he and Heany had produced a document, headed grandly: 'Memorandum of Agreement between Cecil John Rhodes, Maurice Heany and Frank Johnson'. It stated that the two young adventurers would raise a force of 500 men to 'carry by assault all the principal strongholds of the Matabele nation, and generally so to break up the power of the Amandebele that the British South Africa Company might conduct its operations in peace and safety'. For this service Johnson and Heany were to receive £150,000 and 50,000 morgen* of land.

There has been much controversy among Rhodesian historians over this alleged plot. Johnson's version of it was excised from his 1940 autobiography, *Great Days*, at the request of Godfrey Huggins, then Prime Minister of Southern Rhodesia, who feared that it might inflame race relations. But the deleted passages survive. In one Johnson wrote how he had planned to take a force to the Matabele frontier, and then, one night, ride pell mell for Gubulawayo.

> I had an open mind as to the procedure after securing the King and his entourage. We might make a complete job of it by killing Lobengula and smashing each military kraal,

---

* A Dutch measure, equivalent to roughly two acres.

169

before they had time to concentrate or organize. Or – and this I favoured most – I might dig myself in at Bulawayo with Lobengula and his entourage as hostages.

Johnson's highly-coloured version of his life story is suspect, as has been demonstrated by Robert Cary. *Great Days* is shot through with untruths. Mr Cary dismisses this particular story, and he may be right that Rhodes would never have approved such a wild scheme. The original of the memorandum has been lost, and we only have Johnson's word that Rhodes signed it.

But Rhodes did ask Johnson to draw up an invasion plan, and the fact that he gave the military option serious consideration is made plain in a letter by Rutherfoord Harris. This even suggests that the leading British officials in South Africa had given their approval, as had Khama, the Mangwato chief, who was no friend of the Matabele, and whose territory would have to be used as a platform for invasion.

An armed road making party, with Khama's consent and assistance, will commence making a wagon road to Mount Hampden. Permission to build this road will only be asked from Khama, in so far as it runs through his territory, but Lobengula's permission will not be asked, he will simply be informed by Mr Moffat. Make it we shall, and the Government authorize us, should Lobengula attack us, not only of course to defend ourselves but to take what measures we deem fit against him.

If Lobengula looks on in silence and does nothing, the charter will occupy Mashonaland. If, on the other hand, Lobengula attacks us, then the original plan communicated [to Khama, and the missionary James Hepburn, to whom this letter was written] will be carried out to the very letter. He must expect no mercy and none will be given him. If he attacks us he is doomed, if he does not, his fangs will be drawn, the pressure of civilization on all his borders will press more and more heavily upon him.

Further evidence that Rhodes was ready to use force against Lobengula comes from Selous himself. In his only reference to the episode, he indicated in an interview with the historian Basil Williams many years later that when he arrived in Kimberley Rhodes had actually accepted Johnson's plan.

Selous had abhorred militarism in Prussia, and liked it no more in his own countrymen. 'I am not a fighting man, and neither look forward to the prospect of being shot, nor feel any strong desire to shoot anyone else,' he declared.

To the proposals being bandied around the table by Rhodes and Johnson, Selous said that a raid on Gubulawayo would be a disaster. The proposition that a force of 500 whites could invade Matabeleland and make war on 10,000 warriors was ludicrous. Furthermore, an attack on Gubulawayo would bring retaliation against the traders and missionaries, while the invaders 'would have to fire into kraals killing women and children and so arousing great indignation in England'. All in all, Selous added dryly, 'this would be a bad beginning for the British South African Company.'

It was not simply the inadvisability of confronting the Matabele that Selous questioned. His feelings about Lobengula were complex and conflicting. The Sea-Cow Row still rankled, but he recoiled from unprovoked action to depose the king. He summarized his feelings succinctly in a letter to his mother: 'I abhor the Matabele, yet I would not have them interfered with or their country invaded without a casus belli; but that they should keep Europeans out of Mashunaland is preposterous.' Johnson continued to press for invasion, but Selous's persuasiveness won the day. He told Basil Williams in their interview, in 1914, that Rhodes 'was not pig-headed when good reasons [were] stated'. In the end he 'yielded to these arguments'.

At the same time as entertaining the idea of an invasion through Matabeleland, Rhodes had been considering the possibility of occupying Mashonaland from the east coast, via the Zambesi. In a letter which exposes Rhodes's startling ignorance about conditions on the river, he had suggested a month earlier to his closest business associate, Alfred Beit, that they have built 'a steam boat for the river', for an expedition which would 'make for the head sources of the Mazoe and build a fort on high ground'. This 'would settle the question [vis-à-vis the Portuguese] once for all, and place Mashonaland in our hands'.

Having dismissed the invasion idea, Rhodes now asked Selous about the possibility of an expedition up the Zambesi. His response was relayed by Rhodes to the Duke of Abercorn, chairman of the Company:

> He gave me as his opinion that the expedition was bound to fail: 1st owing to the hostility of the Portuguese, 2nd that from the junction of the Shire as far as Tete in the winter, the river would have barely a foot of water, and 3rd when you landed at Tete you could get no transport service to get you from Tete to the Mashona highlands, and in addition that the fever stricken district of the Zambesi Valley would decimate the expedition.

Selous's alternative to these plans was simple: occupy Mashonaland by the most direct route from the south which avoided the Matabele altogether. There was always a risk, he told Rhodes, that the expedition would be attacked, but he knew of a route which he thought would bypass Matabeleland by a safe margin. It was the one which he had proposed in his letter from Tete to the Selous Exploration Syndicate. The force should muster in the north of Khama's country, but then, instead of charging north to Gubulawayo, as Johnson had proposed, it should turn east, following the Limpopo river to the Shashi, and then strike north across virgin veld to the Mashonaland plateau. The destination would be Mount Hampden, which Selous said was the ideal spot for the first settlement.

The main danger was of an ambush while a path was being hacked out of the dense bush of the lowveld. Balancing this, Selous told Rhodes, was the advantage that the route would not infringe on any chief paying tribute to Lobengula. Also, it was probably too distant from Gubulawayo for the Matabele to launch a full-scale attack.

So far, no agreement had been made that Selous would join in the charter enterprise. Indeed, it now appeared that he might still be a threat to it. One of the conditions of the charter had been that there should be no unseemly squabbling with rival concessionaires. Rhodes's instructions from Whitehall were that he should settle with anyone who could show just title to a mineral concession in Zambesia. It would cost him a fortune to eliminate such claims, some of which were valid – like the concession of Fairbairn, Phillips and Leask, which he bought for £20,000 – and some fatuous.

Now here was Selous, flourishing the Mapondera concession, and pointedly making clear to Rhodes his intention to write articles in the British press confirming his opinion that a large part of Mashonaland – including the area for which he had the concession, and Mount Hampden, the proposed settlement – was completely independent of Lobengula, and therefore outside the remit of the charter.

Rhodes wrote to Abercorn: 'I saw at once the danger of our position if a series of articles appeared in the papers from a man of Selous's position claiming that Mashonaland was independent of Lobengula . . . a campaign conducted in the press by Selous would have been most detrimental to our charter.' Rhodes set to work, first to discourage Selous from this course, then to recruit him for the Company. The high-pitched voice and logic were, as always, insistent – the charter was the only hope for a British Mashonaland, Selous's concession was worthless. But Rhodes's legendary powers of persuasion did not work immediately, as he wrote to Abercorn:

> It took me a long time to show him that if he could prove Mashonaland to be independent of Lobengula it would not help the Mashonas but simply would be helping the Portuguese claims and therefore that he would be helping the Portuguese to get the country.

Eventually, however . . .

> when he saw that the only hope for the country was the success of the charter he agreed to throw his lot in with us and proposed with Mr Johnson . . . to form an expedition and go in and occupy the country for the Charter. He agreed to abandon his concession when I told him it was not worth the paper it was written on. Johnson, Heaney and Barrow [sic] had also shares in this concession. They agreed to tear up their scrip; they deemed it fair if I could give Selous something for the time and labour he had spent; I gave him personally 2000 pounds out of my own private fund, but on

173

the distinct understanding that it had nothing to do with his concession and that I recognized it in no sort of way. There were also two companions with him [Burnett and Thomas] and they received 750 pounds each . . . I think they had been away altogether 8 months on the expedition and had been through the most unheard of difficulties.

Logic had prevailed in Kimberley, but not harmony. The clash between Johnson and Selous was not simply one of attitude, but of personality and temperament. When crossed, Selous was capable of a chilly imperiousness, and Johnson, who had been determined to put up an impressive front before Rhodes, evidently came away crushed and resentful. He and Selous had never got on, but from now on their dealings would be marked on Johnson's side by an acrimony which became serious enough to threaten the pioneer expedition. Henceforth, he was out to get Selous.

His main effort was his attempt to destroy Selous's reputation, long after he was dead, in *Great Days*. Johnson portrayed Selous as a shrill, obstinate and overweening pedant, whose importance to the Mashonaland adventure had been greatly over-estimated and who was more a nuisance than anything else. Johnson's version was that the plan for the occupation of Mashonaland was his alone. In one passage, often cited in biographies of Rhodes and histories of the era, he related a chance meeting with Rhodes over breakfast in the Kimberley Club, on 22 December, at which he supposedly proposed the 'safe' route to Mount Hampden, and drew up a detailed plan for an expedition of 250 men and 117 ox-wagons, along with an accurate costing.

The story, or at least its central strand, is nonsense. Johnson probably did breakfast with Rhodes on 22 December, when he presented an estimate of costs as a contractor for the expedition. By then Rhodes had approached Colonel Sir Frederick Carrington of the Bechuanaland Police to lead the expedition, with Selous as guide, and had recoiled on being told by Carrington that 2500 men would be required, entailing a cost of more than £1 million. At this stage, Johnson said that he, Heany and Borrow (no mention was made of their recent partner, Selous) could occupy the country with 250 men at a cost of £94,000, and Rhodes promptly appointed them contractors. The rest of Johnson's story was simply an attempt to steal the main credit from Selous.

A more accurate summing-up of the Kimberley Club meeting is contained in a hurried note from Rhodes to Cawston four weeks later which bear the signs of Selous's influence:

> Selous has arranged to take an expedition into Mashonaland and occupy it before July. It is the best plan and we need not now undertake the Zambesi expedition. The policy of the concession should be to develop the trade and strengthen the trading posts. As soon as we are in possession of Mashonaland the effect will be to re-act on the Portuguese ... We hope we will be able to do it without hostilities with Lobengula.

As the train from Kimberley rattled south in mid-December, Selous's spirits soared with the balmy summer temperature. The main aspects of the colonization of Mashonaland had been resolved. Rhodes and Johnson were to deal with recruitment and logistics. His role would be to guide the pioneer column to its destination, and he intended to travel to the Transvaal immediately to do some reconnaissance. From Cape Town he wrote an ebullient letter home:

> The concession the South African Chartered Company has taken over, and altogether I have made more than 2000 pounds cash this year and shall get more when the Mashuna country is opened up. I cannot come home at present. It would be most foolish of me to do so. The Chartered Company wish to employ me, and I think I may now consider myself to be in their service. At present they are allowing me a retaining fee – so much a month – to keep me going until they actually require my services.

It has been suggested by Professor Ranger that the £2000 payment was, in fact, a kind of bribe, and that Rhodes thereby bought Selous's silence on the flaws in the Rudd concession and the charter. It is fair to say that Selous was now on the Company payroll, and that he did not thereafter take issue in public with the charter. However, this was because he had put his faith in Rhodes as one

175

capable of making Mashonaland a British possession. Moreover, the suggestion that, in order to accommodate Rhodes, Selous ceased to argue Mashona independence is untrue. He continued to insist to Rhodes, Jameson and Harris that the Company should make good its title in Mashonaland by securing treaties with independent chiefs. Initially, the Kimberley regime dismissed the idea contemptuously, but, as will be seen, Selous pursued the argument until eventually it brought about a change of policy – even though it brought no benefit to the Mashona themselves.

In financial terms, Selous actually came out of the deal comparatively poorly. He had abandoned his interest in a valuable concession for a fraction of the amounts being paid by Rhodes to others. George Phillips, who received more than £7000 for his share of one of Lobengula's concessions, retired on it to Kensington, where his fondness for champagne and brandy contributed to his early death. Johnson, Heany and Borrow were left with something in the order of £20,000 each as Rhodes's contractors.

Selous's unworldliness revealed itself again, in a way he found more embarrassing, in the wrapping up of the Selous Exploration Syndicate. He and his partners had merged their interests with the Company, but the syndicate's backers wanted a *quid pro quo* for giving up their claims under the Mapondera concession. Tom Anderson, the chairman, wrote to Rhodes suggesting that he make some 'equitable proposal', with the veiled threat to have Selous's views on the Rudd concession raised in the House of Commons.

Rhodes's shrewdness in emphasizing that his payment to Selous was 'for the time and labour he had spent' on the Zambesi journey, rather than because of the value of the concession, now became apparent. He replied to the syndicate dismissively. 'I said we would in no way recognize their concession but that as a party was going into Mashonaland, I would recommend the Board to allow them to send in prospectors with the party to mark out 100 claims on halves with the Charter.' This offer was rejected, and for more than five years skirmishing continued, with Anderson offering to settle for £10,000 cash, and Rhodes offering shares in the Company at par, while complaining of 'this incessant blackmail'.

Finally, in 1893, as Selous was on his way home to England after the Matabele War, Anderson intercepted him in Cape Town. From

176

Anderson's subsequent letter to Rhodes it would seem that Selous was thoroughly uncomfortable at the meeting:

> He was perfectly astonished to hear we had received no settlement from the Chartered Company and wished at once to use his influence with you . . . but being too busy at the time with the Governor and having to leave immediately for England he promised to write to you after his arrival home. I have since heard from him that he has done so and has asked you to bring about a settlement with us.

Whatever Selous wrote, it was ignored by Rhodes. Anderson received no reply, and soon afterwards the Selous Exploration Syndicate passed into history.

CHAPTER THIRTEEN

《‹•›》

Pioneers on the Selous Road

On the morning of 13 September 1890, a column of a few hundred mounted men in brown tunics and grey breeches, with slouch hats jammed on their heads, jingled to a halt on a plain roughly 1660 miles north-east of Cape Town. It must have seemed an uninspiring end to a long and dangerous journey. A solitary kopje, or hill, lay a mile or so to the south, while to the north the landscape stretched away flat and almost treeless to the horizon. The rains would start soon, turning the veld into lush pasture, but now it was brown and stubbly at the end of the dry winter. A rough flagpole was erected, the men shuffled to attention, and the Union flag was run up as two seven-pounder guns boomed the announcement to the empty plain that Mashonaland had become the latest of the Empress Victoria's foreign possessions.

Nothing in his life gave Selous more satisfaction than guiding the British South Africa Company's Pioneer Corps in the peaceful occupation of Mashonaland. He carved a road which was beyond the reach of the Matabele, but which was through total wilderness, so that one pioneer officer, Captain Henry 'Skipper' Hoste, later remarked, 'Without Selous we would certainly have lost our way.' This route, which for years was the main road into the country, was known as the Selous Road, and after his death his brother Edmund wrote to *The Times* that he had once confided the hope that this name would survive. (It did not.) 'My brother's wish thus revealed must, I am sure, be a deep one, for he was not wont to express pride in anything which he himself had accomplished.'

From his meeting with Rhodes in Kimberley, he returned briefly to Cape Town before going up to the Transvaal on a reconnaissance trip. His main purpose was to get information from a hunter named

178

Carter who knew the lowveld region through which Selous intended to take the pioneers. Carter, who lived in the Zoutpansberg district of the northern Transvaal, gave him useful information on lowveld conditions, before providing Selous with even more valuable intelligence: the Transvaal Boers had long cast an expansionist eye towards Mashonaland and, hearing of Rhodes's charter plans, had started organizing a trek of their own in an attempt to get there first. Selous spoke to a few Afrikaners of his acquaintance who confirmed the story. A force of 1500 Transvalers, mainly from the Marico district, were preparing to march into Mashonaland under the leadership of two prominent Boers, Hans Bezuidenhout and Barend Vorster.

Selous despatched a message to Rhodes. Immediate action was imperative, as the charter force was far from ready to move. Rhodes had earlier told Knutsford: 'You cannot allow a single Boer to settle across the Limpopo until our position in the north is secure.' Now, supported by Sir Henry Loch, Britain's new High Commissioner at the Cape, Rhodes wrote to President Kruger of the Transvaal. They met on 12 March 1890 at Blignaut's Pont on the Vaal river where a deal was made: Kruger was to be given a free hand in Swaziland, but would stay out of Mashonaland. This effectively ended Boer ambitions north of the Limpopo.

While Selous was in the Transvaal, an ugly little charade was being played out at Gubulawayo. Jameson's morphine and charm had started to work on the gouty king. This process was given a nudge by Whitehall, which agreed to demonstrate the splendour of the Great White Queen. The result was the most bizarre diplomatic mission ever received in Matabeleland.

Early in January of the new decade, Captain Victor Ferguson and three fellow members of the Royal Horse Guards, resplendent in scarlet serge, glittering cuirasses and plumed helmets, clanked up to Lobengula's mud and thatch kraal to present gifts from Her Majesty. The scene was recorded by Henry Borrow, in his capacity as a special correspondent for *The Times*. By now the king's gout was so bad that he was 'seated in a bath chair in a cattle kraal, wrapped in a coloured blanket, his feet swathed in dirty flannel bandages. As he sat in the midst of dirt and discomfort, skulls of slaughtered bullocks and mangy dogs, he looked the picture of an African savage.'

179

The king was evidently impressed by the gloriously-attired guards, and Jameson interpreted a message from Queen Victoria in such a way as to leave no doubt that she endorsed Rhodes's mission. Jameson's account of what happened next was that he showed Lobengula a map with the proposed route and asked if the wagons might go east. According to Jameson and Johan Colenbrander, the guide with him, the king not only agreed, but said he would supply 100 warriors to help Selous cut a road. It was February 1890.

With opposition from the Matabele and the Boers supposedly dealt with, preparations went ahead. Recruiting and equipping commenced in Cape Town and Kimberley. The pioneers were signed up by Johnson, as contractor to the British South Africa Company, although Rhodes took an active part in the selecting, making places for young men to whom he took a liking, and for members of the best Cape families. Rhodes's name and the air of a great adventure drew more than 2000 applications for the few hundred places, including Selous's earliest friend in South Africa, Frank Mandy, who was made an officer.

The pioneers were a microcosm of South African society. They included doctors, farmers, clergymen, engineers, the sons of aristocrats and the sons of artisans. They were drawn from Afrikaans as well as English families, and were young, fit and well educated. Johnson, who was hardly objective, called them 'the finest body of men ever got into uniform'. The radical MP, Henry Labouchère, who loathed Rhodes and all his works, denounced them as 'border ruffians of Hebraic extraction'. Philip Mason, an historian, saw them as romantics, 'with the strenuous Puritan romanticism of the Victorians, of Charles Kingsley and Arnold of Rugby'. Robert Blake was probably closer in describing them neither as heroes nor villains, but a mixed bag, drawn by Rhodes's charisma and the chance of making a fortune.

Selous, meanwhile, had returned from the Transvaal to Khama's country, where the Pioneer Corps was to muster. A supply chain was established from the Cape up the Missionary Road as far as Palapye, a forward base in what was British Bechuanaland. By late March, Selous was ready to start cutting a road to the Macloutsie river, on the edge of territory disputed between Lobengula and Khama, from where the expedition would set out.

Selous had been sceptical all along that Lobengula would willingly acquiesce to the occupation, let alone that he would help by providing 100 men for cutting the road as Jameson and Colenbrander maintained. It therefore came as no surprise when he rode into Palapye to find no sign of either the promised Matabele or of Colenbrander. Selous decided to ride to Gubulawayo with Sam Edwards, a hard-bitten old trader, 'to find out for myself if Lo Bengula was really prepared to cooperate'.

The version of Selous's last meeting with Lobengula which came to be accepted in Kimberley, was that the hunter went into Gubulawayo with the subtlety of an enraged bull-elephant, and wrecked the delicately balanced arrangement which Jameson had secured. The genesis of this story was a secret telegram from Borrow to Jameson, sent at Frank Johnson's instigation, reporting that Selous had gone to the royal kraal intending 'if possible to upset the arrangements you made'. Johnson backed this up by complaining directly to Rhodes himself that Selous was taking matters into his own hands, adding: 'It is impossible [to] allow officers [to] act in [a] manner not only independent but foolish and ill-advised.' The fact that Selous had previously betrayed his irritation with Lobengula's procrastination, and his well-known detestation of the Matabele, gave credibility to the theory that he behaved intemperately. However, there is good reason to doubt the accepted Kimberley story, and to suggest rather that there may have been a basic flaw in Jameson's account of what had passed earlier between him and Lobengula.

Selous arrived to find the Matabele capital crackling with tension. Rumours were rife of invasion from the south, and the warriors were becoming ever more insistent in their demands to be allowed to bathe their assegais in white blood. Amid this turmoil, he met Colenbrander and immediately taxed him with failing to deliver the Matabele labourers as promised. In reply, Colenbrander could only refer him to Lobengula.

The king received Selous warmly, being 'evidently pleased to see me again' after a gap of two years. More remarkable, however, was that Lobengula flatly denied Jameson's story that he had agreed to allow a new road to be made to Mashonaland, or that he would send men to help make it. He told Selous: 'There is only one road to

Mashunaland, and that goes through my country.' He made it clear, too, that any attempt to build a new road would be resisted.

It is evident that Selous felt himself in an uncomfortable position. Although committed to the Mashonaland adventure, and hence the British South Africa Company, he believed the king's story that he had not given Jameson permission for a road. Furthermore, he found that some of his old acquaintances at Gubulawayo were far from sympathetic to the idea of a white trek which would overthrow the established Interior order. Sam Edwards, the crusty old trader who had accompanied him to see Lobengula, was one who regretted the challenge to the king's authority. Some of this attitude – the affection that the old hands had always felt for 'old Ben' – was rekindled in Selous in the two days he spent with the king. Later he recalled they talked 'on many subjects, especially game, for [Lobengula] loved to talk about wild animals, having been a great hunter in his youth'.

Finally, the king said: 'Rhodes has sent me many "mouths" . . . But I am Lo Bengula and I want to see the big white chief himself. Selous, take Rhodes by the hand and come back here with him. I will then settle my business with him very quickly.'

Selous was sufficiently moved by this appeal to make an extraordinary journey. Mounted on a horse called Mars, he raced more than 600 miles from Gubulawayo to Kimberley in eleven days, covering more than 100 miles in one day alone. From Palapye, he dashed off a note to his mother: 'I am going to try and persuade Mr Rhodes to accompany me back to Bulawayo. Lobengula promises to come to an understanding with Mr Rhodes as to the opening up of Mashunaland.' It was a vain hope. Fast though he travelled, news of his mission preceded him to Kimberley, probably through a telegram from Denis Doyle, the Company's agent at the royal kraal, sent from Palapye. Rhodes left Kimberley a couple of days before Selous arrived, a coincidence which he found suspicious. Many years later he told Basil Williams that 'hearing of [my] coming [Rhodes] had gone off to the Orange Free State to avoid giving an answer to Loben'.

The idea of a diplomatic mission by Rhodes got no further. When he returned to Kimberley, he again asked Jameson to step into the breach. Early in April, the doctor wrote languidly to his brother:

'Selous is here and in conjunction with some incompetence up above seems to have got my previous arrangements in a bit of a mess.' The following day Jameson wrote again: 'I am going to try and get things back to the point I left them. Selous goes back with me; but probably only as far as Palapye – as he is not persona grata with Loben, and I am sure I can do better alone.'

It may be that Jameson still believed the fiction that Selous was not welcome at the royal kraal, but he did not say so to the hunter himself, and it seems rather that he did not want Selous in the way when he was dealing with the king. On the ride back, Jameson told Selous to stay in Tati, on the grounds that Lobengula might take him hostage in order to thwart the expedition. It was an implausible notion, and Selous sensed the fabrication, but he could only register his disappointment. 'As he was my superior officer I was bound to obey.' Jameson, although he spent five days back at Gubulawayo with his hypodermic and morphine, never did succeed in getting consent for the expedition. Finally, he told the king flatly that a large armed force with a hundred wagons would start for Mashonaland within the next few months. Then he summoned the white traders and warned them of the Company's plans, while advising that if there was trouble with the Matabele they would have to fend for themselves.

Selous never saw Lobengula again. Once the possibility of a visit by Rhodes had been discarded, he put the recent events at Gubulawayo to the back of his mind, and started cutting a road to the Macloutsie. He managed to convince himself that the situation actually represented an improvement. 'We knew exactly where we were, and realized fully that the new road to Mashunaland would have to be made not only without the assistance of Lobengula, but in despite of him and all his tribe.'

This view was not shared by Sam Edwards, who had been at the last meeting with Lobengula. Two months later, as the pioneers were mustering at the Macloutsie, Edwards wrote to the Gubulawayo trader James Dawson:

Many thanks for your last letter in which you told me that you were intending to put your house in order 'for tomorrow we die' . . .

I received a letter from Selous last night. He completely ignores the idea that he ought to have kept his word and laughs at my punctilious notions of honour.

Edwards's cryptic reference raises more questions than it answers, but it is evident that he was upset about Selous's association with the expedition. The changes sweeping north with the tide of imperialism were overtaking not only the natives, but the white tribe of the Interior too. The old fraternity of hunters and traders was, at last, breaking up.

Animosity continued to fester between Selous and Johnson at the advance camp on the Macloutsie. Their differences were aggravated by the extremely ill-defined chain of command which Rhodes had established. Johnson, insisting on military formalities, had been given the rank of major, and, as Rhodes's contractor, had the responsibility of delivering the pioneers to Mount Hampden. Selous, although only a captain, was 'intelligence officer' and guide, and had absolute authority over how they should get there. The situation was not clarified by the attachment to the expedition of two civilians with special status. One was Jameson, who was naturally deemed to speak for Rhodes himself. The other was Archibald Colquhoun, an oriental explorer and civil servant, who was charged with establishing and heading a civil administration once Mashonaland was reached.

The air of hectic confusion surrounding the expedition worried Sir Henry Loch, the High Commissioner, who was less in thrall to Rhodes than his predecessor, Sir Hercules Robinson. Loch told Rhodes he was trying to cut too many corners and insisted that in addition to the advance force of about 200 pioneers, there should be a back-up military contingent of 500 men against the possibility of trouble with the Matabele. This force, to be known as the BSA Company Police, was to be commanded by an experienced army officer. Loch's choice was Lieutenant-Colonel Edward Pennefather, an able if choleric dragoon. Second in command would be Captain Sir John Willoughby, another cavalry officer, who was to play a more prominent, if less reputable, part in the South African story.

Johnson was unhappy to find he was no longer the senior officer, but made up for it by pulling rank on his juniors. He complained continually to Kimberley about Selous, who he said was 'averse to orders'. In one particularly ill-tempered despatch to Rhodes, Johnson wrote: 'Selous is inclined to give trouble and is more bother to me than all the Matabele.' When Harris wrote to him with a list of needs for 'the Selous Road expedition', Johnson replied icily, 'by which expedition I presume you mean the company's Pioneer Corps'.

Selous did not take well to Johnson's idea of military discipline, but it seems that the contractor did not endear himself to many of the men either. One, Adrian Darter, described him as 'a short thick-set, furtive-eyed dark man with the lungs of the Bull of Bashan'. Selous, on the other hand, was 'our hero', Darter wrote. 'The magnetism of the man is in his mild serene speech.'

The feud was bad enough now, while the force was still gathering on the Macloutsie, but Colquhoun and Pennefather realized it would spell disaster if the column should run into real trouble. Colquhoun, who sensed that Johnson was up to mischief, wrote to Harris: 'Selous is very valuable. If Johnson should write anything against him, ask Rhodes not to believe it.'

The issue was resolved just as it was threatening to get out of hand. Pennefather, too, had taken to Selous, having been introduced by him to the exhilaration of chasing giraffe on horseback. He decided to detach Selous from the column, and gave him *carte blanche* to carry out the road-cutting independently. The next time Johnson fired off a command – 'on receipt of this you will be good enough to proceed to this camp as fast as possible' – Selous replied with cool satisfaction: 'I received your order yesterday. However circumstances have occurred which render it impossible for me to comply with them.'

Thereafter everything went more smoothly. When the column reached its destination Pennefather wrote:

> It would have been folly on my part to have interfered with Selous. He is a man with a wonderful knowledge of country and of great tact in dealing with the natives, and any information given by him is absolutely reliable. And as to the

185

way in which he carried out his work, I never knew a man more conscientious in his duty.

Johnson differed to the end. He wrote of Selous in his memoirs: 'It is represented that he played a far more important part in the work of the expedition than he did in actual practice.'

The column lined up on the banks of the Macloutsie on 24 June 1890. There were about 200 pioneers and almost double that number of BSA Company Police, both groups wearing the distinctive brown and grey uniform. Black ancillaries, including drovers, labourers, batmen and cooks, added around 400 to the complement. The base camp was a dusty melee, for in addition to the men there were hundreds of horses and more than 1000 cattle to draw the wagons. Fighting men were armed with Martini-Henry rifles, and the firepower was boosted by four Maxim guns and two seven-pound field guns. The equipment included a naval searchlight, powered by steam engine, which was intended to impress the Matabele with the whites' supernatural powers as it played across the night sky.

This extraordinary cavalcade was inspected by a British army officer, Major-General Paul Methuen, representing Sir Henry Loch. Jameson's biographer, Ian Colvin, gave this account of his parting words to the departing imperial force:

Methuen: Gentlemen, have you got maps?
Officers: Yes sir.
Methuen: And pencils?
Officers: Yes sir.
Methuen: Well gentlemen, your destiny is Mount Hampden. You go to a place called Siboutsi. I do not know whether Siboutsi is a man or a mountain. Mr Selous, I understand, is of the opinion that it is a man; but we will pass that by. Mr Selous is of the opinion that Mount Hampden is placed 10 miles too far to the west. You had better correct that; but perhaps on second thoughts, better not. Because you might be placing it 10 miles too far to the east. Now good morning gentlemen.

A trackless wilderness of 460 miles lay ahead. Selous felt this had not been adequately grasped by a number of the organizers, including Johnson. 'The idea seemed to be that when everything was ready a trumpet would be blown, and the advance would then be made along known roads,' he wrote. In fact, the first stage of the trek would be through territory which not even he had ever travelled before. And in cutting a wagon track from the Macloutsie to the Tuli, he had seen just how thick the lowveld mopane bush was, and how hard the going would be.

A Matabele attack remained the paramount concern, however. Intelligence reports indicated that Gubulawayo was on the boil. Pressed by the indunas, Lobengula had stated categorically that he would not allow the road to be built. Nevertheless, he delayed, while issuing orders for new shields and sandals to be made, the usual preparation for war. Some of the white traders, under constant insults from the amatjaha, packed up and left.

Selous's natural tendency to worry was exacerbated by the possibility of an ambush. From the advice he had been given by Boer friends like Cornelius van Rooyen, he feared that the pioneers were too few. The Boers had more experience than anyone of driving ox wagons into hostile territory, and they believed it would take 2000 men to be reasonably sure of repelling an all-out attack. The force was a quarter that size. Selous believed that a concerted Matabele attack might well annihilate the pioneers.

On 5 July, an advance guard consisting of Selous, Jameson and 100 or so militiamen, crossed the Tuli river into Matabele country. Out of the bush came a small band of warriors in the panoply of war – hairdress, shields and assegais – with a letter from Lobengula: 'Has the king killed any white men that an impi is collecting on his border? Or have the white men lost anything they are looking for?' Jameson replied: the whites intended no threat to the Matabele, but were proceeding to Mashonaland in accordance with the king's original agreement.

A few days later, with a great clamour of lowing beasts, drovers' cries and cracking whips, the main column – a two-mile caravan of wagons, oxen, horses and men – followed across the Tuli. A force of about 100 BSA Company Police under Sir John Willoughby came up as a rearguard a few days later.

The first stage was clearly the most perilous. This consisted of the lowveld bush which stretched ahead, menacing and impenetrable, for about 250 miles. Thickets of mopane trees reduced visibility in places to no more than twenty yards. Through this steamy jungle a wagon track had to be hacked out, rivers forded and the high plateau reached before the onset of the rainy season, which might come as early as September, and which would leave the wagons bogged. Once they got to the plateau, they would be able to cover the final 200 miles to Mount Hampden over open country in relative safety, but Selous was certain that if they got into any difficulties in the lowveld they would be attacked. This made it vital that his route be adequately prepared for the wagons and, above all, that it should be direct. To get lost would be fatal. He checked maps and compass readings constantly and rode out in search of local tribesmen who might act as guides.

Heat and the sense of peril were oppressive as they hacked their way forward in these first weeks. Men never wandered far from their horses, and rifles and bandoliers were kept at hand. With visibility so restricted it was easy to imagine the shapes of Matabele between the mopane branches, and rumours were rife. Trooper William Armstrong wrote in his diary: 'Fighting said to be imminent. Small parties of Matabele all around. No bugle and no talking. Five men on top of each wagon. Every day we expect to be attacked.'

Matabele scouts were, in fact, following the lumbering wagon column. At one point, panic swept through the ranks of the black auxiliaries, and wagon drivers and herdsmen deserted in some numbers. Khama, ever friendly to British interests, especially when there was a chance to score against Lobengula, came to the rescue. By sending a force of 200 men to join the pioneers, he probably prevented a mass desertion by the auxiliaries. Selous believed that this contribution was decisive, and thought it shameful that the Company never saw fit to acknowledge it.

Henceforth, Selous, with about forty blacks, operated in advance of the column. He set up an intelligence unit of mounted scouts, drawn mainly from Khama's men, who rode out ten miles or so from the column looking for signs of Matabele. This was Selous's element and he was content despite the gruelling routine. Road-making was not quite as simple as Pennefather described. ('You cut a path through the bush wide enough for a wagon to go along. Then you drive your wagon along and the road is made.') There were many areas where the ground was not firm enough for the two-mile column of wagons, and trees had to be cut and laid to 'corduroy' the track.

In mid-July, Jameson wrote to Harris: 'The men are working well and keen to get on; but it is pretty hard work for them, as so far it has been horribly thick bush . . . it will be as much as we can do to get in before the rains commence.'

Relief was all the more welcome for being rare. By the Umshabetse river they had covered the first, and most difficult, stage of sixty miles, and Selous and his men frolicked in the warm, muddy water. Emerging refreshed and dripping, he sat down on the bank and wrote a letter home:

> If we can get just two hours' notice of the approach of the Matabele, just sufficient time to have all the wagons put into laager on the old Boer plan, Lobengula's men can do nothing to us as we have several Maxim guns. If they attack us in laager they must suffer fearful loss. Do not be downhearted, dearest mother. I sincerely hope there will be no fighting, and even if there is I stand as good a chance of escaping harm as anyone else. Now good bye my dearest old mother. If this expedition goes through successfully, you will soon see me in England.

He was offering a reassurance that he did not feel. That night a hyena set up an unearthly racket, circling the camp while howling and shrieking, 'like a fiend alternately wailing and rejoicing'. Selous was not a superstitious man, but the last time he had heard anything like it had been the night his friend French got lost, never to be seen again. 'The hideous serenade stirred sad memories within me, and almost made me think that an African banshee was wailing and crying round us, and forewarning us of woe and disaster to come.'

Still, the wagons rolled on without incident, and Selous was enormously relieved to find soon afterwards a Banyai tribesman who had worked for him as a guide in 1873. By the end of July, the road had been cut to the banks of the Lundi river. They had covered about 200 miles in less than five weeks since leaving the Macloutsie, and their goal was within reach.

The problem which now most concerned Selous was finding a route for the wagons to climb the escarpment to the Mashonaland plateau. From the Lundi he set out with four companions on 2 August, and for the next two days they skirted the plateau, until he found what seemed to be a pass ascending gently through the broken country:

> When the sun went down we were still in the pass, but as I felt sure . . . we were now only just below the edge of the plateau, I asked Nicholson to look for a suitable spot to pass the night . . . and cantered on by myself up the pass. About a mile ahead stood a small rocky hill whose summit rose well above the broken ridges by which I was surrounded. This hill I climbed, and my feelings may be better imagined than described when I say that I saw stretched out before me, as far as the eye could reach, a wide expanse of open grassy country, and knew that I was looking over the south-western portion of the high plateau of Mashunaland.

Selous felt 'a weight of responsibility, that had at times become almost unbearable, fall from my shoulders'. Excitedly, he and his companions returned to the camp on the Lundi, where he was assailed by questions. But even at this stage, he remained on edge. 'Skipper' Hoste, who had been with him throughout the road-building, recalled that Selous was relating his discovery in the orderly tent when a din erupted outside. Selous leapt to his feet, exclaiming: 'My God, they've caught us on the hop.' They dashed from the tent, revolvers in hand, only to find that the racket had been caused, not by a Matabele attack, but by a mob of men and dogs chasing a hare through camp.

On 6 August, Johan Colenbrander arrived at the Lundi with a final warning from Gubulawayo. Lobengula told Pennefather to turn back, 'unless you think you are strong enough to go on'. It was a last bluff, and everyone knew it. The message had been written more than two weeks earlier, and the moment for an attack had passed. Pennefather sent back a note that he had orders to proceed, and he would do so, irrespective.

It was at this point, rather than in the Matabele War three years later, that Lobengula's grip on Zambesia was broken. But through consummate brinkmanship he had preserved peace, playing for time until he knew it would be too late to attack. Selous recognized this, though he could perhaps have been more appreciative. He wrote that the king 'had a very difficult part to play, and it is wonderful that he managed to restrain his people as he did.' The young pioneer, Adrian Darter, put it better: 'Loben is the lion that would not devour us.'

By 14 August the column was on the plateau, and the spirits of the men lifted. At what became Fort Victoria, the biggest settlement on the new road, the corps relaxed for a few days, playing games of cricket and football. They had come up about 1000 feet, and breezes cooled the plains as the wagons rolled on. Colquhoun recalled:

> I remember the bivouac at night, when we took our well-earned rest rolled in our karosses and mackintosh sheets, the camp fire flickering and a savoury steam going up from cooking pots. The troopers round the fire sang lustily in the still African night, while the smoke and scent of their pipes, charged with the Boer tobacco which is good only on the veld, but unsurpassable there, filled the air with a peculiar pungency.

On 1 September, when they were less than 100 miles from their destination, Selous found some of his old wagon tracks which ran all the way to Mount Hampden. But now, with the prize in sight, he was deprived of the chance to join in the final savouring of success. Colquhoun had work to do as the new administrator, and decided to break away from the column to try to secure a treaty with the Manica chief Umtasa. It was a laudable objective, and demonstrated that Colquhoun meant seriously to reach an accommodation with native chiefs. The upshot, however, was that Selous was ordered to go too, and he was bitterly disappointed not to see the expedition to its end.

Ten days later, on 13 September 1890, the Union flag was raised a few miles south of Mount Hampden. Johnson said he thought the kopje, with the stream of the Makabusi nearby, was a better site. The place was named Fort Salisbury, after the British prime minister. The British South Africa Company expedition had been completed.

*

The new territory took a long time to fulfil the faith that had been placed in it. Some, as we shall see, would argue that it never did, although Selous never abandoned his belief that it would prove one of the most worthy in the imperial crown. A letter to his mother, with its tone of bashful pride, captures his feelings at this time:

This Mashonaland is really a magnificent country. It is simply marvellously well watered, the whole country being intersected in every direction by a perfect network of hard-running streams of crystle clear water. In the valleys the grass is always green. There is no other part of South Africa that can compare with it, and probably few parts of the world.

If only gold is found in fair quantities it will be all right, as a population will then flock up here and means of communication will be at once opened up; but if the gold is a failure, I fear the country will only go ahead slowly; for English and Scotchmen are not content nowadays to merely live in a fine country with a beautiful climate if there are no markets for produce and therefore no chance of making money.

So far everything has gone off so successfully that it seems like a dream and I have played a not unimportant part in it all, I am proud to be able to say. The road to Mashunaland is now being called the Selous Road and I hope the name will endure, though I don't suppose it will. An old Boer hunter whom I know well, and whom I saw just before the expedition started, said to me in Dutch 'I think the expedition without Mr Selous would be like a swarm of bees that has lost its queen and doesn't know where to go.'

But it is too bad of me to sing my own praises in this style, yet in the matter of the road I do feel most proud at the share I had in putting it through.

No native troubles are to be apprehended except from the Matabele, and with good management they ought now to be avoided . . . The [Mashona] are few and scattered and a very harmless, peaceful lot. They all seem delighted to see us and make use of such expressions as 'now that the white men have come into the country we shall be able to sleep' meaning that they will no longer live in perpetual fear of the Matabele and Gaza Zulus.

Almost exactly eighteen years after Selous's first visit to the territory, Mashonaland was British.

CHAPTER FOURTEEN

《•》

Sort of a Company Man

Selous remained a servant of the British South Africa Company for another two years. He served his employers well, as a diplomat securing treaties with native chiefs, and as an advocate extolling the virtues of the new territory to the British public. Rhodes paid tribute to his 'unique assistance', although Selous's treaty work was valued less highly than the optimistic gloss which he applied to the problems of Mashonaland in his writings.

But once the British flag had been raised in Mashonaland, something went out of his commitment to the Company, and his role in the next phase of the imperial advance was a relatively minor one. He is hardly to be seen in the buccaneering adventure by which Rhodes sought to seize the Portuguese port of Beira, and while the figures of Jameson, Sir John Willoughby and Captain Patrick Forbes were occupying the centre stage of a swashbuckling drama, Selous was generally to be found off on 'diplomatic work' in the bush.

There is an element of time-serving about the years of 1891 and 1892 in Selous's life. For years his family had been urging him to come home, and for the first time he himself felt a genuine desire to return to England. 'I am anxious to get home,' he wrote to his mother. 'Having passed the best part of my life in the wilderness and among savages, I should now like to see something of civilized countries with perhaps an occasional trip into an out of the way place.'

The counter-attraction was the opportunity to make money. Already, in the first year of his association with Rhodes, his financial position had been transformed. As the pioneer column neared its destination, he received a cheque for £3858.10s. from Frank Johnson. This sum seems to have been a resolution of the Selous

Exploration Syndicate's business, as well as payment for Selous's services guiding the pioneers; almost certainly, it included the £2000 from Rhodes for the Mapondera concession. It was a large sum, and, with shares in the Company – which were being issued to all pioneers – Selous could look forward to a comfortable life in England as a bachelor.

The prospect of further benefits decided him against an immediate return home. In addition to his salary, he told his mother, he might come by 'other advantages that may turn out much more valuable', such as land and more shares. It would be foolish to throw away the opportunity when 'if all continues to go well with the Chartered Company I may take quite a good deal of money in the next year or two.' In the flush of his new-found prosperity he even wrote to his mother expressing an interest in buying Barrymore House, the family home on the Thames at Wargrave, after Frederick's death.

During the march north, Selous had raised the issue of the Company's treaty policy, arguing yet again the inadequacies of the Rudd concession as a basis for colonizing Mashonaland. He persuaded both Colquhoun and Pennefather that for the British claim to be legitimized, treaties would have to be secured with the 'independent' eastern chiefs. Colquhoun was a particularly important ally, and an unlikely friendship developed between the abstemious Selous and the Company's administrator, a burly *bon vivant* with a walrus moustache and a fondness for champagne, pâté de foie gras and good cigars. Taking up the treaty issue, Colquhoun wrote to Kimberley:

> Selous maintains as you know, that (a) east of the Sabi and (b) north and east of the Hunyani, the Matabele have no real claim whatever, and that such claims would not stand investigation. I cannot answer for (b) at present, but I can for (a) . . . There are chiefs who acknowledge no-one's authority. They have certainly never been under Matabele authority.

The response from Harris in Kimberley was prompt, and brutally to the point: 'Despite anything Selous or anyone else says to the contrary, Lobengula alone will be recognized, so it is impolitic as

195

well as useless to waste time or money on the so-called independent Mashona chiefs.'

Even Harris in his cynicism acknowledged one exception to this rule, however. This was the Manica chief Umtasa, whose territory was in the highlands lying between the Mashonaland plateau and the Portuguese presence on the east coast. Umtasa's kraal was a mere 100 miles from the sea, and although he gave a nominal allegiance to the Portuguese it was thought he could be easily persuaded to acknowledge a new master. After he had obtained a foothold in Manicaland, Colquhoun's orders from Rhodes were to 'endeavour to secure the right of communication with the seaboard'. Rhodes's eyes were on the Portuguese port of Beira, which was only 350 miles from Fort Salisbury, compared with the 1700 miles to Cape Town.

Selous and Colquhoun left the pioneer column on 3 September. They rode directly eastwards over gently undulating, open country, broken by rocky hills and msasa trees. After a week in the saddle, they started ascending the craggy Manica highlands. This dark, moody landscape, similar to parts of Scotland, was new to Selous. He thought it 'the most beautiful country I have yet seen in Africa'.

Umtasa had survived for his seventy-odd years through a highly-developed sense of when to agree with powerful strangers. His was an uncomfortable neighbourhood. To the east dwelt the ferocious Gaza Zulus. But his principal dread was of a half-caste Goanese, Manuel Antonio de Sousa, also known as Gouveia, who enjoyed Portuguese patronage and had established a brutal fiefdom between the Sabi and Zambesi rivers. Umtasa nevertheless welcomed his British visitors warmly, asserting vehemently that he had never willingly accepted Portuguese authority, and had signed no treaty with them.

The appearance of the Manica ruler was described by Colquhoun:

He appeared attired in a naval cocked hat, a tunic (evidently of Portuguese origin but of ancient date), a leopard skin slung over his back, the whole toilette being completed by a pair of trousers that had evidently passed through many hands, or rather covered many legs . . . He was preceded by a

his diary: 'Glorious country. Riding ahead with Mr S, envied nobody at home. Dinner – antelope, rice, honey, jam, potatoes, milk and nuts.'

A week later they reached Mutoko's country, where negotiations were opened with a high priest known as the Lion God, who had to be propitiated with gifts to gain an audience with the chief. Over the next four days Selous was summoned to indabas with various groups of tribal elders, who asked about his mission. With a better grasp of treaty implications than was common, they interrogated him keenly.

'I was at last permitted to interview the venerable old chief,' he reported later. He and Armstrong were summoned to a vast granite kopje, which was Mutoko's stronghold, and, leaving their horses tethered at the bottom, they ascended through an army of about 1000 men, armed with guns, assegais and bows and arrows. Armstrong thought they seemed 'very warlike people indeed'. Selous agreed. At the top, 'we found that a kind of arbour of boughs had been erected, beneath which sat Mutoko and other elders'. The chief was very shrivelled and infirm, and Selous believed him to be 'nearly, if not quite, a hundred years old'.

The chief was nevertheless clear enough in his thinking. He asked why – if he agreed to grant the Company a concession – it was necessary to sign a piece of paper. Selous repeated a familiar explanation: white men had come to the country to stay; but if the chief made a treaty, they would live in peace and he would receive the protection of English soldiers against his enemies, the Portuguese. Mutoko finally agreed to sign, but his hand was so shaky that Selous had to hold the pen as he made his cross.

As Selous and Armstrong descended from the kopje, the warriors roused themselves to a state of high excitement, brandishing their weapons in mock combat while shouting reassuringly, 'shamwari, shamwari' (friend). 'It was a very savage scene,' Selous reported to Kimberley, 'and I must say the performers looked as though they would thoroughly enjoy sticking an assegai into somebody.'

The Mutoko treaty brought a large area north-east of Fort Salisbury, with mining permission, into the Company's sphere, and Selous reflected contentedly on an important task fulfilled. In his report he could not resist emphasizing another point: 'The majority [of Mutoko's people] do not even know the name of Lo Bengula or the Amandibili, which is not very surprising, considering that no impi of Lobengula has ever penetrated to within several days' journey of the western border of Mutoko's country.'

Over the next few months, Selous followed this up with treaties with the chiefs Maranke and Makoni, and by cutting a road from Fort Salisbury to Manicaland, which remains the foundation of the modern Harare–Mutare highway. Again he was accompanied by Armstrong. The chirpy and enthusiastic young Yorkshireman, still aged only twenty-two, had brought a welcome shot of youth back into Selous's life. Although not quite forty, Selous was showing signs of world-weariness. He wrote home: 'He is a first-rate fellow and enjoys the life thoroughly as everything is new and strange and interesting. To me there is no more novelty in anything out here.'

All the same, an exhilarating encounter with lions one night on the Revue river must have stirred his blood. A pride of five, which included a suspected man-eater, had depleted Selous's team of oxen, and in a night stake-out he and Armstrong set an ambush from a 'hide'. They shot two of the lions, and thought the night's business was over when . . .

> We both heard an animal breathing alongside of our shelter, within a few feet of us, and the next instant a gentle shake given to the hut, and a noise as of one of the loose branches with which it was covered being torn off, let us know there was another lion in our neighbourhood. It was soon evident to me that the animal was looking for an entrance to our shelter, for, after tearing off a few more boughs, it got to the place where we had crept in, but which was now blocked up with poles . . . This was a little more than I had bargained for, and at the risk of incurring the charge of inhospitality, I resolved to try to keep our visitor outside in the cold.

In the inky blackness Selous could see nothing, only sensing the lion's whereabouts, but pointed his rifle between the branches and fired. He recounted: 'The report was answered by the most terrific grunting roars it is possible to conceive, uttered, as they were, within six feet of our ears. I am sorry I had not a phonograph with me in order to preserve these powerful expressions of the feelings of a wounded lion. Suddenly released in a London drawing room, I feel sure they could not fail to produce a very marked effect.' The mortally-wounded creature thrashed about for hours before crawling off to die. Selous never found the carcass, but from the lion's attempts to break into the hide he felt convinced that it had been the same animal which two months earlier, in the same district, had eaten a member of a BSA Police patrol.

The sequel to Selous's mission to Manicaland could have come from the pages of a Gilbert and Sullivan operetta. Hearing about the British treaty, the Portuguese authorities despatched Colonel Paiva de Andrada and his enforcer, Gouveia, to bring Umtasa back into the fold. Not surprisingly, they quickly persuaded him to hoist the Portuguese flag again. No sooner had he done so, however, than Captain Patrick Forbes arrived with a small force to reassert the Company's position. In what came to be known as the Manica Incident, Forbes, on 15 November 1890, entered the kraal of the old chief, by now thoroughly bemused, and arrested de Andrada and Gouveia. Protesting against this clear violation of the Anglo-Portuguese accord, they were led away and sent down to Cape Town.

With the Portuguese demoralized and leaderless, it seemed to Forbes that the way to Beira lay open. It is clear too, from his despatches to Colquhoun, that they had both been encouraged by Rhodes to make a filibustering raid on the port if the chance arose, and that Forbes now made preparations to proceed. But in the meantime London and Lisbon had agreed that the frontiers established by the August convention should remain fixed for six months. On being advised of this by Kimberley, Colquhoun ordered Forbes to withdraw. The administrator was blamed by armchair fire-eaters for losing Beira for Rhodesia, but in fact Forbes had already decided that trying to seize the port with forty men would be over-ambitious. He confined himself to consolidating the Company's hold on Manicaland by seizing the Portuguese stockade of Massi Kessi, a short march east of Umtasa's. In a skirmish here a few months later, a Portuguese attempt to regain the stockade was ignominiously repulsed.

During these events, Selous, no doubt also encouraged by Rhodes, supported the Company's position in the British press. A year before he had written a letter to *The Times*, running to almost 5000 words, calling on British public opinion to check, and counter, the Portuguese, who he said were attempting 'to re-establish their ancient supremacy' in Africa. A second article, for the *Daily Graphic*, was lost in the mail, but another was published by the *Manchester Guardian* in January 1891, at the height of the Manica furore. In it Selous paid tribute to Colonel de Andrada and his associate Baron de Rezende, as 'men imbued with the spirit of the old Portuguese navigators', while calling for 'this feeble, decaying power' to submit to 'the tide of enterprise which has already opened up Mashunaland and Manica to the world, and now demands an outlet to the Indian Ocean'.

It was not to be. A new Anglo-Portuguese convention was ratified in July 1891 which, while it incorporated Manicaland in the British domain, made further adventurism by the Company in pursuit of a port for Mashonaland out of the question. Rhodes, inevitably, was dissatisfied, but the Company had acquired a great deal more territory than it had any claim to.

The Pioneer Corps had been disbanded at the end of the expedition to become the new civilian population of Mashonaland, and almost immediately difficulties developed. The settlers, numbering about 1000 by the end of 1890, living mainly in the vicinity of Fort Salisbury, were unprepared for the shortages and discomforts which immediately arose. No sooner had they arrived than the rains started in what was to be one of the wettest seasons ever recorded in Salisbury. Mud and thatch huts leaked copiously, and became infested with rats. Malaria swept through the new settlement. Food was hard to get and expensive. Even the traditional pleasures of the Interior were denied the settlers, as Colquhoun had banned alcohol.

The main grievances, however, concerned the gap between the settlers' expectations and reality. Although the Company had promised every man a farm of 3000 acres, it had no authority to grant valid land title, and it was not until the following year that the plots which had been staked out with abandon by the new arrivals were legally allocated to them. More important was the failure of the gold diggings to produce the instant wealth that had been predicted. It is true that some mines, including one started by Johnson, Heany and

Borrow on the Mazoe, showed quite promising results, but most returns were dismal. On top of that, the Company's 50 per cent levy on all gold claims attracted bitter resentment from prospectors forced to part with half of their hard-won gains.

Selous noted the settlers' disgruntlement, and was himself dismayed at the lack of preparation for the rainy season. The road south became a bog, and Mashonaland was for a while virtually cut off from the outside world. From Selous's remarks to his mother, Colquhoun, as administrator, seems to have borne the brunt of the criticism: 'Ever since the expedition got into Mashunaland last year there seems to have been an utter want of management of any sort or kind ... many people are beginning to hope that the Imperial government will take over the country.'

The distress signals were noted in London, bringing down the value of Chartered Company shares on the Stock Exchange. This affected Selous's holdings, obliging him to revise the earlier optimistic assessment of his financial position. He would not be able to buy Barrymore House after all, he told his mother, and although much looking forward to leaving Africa, he felt compelled in July 1891 to accept another one-year engagement with the Company:

> You must not be disappointed; a year will soon slip away, and then for 'England, Home and Beauty'. They give me 1000 pounds and all expenses for this year's work, and that is a sum that I could not afford to let slip. Besides that I ought not to leave just now as I want to see what to do with my land and gold claims.

Selous's land allocation, in common with the other expedition leaders, was 20,000 acres, almost seven times that of ordinary pioneers. Johnson, Heany and Borrow were buying whatever land they could and offered him around £4000, which he refused, instead putting the land, with his gold claims, into a company started by Sir John Willoughby, second in command of the expedition. By the turn of the century Willoughby's Consolidated Company had acquired 3900 mining claims and more than half a million acres of land. Selous would later return to work in Matabeleland for this concern, but he never farmed his own land in Mashonaland.

The new territory's image in the City of London was dealt

another, and more serious, setback that year with a visit by Lord Randolph Churchill, who had agreed to travel through Southern Africa and write a series of articles for the *Daily Graphic*. The statesman, his days of glory behind him, was sick in body and jaundiced in mind, and seems to have upset almost everyone he met, including Rhodes, who had hoped to impress him. Lord Randolph was accompanied by his own mineral expert and was at least encouraged enough to make some investments of his own. But his public pronouncements sent Chartered shares plummeting even further. 'Mashonaland, so far as is at present known, and much is known, is neither an Arcadia, nor an El Dorado,' he wrote. The mineral prospects 'might yield a small profit to the individual miner', but so far nothing had been found 'as would justify the formation of a syndicate or company, and a large expenditure of capital'. Lord Randolph was not encouraging either about the possibilities for migration. The rainy season, and the diseases afflicting both man and beast, seemed to him to offer 'invincible obstacles to large settlements of white people'.

Amid the crisis of confidence, Cecil Rhodes decided to make his first visit to the country which was already being called Rhodesia after him. At Fort Salisbury he was met by a 'Vigilance Committee', which presented a catalogue of grievances. Rhodes wrote: 'I found a discontented population of about 1500 people and an expenditure of about 250,000 pounds a year on police. Things looked rather bad. Dr Jameson and myself talked matters over, and he said, "If you will give me 3000 pounds a month I can pull through".'

Jameson now took over from Colquhoun. The first administrator retired in August 1891, ostensibly because of ill-health, but in reality because his authority had been steadily undermined by Jameson's influence on Rhodes. Colquhoun had never got on with 'the Doctor', and, without his backing, had little chance to be effective.

Rhodes and Jameson then set off to rally the wavering settlers. At Fort Charter, about eighty miles south of Fort Salisbury, they were met by Selous. In a week they covered hundreds of miles by horse and wagon, and between Rhodes's purse and Jameson's charm they left the settlers happier than they found them.

Gradually the situation improved. Civic buildings sprang up on the plain north of the kopje. Pioneer Street, at the foot of the kopje, became the first thoroughfare. The settlement lost its fort aspect, and became known as Salisbury. Prohibition was lifted and alcohol became available, albeit at a daunting price. Sporting contests, cricket and rugby, were organized, and at the end of 1891 the first race meeting was held. A newspaper, the *Mashonaland Herald*, appeared. A road across the Limpopo was opened up to the Transvaal. In January 1892, Selous wrote to his mother in an optimistic and affectionate mood:

> Time is flitting fast and we are now well into another year. I did not forget your birthday on Dec 24. My own came soon afterwards, and I am now 40 years of age and before the end of this year is out I hope to be in England.
>
> The telegraph wire is now at Fort Charter, and before the end of next month the office will be opened here in Salisbury, and Mashunaland will be in telegraphic communication with the whole of the civilized world. This, if you come to think of it, is really a magnificent piece of enterprise.
>
> The government buildings are progressing rapidly. We now have an abundance of vegetables here. Everything thrives marvellously – potatoes, cabbages, onions, chalots [sic], radishes, lettuces etc. Wheat sowed in August last ripened and was cut in four months from the date of sowing. Major Johnson's agricultural expert pronounced it to be as fine a sample of wheat as he had ever seen, and says he will be able to raise two crops a year. In fact, the country is now proving to be an exceptionally fine one both for agriculture and stock farming, in spite of Mr Labouchere and Lord Randolph Churchill.

Selous had come to another crossroads in his life. The Mashonaland adventure was over, and he had had his fill of Africa for the time being. Ahead lay his return home and the prospect of travel and sport in other lands. He intended to visit America for the 1893 World Fair, and hoped to see Japan as well. He could live quite comfortably as a bachelor on the £330 a year income from his De Beers shares, while his interests in Mashonaland would increase in value as the country developed.

He had one last important service to perform for the Company. For some time he had been working on a second book, to be called *Travel and Adventure in South-East Africa*. It picked up the narrative of his experiences where *A Hunter's Wanderings* left off in 1880, and, like that book, it concentrated on hunting and adventure stories. But in the last months of his employment, Selous spent his spare time writing a final section, about the pioneer expedition, and on the prospects for Mashonaland. These chapters amounted to a counter-attack on Churchill's judgment, and a ringing endorsement of the Company's administration.

His most earnest desire, he wrote, was that he might live to see the territory, 'endeared to me by so many stirring reminiscences, grow and increase in prosperity until it has become a rich portion of the British Empire'. This fondness clouded his faculties. Having invested so much of himself in the new colony, he had not the heart – nor perhaps the intellect – to perceive dispassionately the short-comings of the Company's development policy. His blithe statement that 'before the end of this century Mashunaland will take a high place amongst the gold-producing countries of the world', was conspicuously wide of the mark. Even more so was his judgment on Jameson as an administrator imbued with 'a correctness of judgment which amounts to nothing less than genius'.

Within a few years Selous would rue expressing these opinions. Rhodes succeeded in 'booming' Mashonaland on the Stock Market with falsified gold reports until 1895, when the bubble burst, and Chartered Company shares, which had risen from £1 to £7, crashed again. Selous, believing that he had been manipulated to assist the boom, turned bitterly against the Company and became caustic in his public statements on the mineral prospects of the territory, while never abandoning his belief in its agricultural potential. In 1900, he wrote to Theodore Roosevelt, then vice-president of the United States, and a confidant: 'I had hoped that the opening up of Rhodesia would have induced people from the [British Isles] to go and settle on the land. But this hope has not been fulfilled, and I am informed that almost all the British population in Rhodesia is in the towns of Salisbury and Bulawayo and on the mines.'

In the middle of 1892, Selous left Salisbury by his own eastern road for the coast. On his way through what is now Gorongosa

National Park in Mozambique, he shot the last elephant of his life, a magnificent old bull with tusks weighing more than 100 pounds. As he looked back towards the country where he had spent the past two decades, all seemed tranquil, and he had no intention of returning for several years.

In fact, clouds of rebellion and war were looming, presaging what was to be the tempestuous final decade of the century in Southern Africa.

CHAPTER FIFTEEN

Love and War

The year of 1893 was a momentous one. For the first time in his life, Selous found himself both in love and at war. The object of his affections was the teenage daughter of a country pastor. His foes, in a war that drew him back to Africa against all his intentions, were the Matabele.

When the *Hawarden Castle* berthed in Southampton just before Christmas in 1892, Selous was within a few days of his forty-first birthday, and seemed a confirmed bachelor. Whatever liaisons he had formed in the Interior, he had never established a serious relationship with a white woman, and the chance of marriage appeared to have passed. He had become set in his own ways and dismissed the idea of romance. 'At my age marriage would be very risky,' he confided to his sister Sybil.

The idea of settling down was even less attractive. 'I am grown so restless that I shall never, I fear, be able to remain for long in one place,' he told his mother. He would be 'a wanderer to the end of my days', and intended to start a trip around the world soon, visiting the United States and Japan. All these notions were shattered within a month of his arrival home.

The Selous family reunion at Barrymore House for Christmas was overshadowed by the death of Selous's father Frederick in his ninetieth year. But others of the clan had gathered, and stayed to enjoy the Berkshire countryside that winter. In all probability, Selous's sisters Ann and Sybil were there, with their respective husbands, Richard and Charles Jones. That would help explain the presence at Barrymore House of the Jones's cousin, Gladys Maddy, a startlingly pretty girl of eighteen.

There is no record of Selous's first meeting with Gladys, but

208

Millais, who knew him as well as anyone, said he was so affected that he decided to make her his wife there and then. The situation might have seemed faintly absurd – a grizzled outdoorsman of forty-one falling in love with a teenage girl; but Selous had good reason to be smitten. Gladys was dark and slender, with a fine, narrow-waisted figure, while her manner was gay and vivacious. Her prettiness was lasting, and she remained an attractive woman with admirers long after Selous's death. She was one of the very few women who ever managed to charm Cecil Rhodes.

The Church and Gloucestershire figured prominently in Gladys's antecedents. She was the daughter of the Reverend Henry Maddy and Emily Jones, both of whose parents had been mayors of Gloucester. The family was industrious, patriotic – and conservative. Canon Maddy was the pastor in the parish of Down Hatherley, near Gloucester, for fifty years, and Gladys was raised in a rural vicarage. She was no country mouse, though. As the firm mouth and level gaze of her portraits indicate, Marie Catherine Gladys Maddy would grow into a resourceful and resilient woman.

Gladys was evidently attracted to Selous as well. Although on the verge of middle-age, he was still a handsome man of presence and charm, and in excellent health. He had returned to England with his fame enhanced by the Mashonaland adventure; his movements were reported in the press, and he was celebrated as well as prosperous. As one of Gladys's nieces later remarked, 'he must have seemed like a being from another world to the daughter of a quiet country parson.' But perhaps almost as important for a girl of Gladys's background, Selous's modesty and shyness made him a distinctly English hero. And it must have helped that he could make light of their age difference with wry little jokes.

Ann Selous was delighted to find her son in love at last. Gladys's parents, however, were not. Why this was so is not certain. Canon Maddy was not one to leave records on family affairs, his diary being a model of austere brevity. (A characteristic entry runs: 'May 18, 1871. Married. Ascension Day.') It is convenient to ascribe his opposition as the natural reaction of a parent confronted by an eighteen-year-old daughter who has fallen in love with a man more than twice her age. But it does not explain everything. Selous was, after all, a highly eligible man, and the canon had himself been over forty when he married. It is possible that Selous, as he wooed Gladys in the spring of 1893, made a clean breast about his African 'family', and the children whom he had left behind. We know that he did not shy away from the matter, and that he had confided it to his own family.

Whatever the reason, the Maddys remained unenthusiastic about the prospect of a marriage, while gradually coming to accept it as inevitable. They did insist on an engagement of at least a year. Gladys went down to Barrymore House on 25 May, two months after her nineteenth birthday, and there her engagement to Selous was announced.

Selous's absorption with Gladys was not to the exclusion of everything else. Public recognition of his exploits was helped by the way the pioneer expedition had captured popular imagination. He was still referred to in the press as the 'Mighty Nimrod' but a wider appreciation of his work as a traveller, geographer and naturalist was growing. At the Natural History Museum, the specimens he had shot for Gunther were on prominent display, and he was invited to address the Zoological Society. He had finished writing *Travel and Adventure in South-East Africa*, which his new publishers, Rowland Ward, were confident would be a best seller.

A profile soon after Selous's return appeared in the March issue of the *Review of Reviews*. The writer, perhaps taken aback, found the legendary hunter 'an English gentleman who finds his natural level among the cultured and well-to-do classes', as well as 'an inveterate tea-drinker', and added: 'No one who sees him in club or drawing-room would imagine that this was the man who has wrestled with wild beasts in African jungles, who has run mile after mile in his hat and shirt after elephants.' The article went on to describe him as: 'In politics, a Liberal at home and an imperialist abroad,' and compared him with Charles Gordon:

> Like Gordon, he is extremely modest and unassuming, with a kindly soul in him and a passionate devotion to England . . . Both had a passionate hatred of injustice, and a sense of duty which dominated even the instinct of patriotism. Mr Selous, for instance, was, and is, almost Gordonian in his denunciation of what he regards as the injustice of England's

dealings with the Transvaal . . . But Mr Selous differs from General Gordon as a man nurtured on Byron and Darwin differs from a man nurtured on the Bible and Thomas á Kempis.

The culmination of his new celebrity status came when the Royal Geographical Society, in recognition of his work in Mashonaland, presented him that year with the Founder's Gold Medal. This was the RGS's most prized award, the previous recipients of which included Livingstone, Stanley and Speke. Selous responded by giving a lecture to the society, entitled 'Twenty Years in Zambesia', which embroiled him in a public row with Stanley.

Three years earlier Stanley had made the last of his great African journeys, to rescue Emin Pasha, governor of Southern Sudan, during the Mahdist uprising. The venture succeeded in its objective, but the cost was high and the casualties included an old hunting friend of Selous's. This was the whisky heir James Jameson, who died on the Congo river. Stanley had ordered Jameson and two others to wait on the river for supplies while he made a dash to reach Emin. One of the trio, Major Edmund Barttelot, was killed by a local chief, and Jameson died alone of malaria two weeks later. The fiasco of the Rear Column, as it became known, started an acrimonious feud between Stanley and the families of the dead men. The affair was all the more unpleasant for allegations by an Arab interpreter that Jameson had encouraged cannibals to kill and eat a young girl in order to witness and sketch the spectacle. When Selous addressed the RGS he evidently intended to try to rehabilitate his friend's memory. He spoke of Jameson as a fine, brave man, 'who lost his life when left behind on the Congo in the Emin expedition'.

Selous probably did not intend offence, but the notably thin-skinned Stanley took it. A few months later, when Selous was delivering another address, this time to the Royal Colonial Institute, Stanley struck back. The jovial atmosphere that accompanied one of Selous's standard recitations of hunting anecdotes and yarns was swiftly dispelled as discussion was thrown open to the floor and Stanley rose. Without preamble, he plunged in. It would be a good idea, he said, if people who wanted to shoot animals in Africa paid a tax of £10 per head. He believed Mr Selous had shot around 800 head, and would therefore be liable for a tax of around £8000. 'I do not like the idea of people going into Africa to shoot lions and elephants and hippopotami and other game indiscriminately,' he added, especially as animals could feed labourers working on more worthy projects. He concluded with a backhanded compliment that Mr Selous was 'a capital lecturer' who would be much appreciated if he made a tour of America. Then he sat down.

There was an uncomfortable silence, before other speakers rose. If Stanley had expected support from the floor he had misjudged the audience which included a number of South African visitors. One averred that he knew Mr Selous was 'no mere slaughterer of game', but a geographer and naturalist of note. Another thanked Selous 'in the name of Young England for opening Mashonaland to us'. Yet another, in a dig at Stanley, said Selous was 'a great peace-maker' who, if he had ever encountered the Mahdi, would probably have been able to subdue him with tact.

Selous then replied for himself. 'I do not wish to detract from the harmony of this meeting. Mr Stanley seems to me to have spoken without much knowledge of his subject. When a man follows elephants and dangerous animals with obsolete weapons he takes his life in his hands, and I do not think I have ever done anything in Africa to make me feel ashamed.'

The incident was monitored by the press, and Stanley came in for further criticism. To the craggy explorer – 'Bula Matari', or the Smasher of Rocks – controversy was nothing new, but Selous normally flinched from it, and dreaded the idea that he might be misunderstood. Painstakingly, he wrote to the *Pall Mall Gazette* to emphasize that it was not his claim that he had killed 800 animals, but Stanley's. He also wrote to a friend in South Africa.

The other day I gave a lecture at the Royal Colonial Institute, and Mr Stanley took the opportunity of making himself disagreeable at my expense. He of course laid himself open to some very obvious retorts from myself, which I refrained from making as I did not want to be unnecessarily offensive; so I only answered him quietly and told him he did not know what he was talking about. Now I don't want the impression to get abroad in Mashunaland that I was in the wrong in any way, because I was not, and the whole audience were with me and against Stanley . . .

In one sense, at least, Stanley was right. Selous's lectures were becoming a popular entertainment. Minutes of his addresses to geographical societies around Britain suggest a performance that was something like a salon recital: he would go through a repertoire of stories about hunting, narrow squeaks and savage Africa. At the end the audience would usually demand more, and, at a sign from the chairman, he would plunge willingly into another tale or two. In addition to light anecdotes, he started to promote Mashonaland and the Company which, he said, was doing great work in the new colony.

So successful had his lectures become that Selous was about to embark on a tour of the United States when war broke out in Matabeleland.

The inevitable clash had long been delayed, almost to the point where it seemed that it might be averted. Over the three years since the pioneers' arrival a *modus vivendi* between the settlers and the Matabele had evolved which had kept the peace. An unofficial frontier, the Umniati river, was observed by both sides, and when breaches occurred they were swiftly resolved in contacts between Lobengula and Jameson, now officially administrator of Mashonaland. A great deal has been written about the causes of the Matabele War, some directed at proving that it was engineered by Jameson and Rhodes. This argument has been adequately refuted elsewhere. Jameson did anticipate a time when the Company would be strong enough to confront the Matabele, but in mid-1893 the level of military preparedness in Mashonaland had never been lower.

The spark for the war was a raid by a Matabele impi in the vicinity of Fort Victoria, a European settlement roughly halfway up the Selous Road to Salisbury. No whites were harmed, the raid being directed at local Mashona who, by the standards of the time, had done enough to provoke Lobengula's wrath. But the punitive impi went too far, storming through the countryside, seizing white farmers' livestock and slaughtering Mashona indiscriminately. When Mashona refugees took sanctuary inside the fort they were followed into the precincts of the settlement by the Matabele. Settlers' servants were murdered with assegais and knobkerries on the dusty streets of the town and on outlying farms. Warned not to interfere, the whites watched these killings helplessly, although when the commanding indunas called on Captain Charles Lendy to hand over the refugees in the fort, he refused.

Over the next few days the Matabele stayed on to plunder the district until Jameson arrived from Salisbury, summoned the indunas, and ordered them back to Matabeleland. When they did not retire as briskly as Jameson had instructed, Lendy attacked and nine warriors were killed.

The Victoria Incident inflamed both sides, the whites because for the first time they had seen a rampaging Matabele impi at close quarters, Lobengula because the indunas returned to Bulawayo claiming they had been called to an indaba and then treacherously attacked. Moreover, it exposed irreconcilable attitudes. Lobengula might accept the Umniati river as a frontier for practical purposes, but he neither could, nor would, restrain his indunas from raiding Mashona settlements beyond it. The Matabele economy and military structure depended on raiding, and Lobengula had never acquiesced to the notion that the Mashona were no longer his subjects. But the Europeans now saw the Mashona as *their* vassals, and were insisting that the border should be inviolable.

The gathering of the storm has been vividly reconstructed by Philip Mason in his book *The Birth of a Dilemma*, with the help of official papers, and, in particular, letters between Lobengula and Loch, the High Commissioner at the Cape. As the supreme British authority in South Africa, Loch was in a position to prevent the Company waging war, and did his best to avert conflict. But early on he issued an ominous warning to the king: 'My friend . . . these acts . . . cannot be permitted. They will bring on you the punishments that befell Cetewayo . . . I wish to control the anger of the white people . . . but I shall not say stop to them unless you at once withdraw your impis and punish the indunas.'

Lobengula too endeavoured to maintain peace, but he could also be uncompromising. He replied to Loch that he would only return the plunder when Lendy handed over the refugees. To Rutherfoord Harris he wrote: 'I thought you came to dig gold but it seems that you have come . . . to rob me of my people and country as well . . . you are like a child playing with edged tools . . . Captain Lendy is like some of my own young men; he has no holes in his ears and cannot hear.'

Peace initiatives came too late. Rhodes and Jameson had by now resolved on war, and started preparations. Volunteers were offered a farm of 3000 acres and a share of the booty of Matabele cattle. Loch prevaricated, reporting to London that while he felt Lobengula was anxious for peace, he could not vouch for the impis which had taken up positions on the roads leading to Salisbury, Fort Victoria and Fort Tuli. Also, having raised a new military force, the Company could not afford to allow the suspense to persist indefinitely.

Selous had followed developments from England with the keenest interest. At the time of the Victoria Incident he sent a telegram to Jameson offering his services. When the tension continued to rise, he took leave of his mother and Gladys, and sailed for South Africa.

The murder of the Mashona at Victoria confirmed Selous in a hatred of the Matabele which now transcended his lingering liking and respect for Lobengula. It revived memories of an earlier Matabele raid in which an old Mashona chief named Lomagondi, of whom Selous had been fond, was killed. Once an agent of peace, he turned his efforts now to waging war with a clear conscience, even eagerness. The Matabele, he said, were 'an overbearing and cruel people who were as certain sooner or later to come into conflict with the advancing wave of European civilization as gunpowder is to explode when brought into contact with fire'. As voices in Britain, notably that of Henry Labouchère, were raised against the war, Selous closed ranks with the settlers. He wrote later: 'The whites were certainly the aggressors, but they were driven to aggression in self-defence, for it had become perfectly clear that either the colonization of Mashonaland would have to be abandoned, or the power of the Matabele broken.'

After landing at Cape Town, Selous made his way up the Missionary Road, and on 27 September arrived at Fort Tuli. Here, at Jameson's suggestion, he joined a force of the Bechuanaland Border Police under Lieutenant-Colonel Hamilton Goold-Adams. This Southern Column was a force of the Imperial Government, and thus responsible to Loch. Jameson was in command of the Company's forces, which had mustered at Fort Victoria.

No serious fighting had yet taken place, but soon after his arrival at Tuli, Selous was involved in a fiasco which darkened the war clouds, and for which he bore some responsibility. He had just got back to camp after a scouting mission when he spotted an old friend, James Dawson, the Bulawayo trader. Dawson had arrived at Goold-Adams's headquarters with three envoys from Lobengula, who were on their way to talks with Loch at his invitation. It was Dawson's responsibility, as their escort, to deliver them to Goold-Adams before they continued their journey. Instead, a combination of the casual old Interior ways and an almost subconscious manifestation of racial contempt led to a disaster.

Selous told the Reuters agency in an interview that he went over and greeted Dawson and one of the envoys, Ingubungo, a half-brother of Lobengula, whom he knew well. At this critical point, Selous and Dawson went off 'for a cup of tea', leaving the indunas alone. A series of misunderstandings followed: Goold-Adams heard that three Matabele were in camp, and ordered that they should not be allowed to leave. An attempt was made to detain the envoys, one of whom panicked, seized a bayonet and stabbed a guard. In the ensuing scuffle two of the envoys were killed, only Ingubungo surviving.

It was, as Selous said, 'a deplorable accident'. He was, he added, 'to a certain extent responsible for Dawson not having immediately reported his arrival with the envoys to Goold-Adams'. He also admitted that he and Dawson should not have left the envoys alone.

But careless and insensitive though he and Dawson had been, the incident had little impact on the course of events. Skirmishing had already broken out, and Loch had effectively signalled the start of war by authorizing Goold-Adams to advance. Lobengula might reflect bitterly on white duplicity, but events had, finally, spun out of his control.

The next day the Goold-Adams column started its advance on Bulawayo from the south, as Jameson began his movement from the east. Selous just had time to dash off a note to his mother which concluded:

Long before you receive this letter you will know probably whether we have been successful or not by cable. I must take my chance with the rest, and hope to return to you all safe and sound before long and marry my dear little Gladys. Goodbye my dearest Mother, hope for the best and believe in my star.

News was soon received at Barrymore House, but did nothing to allay Ann Selous's fears. It came in a cable from Lord Ripon, the new Colonial Secretary, and was addressed to Selous's brother Edmund: 'Telegram from Sir H. Loch reports successful engagement with Matabele November 3. Selous whilst gallantly defending rearmost wagon received bullet wound in side, bullet glancing along his ribs. He is already moving about.'

Selous had thrown himself headlong into the first of what would be a number of military engagements in his life. Goold-Adams's force had advanced to within about fifty-five miles south-west of Bulawayo, and had come to a place called Mangwe, when distant shots announced that straggling wagons had come under attack. Prompt help, even from one man, was vital. While a mounted column was still mustering, Selous slung on a rifle and cartridge belt, leaped on to his horse and galloped back down the road. He found four wagons being defended by a handful of Bamangwato volunteers against a sizeable Matabele force armed with assegais and rifles. Selous raced up bawling: 'Don't leave the wagons, the white men are coming.'

Dismounting, he started to shoot, while the Matabele turned a warm fire on him. Some of the warriors had muzzle-loaders and their powder was old. The shots made 'a loud buzzing noise which I could hear approach long before they reached me'. This was disconcerting, but the low velocity of the Matabele fire saved his life.

Groups of warriors were working their way up on him, and one bullet buzzed close by his head. After about five minutes of shooting the wagons were almost clear, and Selous decided it was time for discretion. However as he was mounting he was struck by what felt like a hammer blow in the chest. He only just managed to stay in his saddle, but at that moment help arrived as the mounted column galloped up.

It was a slight wound. The ball had hit him three inches below the right breast but was almost spent and had been deflected by a rib before exiting eight inches away. It was not at all dangerous, he assured his mother, although he was stiff and sore. In the subsequent engagement the column had lost four men, while Matabele casualties were considerable.

Neither Selous nor Goold-Adams's column took any further part in the fighting, which was all over within a month. In its advance from the east, Jameson's force settled the issue in two battles. Matabele bravery proved no match for the Maxim gun, which made its grim military debut along the banks of the Shangani and Mbembezi rivers, and was the deciding factor of the war. A white force of about 650 men crushed the Matabele army of around 8000, and Lobengula's two best regiments were virtually annihilated. The Matabele never got close enough to wield their short assegais. Jameson's casualties were six dead, which, added to the four suffered by Goold-Adams, amounted to ten for this decisive phase of the war. Matabele casualties have never been established, but they were many hundreds.

Jameson entered the smouldering ruins of Bulawayo on 4 November to find Lobengula had abandoned his kraal and fled to the north. The king had kept faith to the end with the Bulawayo whites, issuing orders that the two traders who had stayed on, James Fairbairn and William Usher, were not to be harmed. Goold-Adams's column arrived a week after Jameson. Selous, despite his wound, was on his feet and felt quite strong.

Jameson sent a message to Lobengula, who was believed to be about twenty miles north of Bulawayo at the Shiloh mission station, asking him to return and promising that he would be 'kindly treated'. The king replied, 'I will come,' but instead he retreated further north, beyond the mission at Inyati. Jameson decided to send a force to apprehend him.

Selous made every effort to join the ill-fated Shangani Patrol. He told Jameson that he was quite fit enough for hard riding, and that he believed he could persuade Lobengula to take part in an indaba. Jameson, however, who seems always to have wanted to exclude Selous from dealings with the king, forbade him, on medical grounds, saying that irritation of the wound might cause an abscess, and that he needed at least two weeks to recuperate in Bulawayo.

And so Selous, who at this stage was one of a very few white men whom Lobengula might still have trusted, was denied the chance to parley with the king.

It would be pleasant to record that amid the ruins of the kraal which had been a focal point in his life, Selous was touched by the downfall of Lobengula. He might have recalled their first meeting here, when the king had guffawed at the idea of a teenage boy shooting elephant, or, twenty years later, the final meeting when they had again talked of animals and hunting. Sadly, there is no sign that he did any such thing. Selous's romantic impulses, his love of honour and the grand gesture, were always subdued when it came to the Matabele.

From Bulawayo he wrote to his mother that he would 'come home and marry Gladys, unless the wear and anxiety have made me look so old that she will not have me'. The campaign had 'gone off in the most wonderfully lucky way for our side', while the Matabele generalship had been appalling and the impis had missed numerous favourable chances to attack. He wrote:

> On the two occasions when they attacked the laager, the machine guns simply mowed them down, and they never had a chance. No one knowing their abominable history can pity them, or lament their downfall. They have been paid back in their own coin . . .

His final word on the end of an era was, if not exactly compassionate, at least eloquent:

> So you see the fair-haired descendants of the northern pirates are in possession of the great king's big kraal, and the Calf of the Black Cow has fled into the wilderness.

The pursuit group, under the command of Major Patrick Forbes, consisted of fewer than 200 men, including a force from Fort Victoria led by Captain Allan Wilson, and a smaller group under Captain Henry Borrow. They set out from Shiloh on 25 November, and a week later had reached the banks of the Shangani river, where they believed they were within a day's march of Lobengula. From here, despite evidence of a large Matabele presence in the vicinity,

Wilson set off across the river with twelve men to try to locate the king. Having done so, he sent back a request for reinforcements, apparently believing he could drive through the straggling bands of Matabele to the king's wagon, seize him and withdraw. In response, Forbes detached another twenty-one men under Borrow to join Wilson. Soon afterwards the level of the river rose, and when, on the morning of 4 December, Forbes heard heavy gunfire from the other side of the river, he was powerless to help. In the space of an hour, the thirty-four men of the Wilson patrol were wiped out, fighting to the last and, according to possibly fanciful accounts, singing 'God Save the Queen' as they died.

Forbes was by now under attack himself and short of ammunition and provisions. Without knowing Wilson's fate, he was forced to start a retreat. Messengers went ahead to Bulawayo with the tidings that the mission had failed and that Forbes was withdrawing. Meanwhile, Rhodes had arrived from the Cape on 4 December and joined a relief column, led by Jameson and guided by Selous – now deemed fit – which started north to meet Forbes a few days later. They set up a camp at Inyati from where Selous and another scout, Charles Acutt, foraged forward and found the bedraggled remnants of the Shangani Patrol on 14 December. These survivors presented a sad spectacle as they straggled into Inyati. One trooper noted: 'It was a most pitiful sight, a sight I shall never forget. The men limping along and the wounded riding on horses . . .'

The remains of Wilson, Borrow and their men were not found for another two months, but there was never much doubt about their fate. Selous had been friendly with both men, Borrow especially, and he was deeply distressed. At the same time, he had misgivings about the role played by Jameson, whose abilities as an administrator he had so recently been trumpeting. Selous was quite shocked at Jameson's lack of emotional response to the death of his men, and contrasted it with Rhodes's reaction. Selous later told Basil Williams that Rhodes 'had really more heart (tho' [was] less sociable) than Jameson', and had been 'much more upset' by the disaster.

Selous also found distasteful the way Jameson now sought to absolve the Company, and himself, from any blame, and to make Forbes the scapegoat. A bold if unimaginative soldier with a rather stiff manner, Forbes had alienated some of his junior officers and found himself the target of whispered recriminations. A Court of Inquiry made no finding, but Sir Henry Loch, the High Commissioner, did and laid the responsibility squarely at Jameson's door. 'The Patrol was far too weak for the duty it was expected to perform,' he wrote.

Selous made his position clear by inviting Forbes to be his best man at his forthcoming marriage to Gladys. In January, he started south from Bulawayo, to be followed a few weeks later by Forbes, whose once-promising career with the Company was in ruins.

Allan Wilson and his companions were the new territory's first martyrs, and the Shangani Patrol became Rhodesia's Isandhlwana, its Little Big Horn. The troopers' last stand, a circle of men blazing away at the advancing waves of Matabele warriors, was depicted in countless tableaux in colonial homes, and inspired some dreadful verse.

Lobengula did not long survive them, although the exact circumstances of his death have never been satisfactorily determined. From the Shangani river, he withdrew further north, reaching the Zambesi. There, a fugitive in his own land, he died within the next few months, probably of malaria or smallpox.

A loyal induna, Mjaan, recounted the king's burial to the trader James Dawson, who recorded it:

> He buried him in all his feathers and finery, with his shields and assegais, and all the rest of the royal paraphernalia. He set him up in a cave in the face of the rock where, after fixing him properly, he stuck his assegai in the king's stomach, and the Calf of the Elephant belched. Mjaan was then satisfied that he had done his work properly, and closed the cave up.

It was left to Sir Ralph Williams, who had been at the royal kraal with Selous ten years earlier during the 'Sea-Cow Row', to provide a fitting epitaph for Lobengula.

> Many of us, long before Rhodes's time, had good cause to appreciate he who, at the head of the cruellest tribe in Africa, always protected the whites and, I will go further, understood an English gentleman. He was a gentleman himself. His fall was inevitable, the march of civilization; but I have often

sighed to see the dregs of the Kimberley 'diamond market' selling in Bulawayo and sneering at the memory of whom not one of them would have dared to face.

The wedding took place on 4 April 1894, and was quite an event in the parish of Down Hatherley. Canon Maddy and his family were much respected, and Gladys was a favourite in the community because of her vivacity and voluntary work. A lengthy report in the local newspaper stated that the nuptial had been the theme of conversation for weeks, and owing to the fame of Mr Selous, the celebrated South African traveller, was anticipated with much interest.

It was a fine day in early spring, and the entire village turned out for a sight of the rector's lovely daughter and her hero back from the war in Matabeleland. The paper's reporter was inspired: 'An overflowing congregation had crowded into the sacred edifice, situated in the midst of sylvan scenery, while from the stately tower the Union Jack was to be seen fluttering in the breeze.' More prosaically, Canon Maddy recorded in his diary that the splendid flower arrangements by Roberts & Starr of Gloucester had cost £4.

Gladys, just turned twenty, had only recently recovered from the measles, but was still a dazzling bride in white serge. Her dark, curly hair was drawn back under a white beaver hat with a large ostrich feather. She wore Fred's gift, a diamond and sapphire bracelet, and a diamond monogram brooch presented by the Chartered Company.

Selous's best man was not, in the end, Forbes, who had been taken ill in London, but the convivial giant George 'Elephant' Phillips, one of his few surviving friends from old Bulawayo days, who, having retired to Kensington in prosperity, was wreaking havoc on a sturdy constitution with his intake of brandy. Phillips had been one of the celebrants the previous night at the Charing Cross Hotel, where friends from Rugby School and Africa held a party for Selous. He was presented with a silver salver and ewer, and, in an evident allusion to the recent hostilities, gave a speech in which he said Rugby had taught him to despise the strong boy who bullied the weak one, but to admire the strong who protected the weak.

Selous and Phillips were joined at the altar by Canon Maddy, who had come to terms with the match and gave Gladys away. The ceremony was conducted by her cousin, also Fred's brother-in-law, the Reverend Charles Jones. Afterwards, the guests strolled across to the rectory for *déjeuner*. The couple had to leave early, however, to start an exotic three-month honeymoon which Fred had planned with the true traveller's enthusiasm. They would take the boat train from Calais, and journey on to Geneva, Milan, Venice, Budapest, Transylvania, then down the Danube to Odessa and on to Constantinople. Along the way he would do some egg-collecting and Gladys could pass spare time with needlework, at which she was exceptionally skilled.

In the soft glow of the late afternoon, Mr and Mrs Selous left the rectory, and as they passed through Down Hatherley, villagers lined the road and waved hats and handkerchiefs in farewell. Gladys, the paper reported, acknowledged the salutation by wishing everyone a hearty ' "goodbye" '.

CHAPTER SIXTEEN

Raid and Rebellions

For the radical MPs in the British House of Commons, the Matabele War confirmed the worst suspicions about Rhodes and the Chartered Company. Leading the public outcry was Henry Labouchère, who denounced 'the most scandalous financial company since the days of the South Seas Bubble', and described its servants as 'border ruffians, murderers, marauders and riff-raff'. Hardly surprisingly, Selous engaged in a venomous slanging match with Labouchère. In the course of it, however, he demonstrated more loyalty to old comrades than good judgment.

Labouchère epitomized the radical of nineteenth-century English politics, championing the oppressed and reviling imperialism and cant. His cheerful iconoclasm frequently provoked outrage, and Selous was only one of his many antagonists. The Queen loathed him, and her son Bertie spoke of 'that viper Labouchère'. Sir Hercules Robinson, former High Commissioner at the Cape, was nearer the truth in saying that he 'wanted to play the Good Samaritan without the oil and twopence'. Nevertheless, 'Labby' was a brilliant debater, and the House was not his only forum. He owned a magazine called *Truth*, in which he campaigned ceaselessly for the great libertarian issues of the day, and fearlessly exposed shady business practices. On the debit side, he revealed a strong streak of anti-semitism. Rhodes, and his connections with 'astute Hebrew financiers', made a perfect target for such ideals and prejudices, although in the end Labouchère came to have a grudging respect for him.

The campaign in *Truth* against the Matabele War made no pretence at even-handedness, for, as Labouchère said, 'there are plenty of my contemporaries ready to publish any statement redounding to the credit of these filibusters.' His main contention was that the Company had provoked the war because it was facing economic collapse and, having failed to find payable gold in the area of its charter, was desperate to prospect in Matabeleland. A series of reports on this theme were followed by a long account published in *Truth* on 15 February 1894. It quoted a claim by Captain Lloyd Francis in a Pretoria newspaper, that he had executed Matabele captives under orders, and that surrendering warriors had generally been subjected to brutal treatment. Francis had been a member of the Shangani Patrol, but was accused by Forbes of cowardice and was regarded by Selous as an unreliable, unstable character, although his allegations may have been true. Less sustainable was a separate report in *Truth* by an anonymous correspondent stating that, in proportion to the period of the Company's presence in Mashonaland, its forces had killed as many Mashona as the Matabele.

Selous was roused to fury by these reports. The deaths in the war of friends like Borrow and Wilson, and Ted Burnett (who, the companion of his trip to obtain the Mapondera concession, had also been killed) made him especially sensitive to Labouchère's claims. The editor of *Truth* became Selous's *bête noire*, the incarnation of the stay-at-home polemicists who he had always suspected would distort and misrepresent the deeds of decent Englishmen abroad.

Selous fired the first salvo in what became a running feud in a letter published by *The Times* a few days after the *Truth* article. He said the allegations were tantamount to saying that Colonel Goold-Adams, under whom he had served in the Southern Column, had ordered that prisoners be murdered in cold blood. 'Such an accusation is too monstrous, too infamous; it makes me mad to see such falsehood presented to the English public as truth.' He questioned why Labouchère was so eager to ferret out 'from every obscure source' any information 'to 'so unjustly disgrace' his countrymen, and referred him to a refutation of Francis's claims by a fellow officer, Captain C. Griffiths. Of these two witnesses, Selous said, 'with both of whom I came a good deal in contact . . . I would believe what Captain Griffiths simply averred rather than what Captain Francis swore to.' Then he turned to a sensitive point:

225

I entirely repudiate the oft-repeated insinuation of Mr Labouchère that I am a paid agent of the British South Africa Company, and simply write what I am told by Mr Rhodes . . . I have many personal friends among the officers and men lately engaged, and I consider it to be my duty to defend them against the foul calumnies which Mr Labouchère is so industriously circulating.

No war, he added, could bear the microscopic inspection of armchair philanthropists, without revealing man's 'innate savagery', but he was quite confident in the outcome of any inquiry. 'I can assure Mr Labouchère that nothing would please me better than that any man who has been guilty of the cowardly and brutal crime of butchering unarmed Matabele should be brought to trial.'

It was a reasonable response, but flawed in one important respect. Selous had described the anonymous report on alleged brutality towards the Mashona as 'abominable falsehoods . . . either prompted by malice or ignorance', and went on, 'As far as I know two women and one child have been killed in Mashonaland by white men since 1889.' He had overlooked a significant incident which rendered this statement false.

Public opinion was behind Selous. The Matabele campaign was seen as having been a swift and brilliant military triumph by a handful of civilians, and was contrasted with the costly Zulu War, in which, at the Battle of Isandhlwana alone, more than 900 British soldiers were killed. It was considered inconceivable that men as gallant as Allan Wilson and his companions could have carried out atrocities. *The Times* weighed in with an editorial stating that Selous had issued 'a direct challenge which can be neither ignored nor evaded'. The allegations in *Truth* were 'so monstrous as to be inherently improbable', and were to be held in 'wholesome contempt' unless substantiated. It concluded: 'Perhaps Mr Selous does well to be angry . . . At all events, he has joined battle with Mr Labouchère. He asks, and is entitled to be heard.'

Labouchère was not long in returning the fire. He could not, he admitted, provide the 'body of direct testimony from witnesses of unimpeachable character' demanded by *The Times* to prove that prisoners had been killed. But gleefully he seized on Selous's blithe claim that the total civilian casualties of white rule in Mashonaland had been two women and one child. He cited an incident in 1892 in which Captain Charles Lendy had bombarded the village of a Mashona chief who had refused to submit to Company justice, in doing so killing twenty-three people and earning himself a severe reprimand from the Colonial Office. 'Does Mr Selous forget the incident?' Labouchère enquired. 'No one who reads the official account of this atrocity can doubt that the Mashonas gained nothing by the substitution of the rule of the Company for that of the Matabele.'

Labouchère continued that although Selous maintained he was no apologist for the Company, his new book, *Travel and Adventure in South-East Africa*, which had been published just before the war started, rather suggested otherwise. Moreover, he added, twisting the knife:

> If he has land or mining rights in Mashonaland, it is his direct interest not only that the charter should not be revoked, but that the Company should be able to fill its coffers by creating the notion that Matabeleland is a valuable possession, that there is gold there in paying amounts, that the climate both in Mashonaland and in Matabeleland is all that can be desired for Europeans, and that settlers will be wise to go there. Whether he has, or has had, shares in the Chartered Company I do not know . . . It is quite enough for me to regard his testimony respecting these countries with the suspicion that I always feel for that of an interested party.

Selous retired bruised from this encounter. He did still hold land and mining claims, and, too late, he saw that coming to his comrades' defence had compromised his own position. It did not help that he had started to revise the high opinion which he had expressed in *Travel and Adventure* about the leading lights in the Company, and especially Jameson, nor that wise heads in the City were becoming cynical about the falsified gold bulletins from Mashonaland. Selous's tub-thumping for the territory in *Travel and Adventure* could be made to seem naive and injudicious, if not worse. Millais wrote: 'Selous was much depressed by [Labouchère's] attacks and resented them bitterly, for he knew he was totally innocent.'

This embarrassment aside, *Travel and Adventure* was enjoying a large success. Its publication had been timely; the dramatis personae of recent events in the Matabele War, Lobengula and Jameson, were prominent on its pages, while the narrative of hunting and encounters with hostile tribes was told with flair. The reviews were excellent and delighted Selous and his new publishers, Rowland Ward. In contrast to *A Hunter's Wanderings*, Selous also considered that he had been well paid.

The book's success launched him on the lecture circuit again. But a few weeks after his exchange with Labouchère in the pages of *The Times*, a speech to the Royal Colonial Institute demonstrated that the debate had touched a raw nerve. He addressed a packed session in the Whitehall Rooms at the Hotel Metropole, and began with an account of Matabele history and of their brutality – an account so exhaustive that his listeners could have been forgiven for surrendering to restlessness or sleep – before he returned to the attack against Labouchère. Now the partisan crowd cheered him on as he excoriated 'the slanders concocted against honourable men', and 'the screechings of the dirty bird that has fouled its own nest'. It was not one of Selous's most dignified performances, and a few of his closer friends, including Rowland Ward, head of the publishing company, advised him to avoid public statements on the subject for a while.

Less than a year after their marriage, Fred and Gladys sailed to Africa. They had bought a house called Alpine Lodge at Worplesdon in Surrey, set beside a stream and amid rambling countryside, which in later years was transformed into the quite grand residence they occupied until their deaths. However Selous had remained plagued by financial worries. He should, in fact, have been quite prosperous, but the collapse of the gold-share boom in 1895 – which affected De Beers shares, on which he and Gladys depended for income – made him reconsider whether he was ready to settle down in England. The upshot was that when he received a letter from Maurice Heany, his former partner, inviting him to help manage a large commercial farming concern in Matabeleland, he quickly accepted.

The Maddy family were much opposed to the idea of Selous taking their daughter to a place where the Matabele had, quite recently, been trying to kill him. But at this stage of their life, Fred made the decisions and Gladys followed. She had just turned twenty-one, to his forty-three. In time, Gladys would learn to assert herself very adequately, and then she would generally stay at home rather than accompany him on his many and frequent travels.

Fred and Gladys left England in March 1895, spending their first wedding anniversary at sea. They arrived at the Cape to find a note from Rhodes for Selous: 'Come at once to Groote Schuur & your wife.' Most of the next two months were spent with Rhodes at his residence, an old Dutch granary set against Table Mountain, which he first rescued from neglect and then, with the assistance of a young architect, Herbert Baker, transformed into a magnificent Dutch colonial mansion. It was one of Rhodes's visions – 'big and simple, barbaric if you like', as he put it – and the grounds, 1500 acres on the slopes of Table Mountain, commanded a view of the glorious cape where the Atlantic and Indian oceans meet.

Gladys was overwhelmed by her first experience of Africa, responding with youthful delight to its beauty. Her gardening instincts were aroused at Groote Schuur, especially by the hydrangeas for which the estate was renowned. Rhodes, who was notoriously immune to female charms, seems to have been enchanted by her. Baker, the architect, records that Gladys was one of the few women Rhodes ever took to, and that he gave her 'the kindest fatherly advice about the difficulties she would experience on the frontier'.

Rhodes was now at the peak of his fame and achievement. On his trips to London he was lionized as few men from the colonies had been before. Whitehall had endorsed his proposal that the conquered territory of Matabeleland be incorporated into the charter, and in May the unification of Zambesia under the name of Rhodesia effectively came into being. Rhodes's accomplishments in the North would alone have been sufficient for one lifetime. But he was also Prime Minister of the Cape, and he had one more of what he called his 'big ideas'. This was a union of Southern Africa, incorporating Rhodesia, the British colonies, the Cape and Natal, and the Afrikaner republics of the Transvaal and Orange Free State.

In these weeks at Groote Schuur, Selous noted Rhodes's habit of brooding when others were speaking. He would sit after dinner among his guests for a couple of hours, meditating while they chatted, then rise, slapping his knees, and go off to bed without saying a word. When he had the floor he would talk animatedly about his plans. Both he and Selous understood, and sympathized with, Boer nationalism, while disliking what Selous called 'the narrow-minded and illogical despotism' of the Kruger regime, and both agreed that Anglo–Boer cooperation was vital to the future of the region. And Rhodes seemed in no hurry. He told Selous his maxim for dealing with Afrikaners: 'You never get anything out of a Dutchman by kicking him, but you will get all you want by patience.' This made his subsequent conduct all the more inexplicable to Selous.

As Fred and Gladys were preparing to leave, Rhodes took her aside and said: 'Your life will be very dull without a good horse – so when you arrive at Bulawayo go to the Standard Bank and you will find a sum of money to get the very best horse you can.' When she did call at the bank, she found Rhodes had transferred £500 to an account for her.

The journey to Bulawayo took another two months, by ship to Beira, and then by ox-wagon up the road Selous had cut in 1891, but Gladys took it all in her stride. Moreover, she enjoyed the wildlife which Fred pointed out along the way, made no complaints about the discomforts of travel, and by the time they reached Bulawayo in August, he must have been feeling much reassured by the way his young bride had adjusted to their new life.

He was astonished at the transformation that had overtaken Bulawayo since Lobengula's fall. On the ruins of the royal kraal a booming frontier town had sprung up. The most prominent building was the new Bulawayo Club. Another focal point, across the dusty street, was the cluster of buildings at Market Square. The town had an air of vigour that Salisbury had still not acquired, for money was being made in cattle speculation, and gold hopes were still high. An optimistic white population had grown to around 1000 men and women, while the Matabele appeared to have accepted their defeat three years earlier. To Selous it seemed that 'everything was *couleur de rose*'.

His job was with the Matabele Gold Reefs and Estates Company

– a subsidiary of Sir John Willoughby's Consolidated Company in which he already had investments – which was being managed by Maurice Heany. Selous was expected to help Heany occasionally with administration, but his main duty was to run an estate at Essexvale, about twenty miles south-east of Bulawayo, an early model for the large commercial farms in Rhodesia.

The Essexvale estate consisted of about 200,000 acres of virgin bush, and again Selous had cause to be proud of Gladys. Their first home was a mud and thatch hut, while they awaited the arrival of a prefabricated bungalow from England, but she made the best of it, declaring that it was beautifully cool in the dry, intense summer heat. She was a dedicated gardener, and once they had chosen a site – which commanded a fine view overlooking a river gorge – she started sowing flowers and vegetables.

By Christmas, they had settled to their new life. About forty acres had been cleared and planted with maize, water melons and fruit trees. Selous also kept about 1000 head of cattle. Local Matabele tended the animals and brought Gladys milk from which she made about ten pounds of butter a week; this was taken into town by a servant who returned with their mail and provisions. Neither Gladys nor Fred spent much time in Bulawayo, only riding in occasionally to see friends and spending the night before returning in the morning. 'We had a very happy three months,' Gladys wrote.

In their self-sufficient idyll, Selous was blissfully unaware of the plotting that was going on in town. This involved not only Jameson – now administrator of the whole of Rhodesia – with whom his relations were cool, but also his employers, Willoughby and Heany. The scheme being hatched led back to Rutherfoord Harris in Kimberley, Rhodes in Cape Town, and, ultimately, all the way to Whitehall. Somehow, through the weeks of December, the comings and goings of groups of armed and mounted men, and the feverish talk of tension in the Transvaal, Selous remained ignorant of the storm that was about to break. He remarked later: 'I was not in the councils of Rhodes, or Jameson or Willoughby, and knew nothing about the coup d'état which was [being] so carefully prepared.'

The background to the Jameson Raid is easily explained. For years, momentum had been gathering among the Uitlanders of the Transvaal – mainly Englishmen, but also other 'foreigners' – for political rights. The reason that Kruger denied them was that the Afrikaners had become a minority in their own country, swamped in the rush that followed the gold finds. Uitlander grievances produced talk of an uprising, and a disastrous temptation offered itself to Rhodes: to advance his plan for a South African federation by overthrowing the xenophobic Kruger Government. Jameson, with a volunteer force drawn mainly from the BSA Company Police, was to station himself on the Transvaal border, and, on the basis of a false plea for help, ride to the defence of the Uitlanders, while they 'spontaneously' rose up against their Boer 'oppressors'.

Harris, whose malign blunderings were finally exposed by the raid, was to help set events in train. One of the steps he took was to send a telegram to Bulawayo. What followed was described by Selous in a letter to his friend John Scott Keltie, secretary of the Royal Geographical Society:

> The first the general public in Bulawayo heard of the troubles was that 144 Englishmen had been shot down by the Boers in the streets of Johannesburg; this report reached this country at the same time as a wire from Dr Jameson calling upon the officers of the Rhodesia Volunteer Force to get together 1,000 men and to be in readiness to march with them immediately for the Transvaal.

The settlers mustered in Market Square. 'There was great excitement and we hardly knew what to believe,' said the Reverend Isaac Shimmin, a Wesleyan pastor. Selous stood up and said if Englishmen had indeed been shot down for demanding political rights, then he would be prepared to ride. Privately, to Shimmin and others, he expressed strong doubts as to the genuineness of the distress message.

His suspicions soon proved justified. Jameson and Willoughby had crossed into the Transvaal on 29 December accompanied by 420 men and the cheers of jingoes everywhere. What he did not get was the anticipated spontaneous 'rising' of the Uitlanders. After a humiliating skirmish with the Boers near Krugersdorp, in which at least seventeen of his men were killed, Jameson surrendered on 2 January 1896.

Selous wrote angrily to Keltie:

Now that we know there was no rising in Johannesburg, and can see that the discontent of the Uitlanders has been exaggerated by certain people to forward their political schemes, there seems to be no justification for Jameson's invasion, and the thinking portion of this community (which is a very small one) of which I count myself one, have no sympathy with the plot to overthrow the Transvaal Government.

All that had been accomplished was 'the transferrence [sic] of all the leading men of this country to Pretoria Gaol'. It had been 'a ghastly business altogether', but bitter though the humiliation for Englishmen, 'it will be infinitely worse if, from chagrin and mortification at Jameson's defeat, the British Government goes to war with the Transvaal.' With a good deal more foresight than Jameson had shown, Selous predicted that it would 'require as many troops to conquer the Dutch in South Africa, fighting in their own country, and with the right on their side, as were employed for the invasion of the Crimea'.

In her meticulous analysis of Jameson's Raid, Elizabeth Longford has helped explain how the success of the Matabele War so turned the Doctor's head that he could have acted in the incredibly reckless way he did. To Jameson it must have seemed that the Boers would collapse in the face of his irregular cavalry and Maxim guns just as the Matabele had. Lady Longford comments: 'Read the story of Lobengula's fall and you see in it a rehearsal for the fall of Rhodes. Many of the same individuals and much the same spirit which destroyed the poor old savage later brought down his conqueror.'

Rhodes was ruined by the raid. He had, in fact, tried at the last minute to stop it, but was let down by Harris. When he heard the news he went ashen and blurted out: 'Old Jameson has upset my apple-cart.' Forced to resign as Prime Minister, he never recovered either his energy or vision, and died six years later of the congenital heart disease which had brought him to Africa.

The raiders fared better. True, Jameson was sent back to England for trial and sentenced to fifteen months' imprisonment, but he was generally treated as a popular hero and served only four months in

Holloway before being pardoned. Astonishingly, he went on to become Prime Minister at the Cape in 1904. Willoughby served eight months before returning to South Africa, and fought the Boers again, in the war which resulted from the raid.

Selous's dealings with the 'Chartered crowd' were never the same again. He had not been taken into Jameson's confidence as it had apparently been recognized that he would be unsympathetic. Selous's abhorrence of controversy made him avoid public discussion of the issue. But the following year, in London, after he had been dogged by a reporter who invaded his hansom cab for an interview, he burst out: 'When the news of the raid came, and the circumstances got out bit by bit I confess I felt very indignant about the whole plot. But I am no politician, and hate all scheming and intrigues.'

Bulawayo returned to some kind of normality in the new year, although the raid had left the town significantly short of able-bodied men, horses and rifles. Another unwelcome side-effect was an outbreak of bellicose patriotism. However, Selous's main concern was how, with Heany in jail, he was going to cope at work. Gladys remained supportive and unruffled as ever; with the happy if incongruous touch of the Englishwoman abroad, she named their prefabricated bungalow on the veld Hatherley Cottage, and made several terraces of flower beds around the verandah.

A sense of grievance among the Matabele had meanwhile been growing for some time. Principal among its causes was the Company's policy towards native cattle herds, which were subject to random confiscation under a specious interpretation of war spoils. Selous thought the policy 'impolitic if not ungenerous'. Even worse was the way it was carried out. He wrote: 'Certain natives suffered wrong, especially owners of only three or four cows, who in some cases lost their all, both in cattle and faith in the honesty and justice of the Chartered Company.' Another complaint was that Matabele chiefs were required to make available men to labour in mines and on farms. The Company's own Matabele policemen backed up this forced labour regime in heavy-handed fashion. On top of all this, an epidemic of the cattle disease rinderpest broke out in the spring, and wiped out many native herds.

Like most of the historical episodes in which Selous was caught up during his lifetime, the Matabele rebellion has been studied from many sides. It has been suggested, for example, that it was a religious-based mass movement. However the earliest theory still rings true – that grievances found expression in a spontaneous reaction, essentially because of the whites' vulnerability. In the words of one of the insurgents: 'There was no organization, it was just like a fire which suddenly flames up.'

The spark was lit on 23 March. Fred and Gladys felt no sense of looming peril, and Fred, who was inspecting cattle for signs of rinderpest, had even felt secure enough to leave Gladys alone for two nights. She was unconcerned, for 'we were on the most friendly terms with all the natives living around us'. On the third morning, several Matabele came to the homestead wanting to buy axes. The Selous kept a store of such goods, and Gladys sold the men axes, and then let them use the grindstone for sharpening. She chatted with them unconcernedly, but noticed that they seemed nervous. 'They would sit watching me work & talk & tell me I was their white Queen – but always wanted to know when was "the boss" coming back.'

When he did arrive back in the afternoon, Selous was deeply disturbed by Gladys's story. That night, she noticed, he brought a rifle to the bedroom. With the morning came news which, as Gladys related it in a letter, must have horrified her parents as they read it, snug in the rectory at Down Hatherley.

> I had breakfast ready when a very good kaffir came running down – 'bring up the horses, bring up the horses'. I could not think what was the matter, but Fred came and said – 'eat what you can, stick a few clothes in your bag, we must ride hard for Bulawayo. The kaffirs are rising'.

The country around them was in flames. Three miners working a claim nearby were dead; Gladys reflected with mortification that they had been hacked to death with axes. At Edkins's store, to the south, seven whites and two Cape coloureds had been murdered. To the east, at Insiza, the Cunningham family, consisting of two men, two women and three children, had been slaughtered.

Selous never understood why he and Gladys were not killed that night as well. 'I should like to think that because we had always

235

treated them kindly, our neighbours shrank from [it]; but after all that has happened I find it very difficult to believe.' In fact, although he detested the Matabele as a people he had always got on well with individuals, and had been on friendly terms with Umlugulu, a local Matabele high priest and a relative of Lobengula. This man, one of four or five leaders of the rebellion, was described by Selous as 'a very gentle-mannered savage, and always most courteous and polite ... By us he was always treated with the consideration due to one who had been a man of importance in Lo Bengula's time.' For her part, Gladys was unlike many pioneer women in being friendly and helpful to local people.

They galloped the twenty miles to Bulawayo. Gladys found it 'a dreadful ride' and shuddered at the memory of passing through a defile between high rocks and trees where Matabele seemed to lurk behind every bush. As they neared Bulawayo, they met two men in a cart on their way to collect Gladys. 'Thank God, no one expects to see you alive,' said one.

Within a week, Selous reckoned, no whites were left living in the countryside. At least 140 men, women and children, more than 10 per cent of the white population of Matabeleland, and well over half those living outside Bulawayo, were dead. As refugees poured into the town with tales of women and children hacked and beaten to death, a terrible hatred was aroused in the survivors. Vulnerable and fearful, Bulawayo went into laager against an attack and brooded on vengeance.

For the first week, Gladys and the other women and children were put up in the Club. She likened it to the Black Hole of Calcutta, 'awful discomfort on the hard boards, sick people, babies crying, women so excited & alarmed'. In the high tension, false alarms were common. One night, a rider galloped around shouting: 'The Matabele are coming, the Matabele are coming.' Another time, Gladys related:

> Five cartridges went off by mistake. We were woken up by cries of 'they are on us'. It may be funny, but we were not in the least bit frightened. I did not seem to care a bit ... The doctor was expecting a confinement in one corner, a miscarriage in another!! Two more ladies very seriously ill – such a

nice state. Then he said, 'and you will be another if you don't take this', and he gave me a very strong glass of brandy and water.

Gladys spent the next five months in the laager, while Selous was attached, with the rank of captain, to the Bulawayo Field Force. This volunteer militia was raised to defend the town pending the arrival of imperial troops, as almost the entire local force of the BSA Company Police had been on Jameson's raid. Soon after settling Gladys in Bulawayo, Selous rode back to their estate with an armed band. Initially he felt no great animosity towards the insurgents: 'Looking at things from their point of view, if they thought they could succeed in shaking off the white man's rule, well, why shouldn't they try the chances of rebellion?' he mused. However, once he had heard the accounts of murder, he too was seized by the desire for vengeance, 'which could only be satisfied by a personal participation in the killing of the murderers'. In his book on the rebellion, *Sunshine and Storm in Rhodesia*, he wrote:

> I don't defend such feelings, nor deny that they are vile and brutal . . . only I would say to the highly moral critic, Be charitable if you have not yourself lived through similar experiences . . . for you probably know not your own nature . . . the murder of white women and children, by natives, seems to the colonist not merely a crime, but a sacrilege.

From the homestead, which was as he had left it, Selous and his men rode to a neighbouring kraal. They found no warriors, only a woman, children and a few stolen cattle, but he ordered that the kraal be set ablaze. When the whites did encounter a band of suspected insurgents, they opened fire, intending to kill them, 'with as little compunction as though they were a pack of wild dogs'. On this occasion the casualties seem to have been minimal. But a few days later Selous's men penetrated into the rocky landscape of the Matopos Hills and fought a skirmish which, he noted with grim satisfaction, 'left a few of our opponents ready for burial'.

For the remainder of March and April, the settlers were on the defensive, while the Matabele, remembering the painful lesson of the Maxim guns in 1893, made no attempt to breach the Bulawayo laager. Market Square was enclosed by wagons and barbed wire and turned into a formidable stronghold for around 1500 men, women and children. After a week or so in the 'Black Hole' of the Club, Gladys and the other women were allowed to go to the homes of friends. Still, fear and rumours of a massed attack persisted. They gathered force through April as impis started to mass menacingly around the town.

After fainting 'once or twice' on the first day, Gladys showed herself to be one of the most resourceful of the besieged band. There was much admiration for the way she had kept her head in the crisis at Essexvale. 'I have been such a heroine – people asked how I was, and said how plucky, riding all that way. I felt quite important.' One of these admirers was a British officer, Colonel Robert Baden-Powell, destined to found the Scout and Guide movements, who thought her 'a fine frontierswoman', and gave a highly-coloured account of her escape in his book for aspiring guides. (Selous was cited as a 'peace scout' by Baden-Powell in the equivalent book for boys.)

Gladys wrote home:

> You need not be anxious as I am quite safe in laager, but my darling Fred may have a very hard time. I know that he will always be to the fore in everything – but I am proud of having such a husband – when you see what babies and fools some of these men are. Why, some are very much worse than the women. I should be most awfully ashamed if I was in any way a relation of some of the men up here. But there, I have a husband that everyone looks up to and respects.

In Kimberley, a force was being mustered to relieve Bulawayo, and early in May the 750 men of the Matabeleland Relief Force under Lieutenant-Colonel Herbert Plumer marched north from Bechuanaland. Meanwhile, the settler militia, which consisted of about 800 men, was confined by its commander, Colonel William Napier, to a policy of skirmishing. This was too cautious for Selous's liking, as the Matabele had been emboldened to surround the town, and by the end of April were estimated to have around 8000 men in the vicinity. Napier felt no compulsion to go on the offensive. Food and supplies could be brought in, as, by some unexplained oversight, the Matabele had left the road open to Tati. One of Selous's duties was to establish forts on the road to keep it that way.

Finally, operations were started to drive the Matabele back, and in one of the resulting skirmishes Selous had his narrowest squeak of the campaign. While on horseback pursuing a group of Matabele, he and another man, a Lieutenant Windley, had got in advance of their fellows. Selous was dismounted when Windley called out, 'Look out, they're coming down on us from the left', and he turned to see a band of Matabele advancing fast over open ground.

Retreat was imperative, but as Selous reached for his horse it shied. Windley rode after it, but the riderless animal was clean away. Selous was now stranded, with the warriors about 200 yards away, running at him while making a hissing sound by which the Matabele intended, and generally succeeded, in striking terror in the hearts of their enemies. When Selous felt in his bandolier he found he had just two bullets left. He set off after Windley at a desperate run.

He was still very fit and lean but – now aged forty-four – no longer in his elephant-hunting prime. The Matabele gained on him. At this critical stage, Windley came galloping back, urging Selous to leap up behind him. Selous feared, however, that if he tried to pull himself up by the pommel it might drag the saddle round, which would doom them both. The Matabele were now within 100 yards. Selous grasped the bridle and ran alongside as Windley put the horse into a trot. Bullets had started to kick up the ground around them. One knocked a heel off Windley's boot. When they had got some way clear, Selous managed to scramble up behind, only to be bucked off and land heavily on his back. Once again the Matabele came on hard, and he had to resume running while holding the bridle. Finally, Selous and Windley caught up with their companions, who repulsed the Matabele with a volley. Selous was 'so tired by the hardest run . . . since my old elephant hunting days, that it was quite an effort to mount'. To Windley he gave heartfelt thanks.

Through a series of other such skirmishes, the cordon around Bulawayo was loosened, and once Plumer's force arrived the end was in sight. The 2000 men, who by now included about 500 volunteers from Salisbury and Gwelo, were put under the command of Major-General Frederick Carrington, whom Selous thought a vast improvement on Colonel Napier. The two main theatres of operation became the plains north-east of Bulawayo, and the Matopos Hills to the south. Here the Matabele retreated and took months to be winkled out, only finally laying down their arms after peace indabas in which Rhodes played a vital part.

Rhodes came to Rhodesia having already been obliged by Jameson's *folie de grandeur* to resign as Prime Minister. He would soon have to stand down from the Chartered Company too. Now, he threw himself into the campaign, marching down with a relief force from Salisbury. Selous was with the column which met him, and noted signs of the strain which he had been under, 'the fast grizzling hair, and a certain look in the face'.

This final phase was the ugliest of the campaign. The white forces moved out into the countryside where they found the gruesome remains of the families that had been murdered in the first week of the uprising. Every skirmish became an act of vengeance. Selous had helped collect the broken skulls of women and children, 'the blood-stained tresses of young Dutch girls', and was shocked to find the blood-lust that was aroused in him. He wrote of one battle:

> Once broken, the kaffirs never made any attempt to rally, but ran as hard as they could, accepting death when overtaken without offering the slightest resistance; some indeed when too tired to run any farther, walked doggedly forward with arms in their hands which they never attempted to use, and did not even turn their heads to look at the white men who were about to shoot them. No quarter was either given or asked for . . . This realistic picture may seem very horrible to all those who believe themselves to be superior beings to the cruel colonists of Rhodesia . . . but it is possible for a man to live a long life without ever becoming aware that below the polished surface of conventionality there exists in him an ineradicable leaven of innate ferocity.

Rhodes apparently experienced similar feelings. He would urge soldiers to show no mercy, and after an engagement would repeatedly count Matabele corpses. Gladys, who had liked 'the natives', was also affected by the harshness of the mood. 'How awfully they have cut up the white men, women and children –

makes you long to be a man. What savage brutes these natives are.'

There are refrains in all this of a much later conflict in Rhodesia, the guerrilla war of the 1970s. It is easy to see how Selous's book on the rebellion, *Sunshine and Storm in Rhodesia*, became not only one of the seminal works of the country's history but, in its frank and spare account of bush warfare, created an ideal for a later generation of anti-insurgent forces. To be found in *Sunshine and Storm* are many of the attitudes of UDI Rhodesia – the assumption of racial superiority of white over black, the sense of a small community fighting a battle against impossible odds, and the denunciation of a mother-country clique of 'anti-colonials and negrophilists' playing loose with the truth. However, these parallels, which have tended to link Selous's name with the most reactionary and unsympathetic elements of the UDI attitude, do him less than justice. The Selous Scouts, the irregular military unit which acquired international notoriety in the dying days of white Rhodesia, sullied his name and perverted what Selous had stood for in the Matabele Rebellion.

Yet one more of Selous's cherished assumptions was shattered before peace returned to Rhodesia that year. In June the process of rebellion was repeated in Mashonaland. Once again the murder of isolated groups of settlers provoked maddened retaliation. The white sense of shock was even greater than it had been in Matabeleland. Selous was among those who had fostered the notion that the Mashona had welcomed whites as their saviours from the Matabele. Now he could only throw up his hands in defeat. 'After having spent over twenty years of my life amongst the kaffirs, I now see that I know nothing about them, and recognize that I am quite incompetent to express an opinion as to the line of conduct they would be likely to adopt.'

As order was gradually restored, Fred and Gladys surveyed the wreckage of their dream. Hatherly Cottage had been burned to the ground. Willoughby's Consolidated Company told Selous it could not employ him further. There was nothing for it but to return to England. Gladys wrote: 'We had lost everything – clothes, house – and all our work had been destroyed . . . the only nice thing was the vegetable garden full of cabbages, carrots, parsnips etc.'

One good thing alone had come out of the catastrophe. Fred and Gladys had left England a newly-married couple, untested together.

They returned strengthened by the bonds of a shared ordeal. As Fred put the finishing touches in Bulawayo to the manuscript of *Sunshine and Storm*, he penned a simple, heartfelt dedication, 'To My Wife, who during the last few months has at once been my greatest anxiety, and my greatest comfort'.

So at the end of 1896, Selous turned his back for the last time on the country which he had first seen twenty-five years earlier, over which he had hunted and explored, and where he had helped raise the British flag. He was not an emotional man, and he may have felt no great sense of loss as he and Gladys set their wagon for the coast. But in years to come he would often cast his mind back to these plains where so much of his life had been spent. And then, in an armchair in Surrey, he did feel longing – for the sight of an elephant herd wading out into the Zambesi, and the scent of a wood fire on a star-bright night.

CHAPTER SEVENTEEN

《‧》

A Home in Surrey

The England to which Fred and Gladys returned at the end of 1896 was a country at ease with itself, powerful abroad and untroubled at home. Victoria's Diamond Jubilee was about to be celebrated with a pomp and pageantry befitting her empire. Gladstone's Liberalism was on the wane, and Lord Salisbury was back as Prime Minister. Keir Hardie, founder of the modern Labour Party, had won a Commons seat, but the suffragette movement was in its infancy. Rudyard Kipling was at the zenith of his powers, and popularity, while Bernard Shaw had just become drama critic of the *Saturday Review*. Yorkshire were the County Cricket champions; Dr W. G. Grace, enjoying a golden evening to his career, had recently become the first batsman to score 1000 runs in May.

Despite spending more than half his life abroad, Selous remained an Englishman to the core. He had finally come home, and it was not long before he acquired the identity of the country gentleman which he would preserve to the end of his life. He took up egg-collecting again, and could often be seen striding in the fields around Worplesdon, wearing tweed or corduroy plus-twos and a deerstalker hat. He shot grouse – astonishingly badly – at the estates of aristocratic friends, and played cricket for the local eleven. He attended dinners of the Shikari Club, by whose members he was treated with great deference, and sometimes he dined with friends at the Royal Colonial. Once he was invited by the Queen to Balmoral, but declined because he 'couldn't bear all that fuss'. Gladys, who was still sociable and outgoing, must have been dreadfully disappointed.

It was not all gentrified conviviality. Even as he and Gladys stepped off the ship at Plymouth, newsmen were waiting to question him on Labouchère's latest diatribe about events in Matabeleland.

243

Fortunately, he had been briefed by his publishers, Rowland Ward, to expect controversy, and he managed to contain himself, but only for the time being. His new book was laced with biting references to his old adversary: 'Truth – the everlasting Truth which we are told is great and will prevail – is one thing, whilst Mr Labouchère's Truth, sold at all bookstalls at 6d a copy, is quite another.' And: 'Mr Labouchère has professed himself "sorry for the women and children who have been killed." Sorry – only sorry! Wonderful indeed is the serenity of soul that enables that noble nature to view all mundane affairs from the same cold, passionless plane, whether it be the cruel murder of an English settler's wife and family, or an accident to a friend's bicycle in Hyde Park!'

Sunshine and Storm in Rhodesia was rushed into print by Rowland Ward and was on the bookstands within a few weeks of Selous's return. Despite the grim subject matter, it is, because of its candour, one of his most attractive works, capturing the atmosphere and bewilderment of a brutal clash between alien peoples. At the same time, Selous declared unequivocally his independence from the Chartered Company, and criticized Jameson both for the raid and for administrative bungling which contributed to the uprisings. The final chapter was both an eloquent plea for understanding of the Boers, and a prophecy that a war between Boer and Briton would be 'a calamity of incalculable dimensions to both countries'.

The first edition sold out almost immediately, and was quickly reprinted. This further literary success, following that of *Travel and Adventure*, brought Selous a new status in England as a writer, while his work was now being read by the avid hunting fraternity of the United States. A new generation of admirers included a rising politician, Theodore Roosevelt, another keen hunter. From now on, writing provided Selous with a regular additional income. So did lecturing. Not long after returning to England he was 'travelling every day and lecturing every night ... yesterday Halifax, today Swansea'.

He saw these additional earnings as indispensable. Although he and Gladys now lived with every sign of prosperity, he was usually anxious about money. In Millais's words he was 'a man who knew no more about business than a child'. Sound advice helped get his investments on a more stable footing, but any fluctuation in the share market – particularly gold shares in which he had invested heavily – started him worrying about money again. At such times he would become irritable and depressed, and his correspondence contains frequent references to financial losses.

He would make occasional plans to economize. These sometimes restricted his travel plans, and the luxuries which he and Gladys permitted themselves. Nevertheless, the Selous were able to afford major additions to the Worplesdon house, which was renamed Heatherside and steadily transformed into a substantial residence. During a later bout of worry, Selous thought the property might have to be sold, but by then Gladys had put so much into it that he realized it would break her heart to leave. In the absence of evidence about the cause of this fretfulness, and the fact that despite it he and Gladys continued to live in comfort and style, we can but conclude that much of it was self-induced, a legacy of years of indebtedness. Inheriting his parents' estate on the death of his mother in 1913 finally put an end to Selous's financial concerns, and ensured that after his death Gladys was well provided for.

Heatherside was something to which they could both give their energies. Gladys was a fine home-maker, and turned her gardening talents to dahlia-growing, as well as an orchard, and the lawns which ran down to a stream surrounding the property. She kept the house spotless, and visitors noticed the scent of furniture polish, and fresh flowers in the large drawing-room overlooking the garden.

Fred's main contribution was a large outbuilding, which was primarily a trophy room but which he preferred to call 'the museum'. It contained mementos of a lifetime of hunting and collecting, from the chamois which he shot in Bavaria at the age of eighteen, to what he thought the 'gem of gems' of his trophies, the 45-inch horns of a kudu bull, which for a time were the longest known pair. Any visitor who expressed an interest would be taken down to the museum and be treated to a history of the specimens. Once a group of boys was sent down from Rugby, to meet the famous old boy and look over the museum. As they were shuffling in Selous chuckled to hear one lad whisper, 'Fancy bringing us all this way to see this little pip-squeak of a man!'

The contrast between the legend that was forming around his name and his appearance was often remarked upon. People meeting him for the first time expected a figure larger than life – the incarnation of Allan Quatermain, or a swashbuckling combination of Buffalo Bill and Charles Gordon. What they found was a trim, dapper man, about 5 feet 9 inches tall, of some presence but with a seeming reluctance to relate his adventures. A contemporary recalled: 'In no way did he resemble the popular conception of himself. It was difficult to induce him to speak of his achievements with the gun save when lecturing. He was not demonstrative; in fact he suffered a little from shyness and in consequence his greeting was somewhat tepid, but when he had gauged his visitor he thawed and became the model host.'

The gentleness of his manner – some friends saw it as being something quite feminine – could also be misleading. At one social gathering, Selous was talking to a woman about butterflies, in which he had rediscovered an interest. She eventually became bored, and said irritably: 'I want to talk to the big game hunter.' 'But madam, I am the big game hunter,' he replied apologetically.

The modesty was no facade. Once he had started on a story, he told it plainly and without affectation, but he had no illusions about his hunting prowess. He told a friend it was 'bunkum' to call him the greatest of hunters. 'Because I have hunted a lot, that is not to say I am a specially good hunter.' This was a refrain he took up in a lecture to the Imperial Institute, when he remarked that nothing had caused him such annoyance or embarrassment as the names by which he was known in the press – the 'Mighty Nimrod', or the 'Great Hunter'. There had been occasions, he said, when he wished he could have sunk into the ground after missing a rabbit in front of a Scottish gillie who had no doubt been told he was 'the great hunter Mr Selous'.

It was, nevertheless, through his interest in sport and natural history that he now started to form a range of lasting new friendships which formed a very significant aspect of this third and final phase of his life. The friends of the old Interior days had almost all passed on; his contacts with the Chartered Company had been ruptured; those who sought his friendship now honoured him as the sole survivor of that bygone age of muzzle-loader hunting in South Africa. On his side, despite, or perhaps because of, having spent so much time alone, Selous showed a great capacity for making new friends at an age when many men might have ceased to bother.

One of the most important of these new friends was John Millais, a man some fourteen years his junior, who had been inspired by Selous's writing to make a hunting trip to Southern Africa, and produced a classic account of his own, *A Breath From the Veldt*. He met Selous in 1897 and became an intimate friend and confidant. A year after his death, Millais wrote a biography, *The Life of F. C. Selous*.

Others within this circle were Heatley Noble, who coined the description of Selous as 'the hero of a thousand hairbreadth escapes', and with whom he went on egg-collecting expeditions to places as diverse as East Anglia and Iceland, and H. A. Bryden, a fellow hunter-naturalist. His sporting friends included Sir Beville Stanier, who had an estate in Shropshire which was renowned for its partridge shooting, and a jovial character named Sir Philip Brockle-hurst. Long afterwards, Millais recalled weekends spent grouse-shooting at the Brocklehurst estate, Swythamley in Derbyshire, as 'some of the best of life'.

Selous took to the shotgun with enthusiasm, but rather less talent than he had demonstrated for a muzzle-loader. Millais was forced to admit that, 'at first he was a very poor performer', and after a particularly inept performance the 'Mighty Nimrod' would come in for a good deal of teasing. But when the ladies had retired, and the men were gathered round a good fire with the port, Selous would be prevailed upon to relate his early elephant-hunting experiences with Cigar, or his adventures among the Mushukulumbwe, and the years would roll back.

One of those most impressed by his story-telling style was another of his new friends, Theodore Roosevelt:

What made Selous so charming a companion was his entire naturalness and lack of self-consciousness . . . He related his experiences very simply but very vividly, and with the atten-tion to detail which marks the born observer and narrator . . . He made us actually see everything that had happened. He acted the part, first of himself, and then of the game, until the whole scene was vivid before our eyes . . . his keen, simple, fearless blue eyes looking up at us from time to time, while

247

his hands moved with a vivacity we are accustomed to think of as French rather than English.

Selous's relationship with 'Teddy' Roosevelt was one of the strangest of his life. The first contact was made by Roosevelt in a letter soon after Selous's return from Africa. But they did not come face to face for another eight years, and then only met a handful of times. As men they were quite dissimilar, and as hunters they did not have much in common either. If his 'bags' are anything to go by, Roosevelt was a fervent, bloodthirsty sportsman of the undiscriminating school. He was a stalwart of the Boone & Crockett Club, contributed in no small part to the near-extinction of the large American deer, and once shocked Selous with an enthusiastic account of hunting cougar with dogs, in which the climax of the action was a gory pack kill. And yet they corresponded keenly for twenty years, not only on their mutual passion for hunting, but on the main issues of the day. Even when Roosevelt became President, he found time to write to Selous, and their first meeting took place at the White House. For his part, Selous unburdened himself to Roosevelt about his distress over the Anglo–Boer War as he did to few others.

They were brought into contact by a mutual English friend, Edward Buxton, who told Selous that Roosevelt, then assistant secretary in the Navy Department, admired Selous's writing and would be pleased to help him organize his long-anticipated hunting trip to North America. Roosevelt did give advice, although arrangements were made through another of Buxton's acquaintances, Willy Moncrief, who owned a ranch near Yellowstone Park. Selous wrote in his first letter to Roosevelt that he hoped to call with Gladys on his arrival in New York, though the trip would not, he confessed, be as extensive as he had hoped: 'Some months ago I thought that I should be able to spend several months in America and Canada and would be able to put aside 1200 to 1500 pounds for the whole trip. But since then I have lost a lot of money and shall have to be as economical as possible.' In the event, a meeting did not take place this time, as Fred and Gladys saved money by travelling to Wyoming via Canada rather than New York.

Selous made a second trip the following year, and again missed seeing Roosevelt. He was also disappointed by the size of the deer he found in the Big Horn Mountains, and wrote accordingly to Roosevelt, who replied:

> Your letter made me quite melancholy – first to think I wasn't to see you after all; and, next to realize so vividly how almost the last real hunting grounds in America have gone. Thirteen years ago, I had splendid sport on the Big Horn Mountains. I was just in time to see the last of the great wilderness life, and real wilderness hunting . . .
>
> I am glad you like to chat with me, even by letter. Ever since reading your first book I have always wanted to meet you. I hope I may have better luck next year than I had this.

Selous's nervousness about money did not prevent him travelling extensively in the years after his return to England. In addition to hunting in the United States in 1897 and 1898, he made egg-collecting excursions to Asia Minor in 1898 and 1899. In between, he crossed the British Isles almost constantly, usually first class. At hand was always the latest issue of *Field*, required reading of the English sporting gentry, to which he continued to contribute; on these occasions he could be quite heated on subjects such as the protective coloration of animals, and the tsetse fly of the Zambesi. He also developed a new taste in fiction, Thomas Hardy becoming the author he most admired, and *Tess of the D'Urbervilles* his favourite novel.

As the nineteenth century ebbed away, Selous had found an enduring and honoured place for himself in his native land. And although an urge to be on the move would afflict him to the end of his life, he had discovered through Gladys that there were rewards to be found by the hearth. Their first son, Frederick Hatherley Bruce Selous, always known as Freddie or Young Fred, was born in April 1898. A second, Harold Sherborn Selous, followed a year and a half later. (By the end of 1900, Gladys was pregnant again, but this child, a daughter, was lost at birth.)

But the measure of contentment which his first years back in Britain had brought Selous, was about to be destroyed by events across the world.

CHAPTER EIGHTEEN

Boer Against Briton

The Anglo–Boer War represented the death of everything Selous had hoped for in Southern Africa. He saw the Afrikaner republics of the Transvaal and Orange Free State as having justice on their side, and his own country as an aggressor. For so patriotic a man that was bad enough, but his anguish was compounded.

Selous foresaw that, whatever the outcome of the war, British influence in South Africa would never fully recover. He had not shown any especial insight into geopolitics before: he had been right about the Matabele, wrong about the Mashona, and too optimistic about Rhodesia. Where this issue was concerned, however, he had real perception. His predictions of a Pyrrhic victory, of the poisonous legacy of Boer bitterness leading to the eventual neutralization of British influence in South Africa – these were as remarkable for their accuracy as they were for being uncommon in British thinking. But being right did not help. Nothing in his lifetime caused Selous so much pain as the Boer War.

The problem was one of loyalties. He had lived among Afrikaners and learned their language. In his own words, he had 'eaten salt and broken bread in many a Boer homestead'. One of his closest friends was the hunter Cornelius van Rooyen, who let him know that he had taken arms against the Crown. Set against this were Selous's own blood ties. A few of his relatives had enlisted to fight the Boers and one, a cousin named Harry Selous, would fall at the Battle of Paardeburg.

Selous's response to this challenge was arguably more coura- geous than anything he had demonstrated before in the face of the Matabele, or of any charging elephant. When he spoke up for the Boers, Selous knew he was inviting hostility, and he was not surprised, though still deeply depressed, at the results. His stand attracted public criticism and led to a final rift with his old Rhodesian associates, including Cecil Rhodes.

Selous had not always been sympathetic to Afrikaners. We have seen that two decades earlier Britain had fought another conflict with the Boers. When that ended in the humiliation of Majuba, and Gladstone returned the Transvaal to self-government under Paul Kruger, Selous had been among those who railed against 'our pusilanimous government'. All the same, he found the jingoistic cries of 'remember Majuba' distasteful. And the longer he knew the Afrikaners, the more he was attracted by the romance of their history, and the better he understood the emotions that had given rise to the Great Trek. In a few phrases, which summed up his attitude, and attracted much ill-feeling, he wrote to *The Times* in October 1899: 'As for the Boers having a contempt for Englishmen as individuals, that is nonsense. They hate the English Government, and knowing their history, I for one think they have ample reason for doing so, but the individual Englishman that they know they take at his real value.'

One monumental change had come about in the Transvaal since the first war, and that was the discovery of gold in 1886. As a result, the northern Boer republic was the wealthiest province in Africa, while the Witwatersrand, in the words of Lord Selborne, Under-Secretary for Colonies, was the 'richest spot on earth'.

That there would eventually emerge some formal confederation of the British and Afrikaner provinces of South Africa under the British flag was no longer doubted by most forward-thinkers. On the Afrikaner side these included Jan Smuts, the brilliant young State Attorney in the Transvaal, and Jan Hofmeyr, the leader of the Cape Afrikaners. Against them were arrayed an older generation, reactionary and often xenophobic, immersed in a history which bred the cults of racial purity and self-sufficiency; above all, there was the shambling but somehow majestic figure of 'Oom Paul' Kruger. The old president was uncompromising about the Transvaal's independence. He had, as we have seen, frequently demonstrated this to the Uitlanders, whom he denied political rights for fear it would open the door to Britain.

The Jameson Raid smashed the small foundations that had been laid for a South African federation. Smuts, who had seen Rhodes as South Africa's greatest hope, denounced his hero and joined the Pretoria Government. Later he described the raid as 'the real declaration of war in the great Anglo–Boer conflict'. Hofmeyr, who had been Rhodes's intimate friend and political ally for fifteen years, said he felt as if he had been deceived by his wife. Kruger, who appeared near his political end at the time of the raid, was given a new lease of life.

The lines of battle were also drawn on the British side. Knowledge of the raid had not been confined to Rhodes and Jameson. The Colonial Secretary, Joseph Chamberlain ('Pushful Joe', the press called him: 'an ambitious and unscrupulous man', Selous thought) managed to persuade the official inquiry that he was guilty of no complicity. However, later research has all but proved that he was involved.*

The new High Commissioner at the Cape was a man of similar mettle. Sir Alfred Milner arrived in 1897 making diplomatic noises designed to soothe Kruger, but determined nevertheless to establish British dominance in the region. In his study of the Boer War, Thomas Pakenham wrote that Milner yearned for the victory 'that would give him a free hand to "break the mould" and recast South Africa, as Cromer had recast Egypt (and, indeed, Milner's hero, Bismarck had recast Germany)'. The view of Milner, and the Johannesburg financiers who sought the same ends, was that only a military victory would be sufficiently cataclysmic to accomplish this. For three years after the raid, Britain moved steadily towards war.

From the beginning of 1899 Selous watched with deep disquiet as the political temperature rose. He was sufficiently familiar with the methods of South African financiers – less Rhodes on this occasion than Julius Wernher and Alfred Beit, the so-called 'gold bugs' of the

---

* In this respect, an interesting light is cast by an unpublished notebook of Basil Williams, Rhodes's first biographer. The notes of an interview with Lord Grey have a section marked 'private' where Williams has written: 'Re Raid, Grey said Chamberlain certainly knew about the force intended to go into TV [Transvaal] – Grey said that for the honour of England it should not come out, just as it was loyally not blurted out by any of the people at the time. The great difficulty was R. [Rutherfoord] Harris – it took a lot of trouble to try and silence him.' Grey's views are significant as he was not only on the board of the Chartered Company, but a friend of Chamberlain's.

Witwatersrand – to recognize how Uitlander grievances were again being manipulated and orchestrated in Cape Town and London. In December 1898, the shooting of a British Uitlander named Tom Edgar by Transvaal police became a *cause célèbre*. An outcry over Uitlander rights was taken up in Britain. All through the last summer of the century, a deliciously warm one in the English countryside, Selous was distracted by South Africa. On a number of occasions he drafted letters to *The Times* warning of what he saw coming, only to crumple up his efforts.

Once, in July, he actually sent off a letter to Moberly Bell, editorial manager at Printing House Square. Selous did not name Milner or Rhodes, but there could be no doubt whom he meant by 'those who, under cover of the plea that they are only desirous of righting the wrongs of the British Uitlanders, really wish, at any cost, to do away with the independence of the Transvaal Republic'. He did criticize by name two old acquaintances, the author Rider Haggard and Sir Sidney Shippard. Both were vociferously antagonistic towards the Afrikaners. Selous also took to task 'that eminent divine Canon Knox Little – who, although he knows no more about the Transvaal Boers than could be learned from the windows of a railway carriage . . . has satisfied himself that they are a very vile people'. This letter was not immediately published. Selous called at Bell's office, and it was agreed that it would be withheld for the time being.

From his knowledge of what was happening in Pretoria we can assume that Selous remained in touch with his Afrikaner friends, and he clearly thought that war might still be avoided. In a letter to Roosevelt, who had risen to Governor of New York and with whom he now corresponded regularly, Selous wrote that moderate Afrikaners like Hofmeyr, Smuts and Abraham Fischer, the State Secretary in the Orange Free State, had influenced Kruger, who 'is doing everything in his power to meet the Uitlanders halfway'.

But a climbdown by the Transvaal was not enough to deter Milner. Kruger walked out of a conference in Bloemfontein with the High Commissioner saying: 'It is our country you want.' The climax came suddenly. A British massing of troops on the borders of the Transvaal and Orange Free State in October provoked a Boer ultimatum. Fleet Street was unanimous: Kruger had asked for war,

253

he should have it. Hostilities commenced on 20 October 1899, in Natal.

The British public had been denied a major war since the end of the Crimean conflict forty-three years earlier, and the soldiers setting off in khaki from Southampton were back-slapped and exhorted to 'Give it to the Boers'. Also taking ship was Winston Churchill, going to cover the war for the *Morning Post*. Music halls and popular verse reflected the national mood. One contribution by Swinburne to *The Times* provoked revulsion in Selous, who protested that it 'seems to have been written with the sole object of embittering feeling against the Boers'. By comparison, Kipling was quite circumspect, and in 'The Absent-Minded Beggar' – which was published in the *Daily Mail*, set to music by Sir Arthur Sullivan, and used to launch a fund for soldiers' families – he even took a gentle dig at the prevailing jingoism:

> When you've shouted 'Rule Britannia',
> When you've sung 'God Save the Queen',
> When you've finished killing Kruger with your mouth,
> Will you kindly drop a shilling in my little tambourine
> For a gentleman in khaki ordered South?

The realities of war became evident soon enough. Within two weeks the British had sustained a sequence of reverses, and a siege had been imposed on the key military depot of Ladysmith in northern Natal. It would not be lifted for another four months, or before the deaths of many hundreds of soldiers.

Selous threw himself vigorously into the debate with letters to the press, in particular *The Times*. The 'Thunderer' had adopted a staunch pro-war editorial policy, declaring it 'a popular war, more than any other in modern times'. Even so, Moberly Bell agreed to publish his letters in the issues of 24 October and 31 October. These letters are a clear and precise exposition of Selous's views. But what makes them especially interesting is their intensity. His writing sometimes suggests a man of meticulous habit and little imagination; here though, is the blazing-eyed advocate whose passion could both stir and surprise his friends.

He did not doubt, he wrote, now that war had started, that British forces would prove superior to the Boers, and he could only hope for a quick end – and victory. (Privately, he predicted to Roosevelt it would take about eighteen months.) But, he added:

> the history of Switzerland, of Scotland and of the United States of America points to the difficulty of permanently crushing a north European people, and to the likelihood of our having to face another 'war of independence' in South Africa in 20, 30 or perhaps 50 years' time, which may be impossible to bring to a successful issue . . . Every Afrikaner worth his salt throughout South Africa will have been converted into the bitter enemy of British rule in South Africa . . . We have entered upon a course which, though it may give us the goldfields of the Transvaal for the present and the immediate future, will infallibly lose us the whole of South Africa as a British possession within the lifetime of many men who are now living. Through arrogance and ignorance Great Britain lost her American colonies, and if arrogance and ignorance prevail in the present conduct of affairs in South Africa, history will repeat itself in that country.

He summed up:

> I believe in my inmost soul that it is not a just war, that it could have been avoided, that it can bring this country no honour, and that it will be the cause of much future trouble.

Selous was wrong about one thing. The Afrikaners' second 'war of independence' started not twenty years later but fifteen, with a rebellion by former Boer generals. It continued through the 1940s, and the rise to power of the Nationalist Party, and ended when South Africa left the Commonwealth to become a republic in 1961. But however just Selous's sentiments or perceptive his judgments, they did not endear him to the public. In the first months of the war, jingoism reached a frenzy as the news from the front brought home the fact that, far from 'giving it to the Boers', the British forces were being taught a humiliating lesson in irregular warfare. Defeat followed on defeat . . . Magersfontein . . . Colenso . . . Spion Kop. By Christmas 1899, the prospect that Ladysmith itself might fall led to an outburst of popular fury against anything that smacked of 'succouring the Boer'.

Selous had known his opinions would not be well received at home. But the next few months must have been harder than even he had expected, for he was out of step not just with popular feeling, but with many of his fellows and peers. He was attacked in the press, most notably by Rider Haggard. This started a brief exchange of fire between 'Allan Quatermain' and his creator. 'I have been an appreciative reader of Mr Rider Haggard's works,' Selous wrote, 'though I have always thought that the personal humiliation he endured at the time of the retrocession of the Transvaal to the Boers in 1881 had somewhat warped his judgment concerning that people.'

Others were also taking issue with Selous, such as Moberly Bell, one of the great opinion-makers of the day. And, as we have seen, Selous's break with the Chartered crowd was now complete. He told Roosevelt that Rhodes had 'preached a jehad against the SA Dutch', and that 'Rhodes . . . and the capitalists who want to control the mining industry' were more to blame than Kruger. In Rhodesia, meanwhile, English settlers were hastening to take up arms against the Boers. Both Jameson and Sir John Willoughby were serving in Ladysmith during the siege, and were outraged that Selous should, as they saw it, have sided with the enemy. Even his closest friends, like John Millais, thought the timing of his letters to *The Times*, when the war had already started, was 'unfortunate'. It was noted in the press that he had 'incurred considerable odium among his old associates'.

The winter settled in, bringing nothing but gloom to the household at Heatherside. Selous was not surprised by the reaction, but it hurt nevertheless. He wrote to Keltie, resigning his seat on the council of the Royal Geographical Society. His letters had 'naturally made me very unpopular' and it seemed desirable to stand down.

British defeats only depressed him the more. Four days before the disaster at Spion Kop, caused by the increasingly desperate efforts of General Redvers Buller to lift the siege of Ladysmith, he wrote to Keltie: 'We hope that all has gone well with Buller and that he has relieved Ladysmith or will do so shortly. If he should fail in this attack God alone knows how long the war will last, and what will be the end of it.' To another friend he confessed: 'The war upsets me so much that I find it very difficult to settle down to any kind of writing work.'

Selous was not entirely alone in his sympathies for the Boers. Ironically, he found himself allied with a group with which he had previously only ever disagreed – the radicals, including Henry Labouchère. There is no record of any meeting between the two foes; Labouchère's opposition to the war was almost reflex, and he took no part in extra-parliamentary activity. However, with another radical MP, Leonard Courtney, Selous started an organization known as the South African Conciliation Committee. The aims of this body were to press for peace, and to foster goodwill between Boer and Briton. Courtney was president, Selous the vice-president. The SACC's charter was touchingly well-intentioned:

> It behoves us, though the minority, to press the truth as we see it with zeal and courage but without temper or exaggeration; remembering that most of those who differ from us have had scant opportunity of knowing the truth and are as high-minded and anxious to judge rightly as ourselves.

The SACC helped channel Selous's energies at a time when he still held out hope that the war might be swiftly concluded, and that such an organization could play a useful intermediary role. Despite the early reverses, there was never any doubt that the British forces would be victorious in the end. As that inevitability struck home among the Boers, it was reasonable to suppose that the Transvaal might sue for peace on the basis of legislative reforms giving the Uitlanders full citizenship.

Selous's hopes must have been lifted by an extraordinary appeal to him from Kruger himself. It was relayed through an Afrikaner friend who wrote to Selous from Pretoria:

> When I told our venerable President I was writing to you he said: 'Tell Selous, I always respected him as a just, brave and capable "Rooinek" [literally, redneck; Afrikaans slang for an Englishman]. Tell him the ONE desire of my heart is even now to see Peace as quickly restored as possible. The eve of my life has been clouded by this great sorrow. I had always

hoped my white hairs should find eternal rest without seeing the two dominant races of our continent shedding each others blood in such an inglorious cause.

'We are even now always ready to hold out the olive branch, we are ready to make fair honourable concessions to correct grievances which can justly claim reform, as long as our sacred Liberty is not interfered with and is respected. I have said.'

This letter, of April 1900, was annotated by Selous, and there can be no doubt that he passed it on to the Colonial Office. Key phrases are emphasized or underlined in his hand, such as Kruger's insistence that the republics would never give up their independence. There can be little doubt either, that Selous would willingly have become directly involved as a go-between if it came to negotiations. But Whitehall was not looking for peace.

Some officials thought Selous's Boer contacts might come in handy all the same, as a secret letter makes plain. It came from Captain George Wemyss, of the Intelligence Division at the War Office, forerunner of the Secret Services. He invited Selous to undertake a little informal spying in the Transvaal.

The authorities, Wemyss wrote, believed that when peace was concluded, certain irreconcilable Boers – *bitter-einders*, as they became known – would refuse to recognize any authority and would continue to wage a guerrilla war. What Wemyss needed was the service of men 'who really know the back country Boers and who enjoy their confidence, to go among them and in a friendly way explain to them . . . There is no intention of confiscating their farms, or of interfering with them so long as they abide by the laws.' He went on:

The difficulty is to get the names of the really best men. If you could help in this matter, I think you would be doing the Boers a genuine service, and on my part I think I could get any information you gave put forward in the right way.

I know you have a strong feeling of sympathy for the men among whom you hunted for so long, and this is my excuse for troubling you.

There is no indication that Selous responded positively to this overture, and the likelihood is against it, if for no other reason than that soon afterwards the last hope for a just outcome crumbled. The British annexation of the republics was, for Selous, the final betrayal.

At the outbreak of war, Lord Salisbury had declared: 'We want no gold, we want no territory.' As the tide turned inevitably against the Boers in 1900, and British troops started to advance over the veld of the Transvaal and Free State, Courtney and Selous sent an open letter to the Prime Minister, reminding him of his disclaimer to territory, and calling on the Government to regain the confidence of the Cape Afrikaners by affirming that the republics would be allowed to retain their independence after a ceasefire. It was a vain plea. By October 1900, the Transvaal and Free State had been annexed.

Even worse was to follow. An increasingly dirty war continued for another year and a half. Resorting to desperate tactics to discourage the elusive Boers, British forces under Lord Kitchener razed and burned farms, and took captive women and children. The concentration camps, in which between 18,000 and 28,000 people died of neglect and disease – Boers and blacks; men, women and children – were the ultimate disgrace of an appalling blot on British history.

Details of these horrors took some time to emerge, but Selous was already in anguish. He unburdened himself to Roosevelt:

> It is a very bitter grief to me not to be able to side with my own country in this war, and I feel it so much that were I a younger man and unmarried I would leave this country and settle in America . . .
>
> I believe that the annexation will eventually bring about the loss of the whole of South Africa . . . The temper of the majority of people of this country is very overbearing and arrogant just now. The jingos reign supreme and I fear there is little hope of moderation in the hour of victory.

Roosevelt, now Vice-President, replied sympathetically: 'How I wish you could be made Administrator of all South Africa. Somehow I feel that you could do what no other man could, and really bring about peace.'

Selous may have derived some comfort from the tributes that came from South Africa. Hofmeyr wrote thanking him for having sent £25 'to help alleviate suffering among the Boers', and commending his stand: 'I highly appreciate your contribution, even more as it comes from an Englishman who has lived so many years among the Boers and has had the courage to testify in public to their merits, however unpopular their cause may be at the moment.' Other letters of appreciation came from Pretoria, 'the heart of the enemy's camp', as one correspondent put it, in praise of 'your plucky and just attitude against a perfect Frankenstein of fanatical jingoism'. Leo Weinthal, a Pretoria journalist, wrote offering moral support 'in your great work'.

But this recognition brought no lasting relief. For one of a proud, patriotic and melancholy disposition, the despair of seeing his last hopes for South Africa destroyed, together with the pain of being regarded as one of the enemy, took a cruel toll. Although at the age of fifty he was almost as fit as ever, the Anglo–Boer War seems to have knocked some of the stuffing out of Selous. The betrayal of the annexation, which put paid to any notion of a compromise, may even have brought some relief, as it took matters completely out of the hands of the would-be peacemakers. By the end of 1900 Selous felt that the hatred engendered by the war was so terrible there was nothing to be done but leave matters in the hands of the militarists. 'England now has another, and a worse, Ireland on its hands in the southern hemisphere,' he wrote to Roosevelt on 12 December.

Over the last year and a half of the war, Selous played no active part. No letters of this period survive, and he became something of a recluse. As always when he was unhappy, he sought solace in the wilderness. He cast himself into the bleak wastes of Newfoundland, venturing into uncharted territory to shoot caribou, and returned purged and refreshed. And he set off again on long egg-collecting trips – to Spain, to Transylvania, and to Asia Minor.

In June 1902, the war ground to its inevitable conclusion with the surrender of the Boers. The Transvaal and the Orange Free State had lost their independence, and the Witwatersrand was under British control. Paul Kruger died in exile in Switzerland in 1904. None of these events brought any reaction from Selous. He had closed the book once and for all on that chapter of his life. Not even the temporary reconciliation of Union in 1910, under the far-sighted Boer leaders Louis Botha and Jan Smuts, could draw him out. It is as if the trauma had turned him forever from South Africa. He never went back.

CHAPTER NINETEEN

Africa Rediscovered

The last stage of Selous's life was dominated by a new wilderness. This was East Africa, which was becoming a European sporting ground at the turn of the century. He made his first trip there in 1902, revisiting it in 1909, with Teddy Roosevelt, and again in 1911. When the First World War started and Selous enlisted, it seemed only natural that the theatre in which he served was German East Africa. It was also appropriate that when he fell in battle he should be buried there. After the pain and disillusionment over Southern Africa, his experiences in East Africa were the balm, and fulfilment, of his final years.

It was not, however, the only plain over which his restless spirit moved. He had described himself before as 'a wandering Englishman with a taste for natural history and sport', and that remained as true as ever during the first decade of the new century. As he passed from his fifties into his sixties, Selous was often at odds with himself. Despite his advancing years, he found himself pulled, all too often, in opposite directions between wanderlust and a desire for the tranquil pleasures of home. The urge to travel was usually the more compelling. If he was not on the move, he was generally preparing, or looking forward to, his next trip.

Besides East Africa, he twice went back to Newfoundland to hunt moose. He also returned to the United States for a second time to pursue lynx and wolf. A trip to Norway secured the new prize of a Scandinavian antelope's horns. One big disappointment was a venture to the Sudan to try to secure a specimen of the giant eland. He came away angry at his failure to get his trophy, complaining of obstruction by local officials. In this time as well, he made numerous egg-collecting expeditions to destinations as diverse as Bosnia,

Iceland, Asia Minor, Scotland, Holland, Jersey and Normandy. If he had been able, there is little doubt he would have travelled even more. As it was, the Ends of the Earth Club in New York elected him an 'active member' when he was fifty-five.

Initially, Gladys accompanied him on his trips, but that stopped after the birth of the boys, Young Fred and Harold. Given the frequency of Selous's movements it is hard to take very seriously his complaint to Roosevelt that, 'I always hate leaving my wife and boys, and the distress I suffer on this account takes away very much from the pleasure of my trips.' But it is evident that Selous's love for Gladys was lasting, and that he was a proud and affectionate father.

By 1910, he and Gladys had been married for fifteen years, and it is possible that differences in their temperaments, and in their ages, had brought about some distancing after the heady romanticism of their early years together. Selous, still a slim, handsome man, although by now quite grey, was increasingly withdrawn from conventional society. Gladys, on the other hand, still only in her mid-thirties, a mature and extremely attractive woman, remained gay and gregarious. His interests, travel and natural history, had little appeal for her more domestic nature, and fondness for gardening and parties. It is also impossible to overlook the fact that even after the boys were sent to boarding school, Gladys chose not to travel abroad with Selous. Also, that she refused to fall in with his recurrent desire to live in Africa again.

This is not to suggest that theirs was not a happy marriage. What little evidence exists suggests that it was to the end a firm and solid bonding. We know, for example, that Selous wrote to Gladys whenever they were apart. But we simply do not have the basis from which to gain any deep insight into the relationship. After Gladys's death all their correspondence was destroyed, either by her surviving son Harold, or her sister Phyllis.

The two Selous boys reflected some of the differences between their parents. The elder, Freddy, was growing into a dark, vivacious and athletic boy. Harold, almost two years younger, was fair and good-looking, but cripplingly shy. Selous was especially proud of Freddy, while Gladys and her relatives seem to have doted on him. The lad captained his prep school football team, and on graduating to Selous's old alma mater, Rugby, proceeded to outstrip his father, not only academically – which was no great accomplishment – but in sporting prowess. Harold, although an intelligent boy, was overawed by his elder brother and it was sensibly decided that he would be better off at another school, so he went to Radley College.

It was not just the attractions of home that prevented Selous from travelling even more, but money worries. Every time the Stock Market dipped, his old anxieties would return. Usually his fears were exaggerated, and the family continued to live at Heatherside in circumstances that today would be regarded as gracious. But the years of 1907 and 1908 were difficult. Gold shares plummeted in value, and Selous was thrown into an agony of worry. He resigned from the Royal Geographical Society to save money, although this drastic step was averted when the governing council voted to name him an honorary life member. He wrote to Keltie:

> I do not know how to express my sense of the very great kindness extended to me. The position is however somewhat embarrassing, as I do not know whether I ought to accept. I have lost a lot of money lately but am still trying for my wife's sake to hold on to this place [Heatherside] which we have made ourselves and which she loves.

A month later Selous accepted an honorary fellowship of the RGS. His influence continued to be felt at the organization. Charlotte Mansfield, the first woman Fellow, said it was in great measure due to Selous that women were eventually admitted. He met her after she had visited German East Africa and proposed her for membership. Although this application was rejected – at which he was most indignant – he later tried again, and was successful. Miss Mansfield seems to have been the only other woman with whom Selous had a friendship once he had married. When she married he sent her a mirror with the message: 'To my sister of the wild, who heard the call and answered it.'

In the face of his financial problems, Selous took up his pen and tried to write his way out of trouble. He made regular contributions to C. B. Fry's *Magazine of Sports and Outdoor Life* – and, in addition to the standard payment, received from the former England batsman tickets to cricket matches, which he loved. Millais records: 'When any great game was fought at Lords, such as England v. Australia, he was generally there before the game began in the members' enclosure, and, much as he detested crowds, he with his wife would sit out the whole three days and watch every ball that went down. On such occasions he seldom spoke.'

His book writing was going through an unprofitable patch. *Sport and Travel East and West*, an account of trips to America and Asia, which was published in 1900, went almost unnoticed. His next book, *Recent Hunting Trips in British North America*, met a similar fate seven years later. Two other literary projects followed. One, an adventure story for boys, was Selous's first, and only, attempt at fiction, aimed at emulating the success enjoyed some decades earlier by Thomas Hughes with *Tom Brown's Schooldays*. Selous discussed the idea with Macmillan & Co., who commissioned the work. Writing started, and part of a manuscript was seen by Millais. But no book was ever published, and whatever existed of *John Leroux's Schooldays* has been lost.

A second book was more ambitious, and more important. Roosevelt, who became President of the United States on the assassination of William McKinley in 1901, had been encouraging Selous to write a volume which combined more of his hunting memoirs with observations on African wildlife. Their friendship, sustained by correspondence for years, had finally resulted in a meeting in 1905 at the White House. Selous was evidently gratified:

> Of course to have been received at the White House by the President of the United States was a very great honour ... but I hope you will believe me when I say that the deep regard I have for you is not because you are president but because you are Theodore Roosevelt, and because all your life, whether as ranchman, hunter of big game, governor of New York, leader of the Rough Riders in Cuba and president, you have always deserved the esteem of your fellow men.

Roosevelt wrote back, urging: 'Now do go on and write that book. Nobody can write the natural history of big game as you can.' From this idea sprang the last of Selous's major works, *African Nature Notes and Reminiscences*, which was published in 1908 with a foreword by Roosevelt. For unknown reasons, Selous had changed publishers again, leaving Rowland Ward – who Millais thought had treated him well – for Macmillan. *African Nature Notes* did only slightly better commercially than its two predecessors, but it was received with critical acclaim and is far from the dry work the title might suggest. For some of Selous's readers, these observations and anecdotes on subjects ranging from the lion and the rhinoceros, to the protective coloration of wildlife and the depredation of game in Southern Africa, are the high point of his writing. For all its easy readability, it is a serious work of natural history and made no small contribution to Selous's enduring reputation as a field naturalist of the front rank. Millais, whose own *A Breath from the Veldt* is a classic of Africana, thought it his best work, although that place is more conventionally accorded to *A Hunter's Wanderings in Africa*.

Despite his anxieties and restlessness, Selous had much cause for satisfaction in these evening years. His health was excellent, and throughout his fifties he maintained the condition of a man twenty years younger, partly by cycling and playing sport. 'I am inclined to put on flesh if I do not get a great deal of exercise,' he wrote to a friend. In winter he played hockey, and in summer cricket for the local Purbright eleven. Millais wrote: 'I played in some of these matches, which were rather of the "Dingley-Dell" type, and it was always a treat to see Fred standing so close in at point that he looked as if he would catch the batsman before he hit the ball.'

In the fraternities in which he mixed – those of the traveller, the sportsman and the naturalist – he was by now revered as an elder statesman, nowhere more than amid the claret and cigar-thick air of the Shikari Club's annual Oaks Night dinner. A contemporary noted: 'When Selous rose to make a speech you might easily tell by the breathless way in which he was listened to, and the applause that greeted him at the end of his task, how great was the honour in which he was held by the most famous sportsmen of his day.'

One question he was invariably asked on such occasions was what animal he had found to be the most dangerous. He had hunted all the so-called 'Big Four' – lion, elephant, buffalo, and rhinoceros – with a muzzle-loader, and told a meeting of the Authors' Club: 'If the quality of sport is to be measured by the danger and excitement it affords, then no sport on earth can equal an encounter with an elephant in one of their strongholds, where the density of the bush is all against the hunter and in favour of the hunted.' Buffalo, too, were fearsome adversaries. Selous would relate how one of these animals had killed a horse under him, and how he had come close to being impaled himself. Once a buffalo had its blood up, nothing short of a thunderbolt would stop it. He remembered shooting a charging buffalo in the chest with a muzzle-loader; the four-ounce ball passed the length of the body, grazing the heart and lodging under the skin of a hind leg. But the animal still managed to get in a blow at a bearer before falling dead.

In the end, however, it was the lion, with its natural camouflage and speed in the attack, that he rated the most dangerous African beast. Savage and cunning, the great meat-eating cat could be a terrifying adversary. After the lion, he put the elephant, followed by the buffalo, which many other experts had at the top of their lists. The rhinoceros, described by early hunters like Cornwallis Harris and Gordon Cumming as a creature of primordial fierceness, Selous considered ponderous and vulnerable.

Selous first visited East Africa in 1902. His attention was drawn to the area by an article in the *Field*, which described a reign of terror by two man-eating lions. The story had all the ingredients that Selous found intriguing: these cunning predators had claimed dozens of victims, preying off labourers building the Uganda Railway through the district of Tsavo in what is now Kenya. So terrible was the toll of the marauders that construction of the railroad ceased for three weeks, until they were killed by an engineer, Colonel J. H. Patterson. It was Patterson who wrote the account in the *Field*, and Selous – who, as he said, had 'put a few lion stories on record myself' – had no hesitation in declaring it the best tale about lions he had ever heard. Patterson subsequently enlarged the story into a book whose publication Selous encouraged, and for which he wrote a foreword. *The Man-eaters of Tsavo* became immensely popular, going through eight editions in three years.

Initially, Selous's experiences in East Africa were a good deal less exciting than his protégé's. After arriving at the port of Mombasa, he spent a week hunting in the coastal region, and noted in a journal: 'Under present conditions hunting in this part of East Africa is certainly not worth the candle.' But after that he visited what is now west Kenya and was excited by the large herds of delicate antelope,

Grant's and Thomson's gazelle, which he found on the plains around Lake Victoria. In December and January he shot seventy-one head of half a dozen antelope species. In this time he spent a few days with Sir Alfred Pease near Nairobi, who related:

> I remember one day being rather inclined to think him tiresome. He said 'Now I want to get a good Kongoni' (Coke's Hartebeest) – we were standing where there were always hundreds, and often thousands in sight . . . I said I didn't know if I could help him, 'they were much of a muchness'. He asked me questions about measurements and weights and so on, most of which I could not answer. I told him there were plenty to choose from, and off he went and spent the whole of a hot day trying to find a 'specimen' worth having. He returned at night with a head and neck, and then the inquisition began again after measuring, and after a time (perhaps he was two hours messing about with his Kongoni head in the evening, after a tiring day, when I wanted him to come in and sit down) he came to the conclusion there was not much difference between his head and the horns lying about of those we had shot for meat.
>
> Some of my neighbours were amazed at this man, whose great reputation had reached them, and had expected to see him galloping after lions and shooting them from the saddle, etc., bothering himself over Kongoni heads.

Selous and Roosevelt had been corresponding about hunting for years. The first hint that the President was considering a trip to Africa himself was given in a letter from the White House in 1908. 'A year hence I shall stop being president and it may be that I can afford to devote a year to a trip in Africa, trying to get into a really good game country . . . Can you give me some advice?' For the next year, Selous devoted himself to planning every detail of the venture – logistics, location, weapons, equipment and provisions.

Early on, it was arranged that Roosevelt, who was to be accompanied by his son Kermit, would stay with Sir Alfred Pease. Selous advised Roosevelt that he should engage an experienced hunter to supervise porters and act as a guide, much as Selous himself had once done for wealthy visitors to Africa. At first the

President argued, saying he was quite able to look after himself. But Selous persisted: 'I believe you will find that such a man was really very necessary.' Eventually he received a letter from the White House: 'I appreciate your wisdom in insisting upon the desirability of my having a man to handle the caravan.' For the job Selous recommended R. J. Cunninghame, a veteran of the Matabele campaigns, now established in East Africa as a hunter. By his support Selous did a great deal to further professional hunting in the area. The Roosevelt expedition created a precedent for prosperous American visitors to Africa to be accompanied by a 'white hunter'. The emergence of men like Philip Percival, who supervised the sporting outings of such celebrities as Ernest Hemingway and Gary Cooper, was in part due to Selous.

For months correspondence between the White House and Heatherside centred on rifle calibres and manufacturers. Selous was less successful in the matter of provisions. Trying to anticipate the tastes of his illustrious friend, he produced a list of groceries that included pâté de foie gras, tinned prawns and French plums. These were crossed out by Roosevelt, who substituted baked beans, tinned tomatoes and tinned peaches, declaring them 'the three most satisfactory foods for camping I know'. Selous's proposal of a gross of bottles of whisky was also rejected. 'I never take whisky on a hunting trip except for sickness,' Roosevelt remarked tartly.

The press had picked up the news that the President of the United States was going to risk his life in tracking and hunting wild beasts in darkest Africa, and there were rumours that an army of reporters would descend on Nairobi. Roosevelt wrote to Selous in alarm with suggestions that would have raised another outcry had they been known: 'Would it be possible to prevent the reporters from organizing a caravan and trying to accompany me? This would be an intolerable nuisance. Do you think I could get the Governor to prevent their going?'

During this correspondence, Roosevelt had said he hoped Selous might join the safari. However, money was tight at Heatherside again, and until the last minute it seemed impossible. Then Selous was invited by another Kenya friend, an American, William Macmillan, to stay at his ranch about twenty miles from Nairobi. When Roosevelt heard he wrote exuberantly: 'Three cheers! I am simply overjoyed that you are going out. It is just the last touch to make everything perfect.' They agreed to sail together to East Africa, and in April 1909 met in Naples.

On the voyage to Mombasa, Roosevelt again found himself drawn to Selous the story-teller:

> There were on the ship many men who loved wild nature and who were keen hunters of big game; and almost every day as we steamed over the Red Sea and Indian Ocean we would gather on deck round Selous to listen to tales of those strange adventures that only come to the man who has lived long the lonely life of the wilderness.

Delighted though Selous had been to help, he shied away from an invitation to join Roosevelt's group. He confided to a friend: 'His party is so large, and I don't want to be with a crowd.' There may have been other constraints, too. Much as he admired Roosevelt, Selous was distressed by hunting practices which were common among Americans, and which he knew Roosevelt had no qualms about. In an account of a hunting trip to Colorado, Roosevelt had once told him enthusiastically about killing twelve cougars with the help of large dog packs. On four occasions the dogs had caught the quarry, and engaged in 'a savage worry' before it was finished off with a knife. Paul Rainey, another American, had acquired notoriety in the English hunting establishment of East Africa by using similar methods.

Roosevelt may have caused his hosts to look at him askance as well. Soon after their arrival in Nairobi, Selous was staying with Macmillan – a man immense in both wealth and girth (he weighed some 330 pounds) – when they were invited to ride over to Sir Alfred Pease's ranch where the Roosevelts, father and son, were billeted. The former President had already been among the game. In the book he later wrote of his trip, *African Game Trails*, Roosevelt wrote: 'I had shot my first lions, and I was much pleased to be able to show Selous the trophies.' What he did not mention was that these 'trophies' included the carcasses of two lions which were no more than cubs. Selous noted the fact in his journal, and although he did so without comment he must have been horrified.

After that, Selous and Macmillan went off on a two-month safari to the Rift Valley and Thomson's Falls. Among the exotic creatures they encountered were some nomadic Boers who had trekked almost 2000 miles by ox-wagon from the Transvaal – and must have been astonished to be addressed in their own language so far from home by an Englishman – and the glorious flamingos of Lake Baringo. Selous failed to realize his desire to kill a black-maned lion, but there was plenty of other excitement. Macmillan stopped a charging lion with a shot through an eye, and another member of the party was severely mauled.

Selous returned home in July, while Roosevelt stayed on for almost another year. By the time he and Kermit left Africa, in 1910, they had amassed hundreds of trophies. Reporters followed the trip avidly, and big-game hunting acquired a fascination for the American public. In May, Roosevelt, his wife and Kermit arrived in England, and on 1 June they visited Heatherside for the only time, staying overnight. He and Selous remained in constant correspondence thereafter, but they never met again.

Selous's second visit to East Africa helped cement a fundamental change in his attitude to hunting. For some time he had been thinking about a need to enforce limitations on shooting, and to establish sanctuaries to preserve endangered species. He might have reflected on his own part in the slaughter of animals like the square-lipped rhinoceros and the buffalo, which had brought these animals to the verge of extinction in Southern Africa. In East Africa the danger was imminent, owing to the increasing numbers of visiting hunters, and because the firepower of weapons was growing all the time. By the time he was appointed to represent Britain at the second Congress of Field Sports in Vienna in 1910, Selous had become a conservationist.

In an article on game preservation for the *African World Annual* soon after returning from the congress, he outlined an approach which became the model for wildlife administration in British colonial territory. This smacked of the poacher turning gamekeeper, but circumstances were changing rapidly, and bore no resemblance to the heyday of hunting as Selous had known it.

The first necessity for the preservation of African game is the prevention of the acquisition of fire-arms by the native tribes, and what is almost as important is the total prohibition of all commerce or trade in the skins and horns of wild animals by them or white men. No hunting or shooting of wild animals should be permitted except under licences.

His own passion for hunting the larger animals had waned. Once urged by Roosevelt to make a trip to India to write about tiger hunting, he replied: 'The fact is I am coming rapidly to the end of my tether as far as big game hunting is concerned.' But his interest in smaller game, like antelope, and the minutiae of natural history, remained undiminished. Trying to explain his enduring love of the chase, and recalling his youth, he told a questioner: 'It was a matter of bread and butter then. It is a hopeless passion now.'

This boyish enthusiasm, which lasted his lifetime, was one of the qualities that most endeared him to the many friends who had brightened his life in England. Despite his years of solitude, his capacity for making strong and enduring friendships had, if anything, grown. Millais, trying to describe Selous's attraction, wrote that he 'seemed to divine from his own experience how other men felt, and with the intensity of human sympathy knew how to encourage and console others in times of difficulty . . . He had a great sympathy with emotional people . . . It was not rare to see him spring from his chair and jerk his head from side to side at any story of injustice.'

As Selous approached his sixtieth birthday, his life was comfortably divided between family and his own gentlemanly pursuits. Proudly he watched Freddy's triumphant progress through Rugby. Almost every day at Heatherside he would step out to look for birds' nests around the commons and in the hedgerows and forests. Apart from the trophies that adorned the walls of the 'museum', there were few links now with his former life in Southern Africa. Cecil Rhodes had died in 1902. Jameson was still alive but in ill-health. Although he lived in London, Selous had never forgiven the raid and seems never to have seen him. Of the old hunting hands, Cornelius van Rooyen, his Afrikaner friend, was one of the few still alive, living at Plumtree in Matabeleland. Like most of the old fraternity, Cornelius was no correspondent, but one letter which arrived at

Heatherside on a winter's day in 1910 stirred in Selous vivid memories. It evidently affected him considerably, and it is one of the few personal letters to him which he kept. The postmark was Queenstown in the Cape Colony, and the author was Patrick McGillewie, one of a handful of living elephant hunters of Selous's generation.

Dear Sir,

I take the liberty of writing to you on the strength of having been a member of the Jennings party in the latter 60s in Mashunaland. I also beg to thank you for the pleasure I experienced from reading your last book 'Nature Notes'. My brother Henry died on the Hunyani River in 1870, the year old Hartley's son, one of the Woods and old Christian Harmse also died of fever. Fred and Tom Hartley are both dead, but a stepson of the old man, Tom Maloney, still lives close to this town. Tom Hartley was killed at Colenso on the Boer side. Old Bill Finnaughty I am told is still in the land of the living at Bulawayo.

John Baillie was my companion in many wanderings in N E Transvaal. This is the man who shot five lions out of a troop of 15 alone on foot with one dog with a double two-grooved muzzle loader 40 gauge. This happened in 1870 at a place called Dornfontein in Waterberg district, Transvaal. This is the best bag with a muzzle-loader I know of. I was told by a Mr Collins in Waterberg that a Boer, Zacharias de Beer, killed 3 lions at a shot with a 4-bore – two lionesses and a three-parts grown male cub. I don't vouch for the accuracy of the story.

Like most wanderers, I sigh for the old days gone for ever. I left the Transvaal in 1880 when old Kruger came to my place and told me war was inevitable and advised me to go to the Colony. I never went back.

I am under the impression we met in Potchefstroom in 1874 or 75 at Gooch's Hotel, and you played a stringed instrument called a zither – I think I am right in this but it is a long time ago. I will now conclude this rambling letter, congratulating you on your powers of description – if I only possessed half of them I might write a few stories of the old happy days. Is Alex Brown of Tati still alive? T. Leask of Klerksdorp is still living, I believe. The Kirtons are all gone. I was George's best man when he married. I heard of 'Big' Phillips's death from someone who knew. The old hands are nearly all gone.

With best regards, Yours faithfully,

Pat McGillewie.

Selous's abhorrence of public attention – or 'fuss' – remained strong. Less well known was his aversion to convention, and respectability, which, he told Millais, was the 'deadliest gag and wet blanket that can be laid on men'. A story related by Millais is evidence that even at the age of sixty Selous retained a trace of the wildness which had enlivened his schooldays at Rugby.

Millais gives no indication when the incident occurred, but it may have been in 1911, as Selous was setting out on what was to be his last African hunting trip and was staying at the old family residence in Gloucester Road, Regents Park. He had ordered a new rifle for the trip, but he was only hours away from departure on the boat train from Waterloo when the weapon was delivered. There was no time for a proper field test, but it was inconceivable that he should set out for Africa with a completely untried weapon. A maid was sent to summon a carriage and all his baggage was loaded for a quick departure. Then Selous went to an upper room, loaded the rifle and opened a window. From the rows of chimneys stretching away to the West End he took aim at one about 100 yards off and fired five quick shots. A glance through field glasses served to reassure him that the rifle was accurately sighted, and that the shots were nicely grouped. Swiftly, Selous packed the rifle, strode downstairs and opened the front door, where he found a sea of anxious faces looking up. A constable was hastening down the street to investigate. A voice from the crowd asked Selous if he had heard any shooting. Yes indeed, the old hunter replied, climbing into his cab. It seemed that the sound had come from somewhere 'up there', he said, pointing vaguely aloft, as the carriage pulled away.

The expedition of 1911–12, full of thrills and incident, was a happy and appropriate coda to Selous's hunting career. His companion was again William Macmillan, the jovial and burly American sportsman who owned a ranch outside Nairobi. Their destination was the Uaso Nyiro river in central Kenya – the area is now part of the Samburu Game Reserve – where they spent some weeks. It was deadly terrain, the thick bush along the river banks offering poor visibility and giving almost impenetrable cover for the local species of big game, mainly lion and buffalo. Selous was unperturbed: it was enough to be back in the African wilderness, and tracking the creatures he loved. Once he followed a lion and lioness for miles, and then came face to face with a big male, which darted for cover before he could get in a shot. On another occasion, he had an exhilarating horseback gallop after a large giraffe in which he was badly ripped by thornbushes. Macmillan took fright when he saw him covered in blood, but Selous was elated and bright-eyed, saying happily that it had been 'just like old times'.

The high point of the trip, however, was a final encounter with an old buffalo bull on 25 March, an experience which Selous treasured, and which he described in an article in the *Field*. It came after he had tracked two bulls all morning for about six miles before managing to get in a snap shot which wounded one of the animals. It then lumbered off into the bush beside the Uaso Nyiro. The situation Selous faced was the most baleful in which the African hunter can find himself: following a wounded and vindictive buffalo into thick bush. As he came up the side of a gully he heard the animal grunt, and knew it was charging.

I had not heard the sound for 20 years but once heard it can never be forgotten. The next instant he was on us with his nose outstretched, half a ton of bone and muscle driven at tremendous speed by the very excusable rage of a brave and determined animal. When I fired, the muzzle of my gun must have been within three yards of the buffalo. The animal fell but was so close that it struck Elani, a bearer who had been transfixed by the charge, a tremendous blow in the side with a horn. Another bullet quenched the last sparks of life in this brave old bull which died as a buffalo should, fierce and resentful to the last. Elani the bearer suffered four broken ribs.

This account was published in the *Field* on 8 June 1912, under the heading 'My Last Buffalo'. Selous complained to Roosevelt that the editor had, 'with a great want of imagination', deleted the word 'Probably' from his own suggested title. 'I have not yet given up all hope of shooting another buffalo or two in Africa.'

As it turned out, the editor was the more prescient.

CHAPTER TWENTY

The Last War

The onset of the most terrible war in European history was regarded by Selous with the natural foreboding of a father with two sons. But he also accepted it with something akin to relief. For this time, unlike the Boer War, there was no doubt in his mind about the justice of his country's cause. Rather, it seemed that Britain was standing up to the Prussian bullies he had instinctively disliked since his youth in Salzburg. Here, at last, was an opportunity to serve the flag with pride. Although he was approaching his sixty-third birthday, the war was only days old when Selous volunteered for active service.

His determination to get to the fighting, demonstrated again and again in the months ahead, seems almost a case of a conscience trying to compensate for guilt arising from the Boer War. However, it was not just a sense of atonement that filled Selous in 1914, but energy and zeal. Despite his age, Selous remained a dynamic force seeking a cause. It was to East Africa that he immediately looked to make his contribution.

He had longed to be back in the bush. After the excitement of 1912 it had not been easy to settle back at Heatherside. Now that the boys, Freddy and Harold, were at boarding school there was little reason to stay in England when there was opportunity, clear sky and unlimited hunting to be had in Kenya. The main obstacle was Gladys. Having once been a pioneer wife, she had no intention of again giving up gracious living, and her own interests and friends. In 1912 Selous mourned in a letter to a friend, the natural historian and author Abel Chapman: 'If only Mrs Selous would be happy there, I would rather live in East Africa than in this country.'

277

Another difficulty was his mother. Ann Selous was now in her late eighties, and as her health deteriorated, Selous was increasingly restricted in his movements. For many years she had been the focus of his affections, and the regularity with which her final illness is mentioned in his letters to friends indicates how much it was in his thoughts. She died in October 1913, at the age of eighty-seven.

All this while his eldest son, Freddy, had been making dashing progress at Rugby. In December, Selous went up to his old school to give an address to the senior boys on wildlife. Freddy was only aged fifteen but one of the most promising of his generation, enormously popular, athletic and bright. Selous wrote proudly to Roosevelt that he was the youngest boy to have won first fifteen colours for rugby football, and was good at boxing too. 'I hope to be able to get him into the East Africa civil service when he is twenty-two.' By the time Freddy left school in 1915 to follow his father to the war, he had captained the rugby fifteen, and was a member of the rowing eight. 'Just a marvellous boy,' said one of the women relatives who adored him.

Britain issued an ultimatum to Germany on 4 August 1914, and at midnight they were at war. Ten days later, as the flower of young Britain raced to recruiting stations to volunteer, Selous wrote to Chapman with ominous foresight:

> I believe this war will be a terrific business and that we shall have to send something like a million men out of the country before it is over, so that sooner or later I think I shall get into the firing line. Freddy will not be old enough to volunteer until April 21st next, when he will be seventeen, and I fully expect that he will be wanted. If I should be eliminated it would not matter a bit as I have had my day, but it would be a pity if so promising a boy got scuppered at the outset of his life.

A week earlier he had heard from an acquaintance in Kenya who was to play a key part in his war career. This was Colonel Daniel Driscoll, an old colonial fire-eater, who had fought in the Burma War almost thirty years earlier, and during the Boer War formed his own unit of irregulars, known as Driscoll's Scouts. Now he was hoping to raise what amounted to a private army, a 'Legion of

Frontiersmen' of around 1000 men with which he proposed to take German East Africa. Selous had a medical check-up which declared him in superb health and 'fit for service anywhere'. Thus armed, he offered Driscoll his services as an intelligence officer.

With the focus on Belgium, East Africa did not rate highly in the War Office's priorities, and those minds that did turn to the impoverished German colony south of Kenya were not favourable to the idea of a British invasion by so ragamuffin an outfit as that proposed by Driscoll. After some preliminary skirmishing, in which German forces actually occupied territory in British East Africa, the War Office despatched from Bombay more than 7000 men of the Indian Expeditionary Force for Mombasa.

Through the battles of the Marne and the Aisne, Selous fretted. When it appeared that Driscoll's plan was going to be turned down he applied directly to the War Office, taking with him his bill of health and volunteering for front-line service. Failing that, he could be an interpreter. 'I could speak French, a good deal of German and make the Flemish understand my South African Dutch.' His case was put to the Secretary of State for War, Lord Kitchener, personally. The response came quickly: his age was 'prohibitive against employment'. Selous fumed to another ageing friend: 'I suppose that neither you nor I will be allowed to serve our country. We are looked upon as useless old buffers.'

For the time being there was nothing else to do but enrol as a member of the Special Constabulary in Surrey.

German East Africa was one of the least promising of the territories seized by the European powers in the Scramble for Africa, having apparently no mineral wealth, and being rich only in its profusion of wildlife. Bismarck took it over in 1885 more to frustrate British ambitions than anything else. But German industry had reaped rewards: coffee and sisal were starting to flourish; and the Indian Ocean port of Dar es Salaam boasted some fine colonial buildings, while the Kaiserhof was the best hotel in East Africa.

The territory was a large one, more than 360,000 square miles, bound in the north by British East Africa, and in the south-west by Northern Rhodesia. A vast central plateau was divided from north to south by the Great Rift Valley, and crossed from west to east by the

700-mile Central Railway which linked the coast with Lake Tanganyika. Another great inland sea lay to the north, Lake Victoria, the second largest of the world's lakes, which formed a 160-mile water frontier between British and German East Africa.

Colonial settlement was no more welcomed by the warrior tribes of East Africa than it had been by the Zulus and Matabele. To impose their authority the Germans recruited tribal mercenaries, forging them into an armed force known as the Schutztruppe. Prussian and African militarism made a formidable combination. The black soldiers, known as askaris, were fearless and merciless, impervious to disease and excellent shots. Their officers were an elite of German Army professionals. Most important, this crack little army was led by one of the most remarkable commanders of the First World War, Lieutenant-Colonel Paul von Lettow-Vorbeck.

Von Lettow started the campaign in East Africa outnumbered roughly eight to one. Nevertheless, he seized the initiative from the outset, becoming the only one of the Kaiser's generals to invade British territory, and at the end was the only one left undefeated. In between, making brilliant use of the principles of guerrilla warfare, he led Commonwealth forces a costly and miserable dance all over East Africa, repeatedly tweaking the tail of the British lion. When he finally laid down arms, two weeks after the armistice in Europe, he had tied up about 370,000 Commonwealth troops with a force which never rose to more than 15,500.

The key to the East African campaign was two corridors between ranges of mountains lying to the south-east of snow-capped Kilimanjaro. Ten days after war broke out, von Lettow darted through one of these corridors, the Taveta Gap, to seize the British border post. Initially nonplussed by such cheek, British headquarters in Nairobi set to work on a strategy. In November a force of 12,000 men, under Major-General Arthur Aitken, confident in their numerical superiority, launched a two-prong counter to crush the Schutztruppe. Force A was to drive through the second of the corridors to the rail-head of Moshi, while simultaneously Force B landed at the thinly-defended port of Tanga, about 160 miles to the south-east. Von Lettow would be caught between hammer and anvil.

The expected walkover instead turned into a fiasco. A landing was accomplished at Tanga, but inexperienced and panicky Indian troops under incompetent commanders were completely out-fought by a German force one-eighth the size, and re-embarked. At Moshi, the British were also repulsed by a much smaller force. Talk at headquarters about the Indian Army making short work of 'a few niggers' was silenced. This was going to be a long haul.

The Tanga fiasco accomplished for Selous what his own lobbying could not. Recruiting policy for East Africa was hastily reconsidered, and Colonel Driscoll was asked by the War Office in December how long it would take to get together his 'Legion of Frontiersmen'. He promptly wrote to Heatherside: 'If I am ordered out – as is very probable – will you come with me?' Selous sent his reply by telegram.

Driscoll's approach seems to have been more that of a laird inviting some old sporting chums to a grouse shoot than a guerrilla commander preparing for a difficult campaign. Word went out through a fraternal network to the colonies and Americas, summoning as colourful and eccentric a band of warriors as could ever have taken the King's shilling. They included a circus clown, a general in the Honduran army, an opera singer, a Texas cowboy, a music-hall acrobat, a lighthouse keeper, a Buckingham Palace footman, the odd barman and French Foreign Legionnaire, and a motley group which Selous referred to as 'the tailors, cobblers and barbers'. His old Nairobi hunting friend, the American William Macmillan, threw himself into the enterprise with zest, although his 330-pound bulk ill-suited him to the sort of hit-and-run skirmishing envisaged by his commanding officer. Driscoll himself was a florid character, born and raised in Burma, whose habit was to utter strings of expletives in a rich Irish brogue, and who was given to impromptu demonstrations of his marksmanship with a pistol. But he was a real warrior too, dashing and resourceful for all his fifty-two years. During the Boer War he had been twice mentioned in despatches and was awarded the DSO.

Selous's age did not bother Driscoll, who had earmarked him for the job of intelligence officer, but it became an issue again when the War Office started taking a proprietorial interest in the officer corps. Driscoll bristled when it was indicated that some of his friends would be replaced by regular army officers. Selous worried that he would be the first to go. However, in February 1915, Driscoll told him that the War Office had approved him for active service, as a company officer with the rank of lieutenant. He had just turned sixty-three.

Gladys was contributing to the war effort too, and in March crossed to Le Havre to work at the Young Men's Christian Association. That same year, Freddy would finish his schooling at Rugby and go straight to Sandhurst. Harold, at Radley College, was only fifteen. Selous worried about them, while never doubting that they should volunteer. As the time drew near for his departure, he also fretted that fate, and the bureaucrats at the War Office, might yet intervene and disqualify him. 'I shan't really feel safe until I am on board ship.'

In May, Driscoll, Selous and the rest of the 'Frontiersmen' – rechristened according to War Office protocol the 25th Battalion of the Royal Fusiliers, but more colloquially known as 'The Old and the Bold' – landed at Mombasa. Soon afterwards they were inspected by General Michael Tighe, the local commander, and his intelligence officer Captain Richard Meinertzhagen, one of the ablest men serving in East Africa, and a trenchant critic of the High Command. Meinertzhagen had met Selous in Kenya and was a keen hunter and naturalist himself. He spotted Selous at the head of his platoon, 'looking very serious and standing strictly to attention'. They were soon deep in conversation on hunting matters and, Meinertzhagen noted in his diary, quite forgot they were on parade, 'much to the amusement of Selous's platoon, who still stood rigidly to attention throughout the discussion'. The conversation was cut short when Tighe told Meinertzhagen curtly that they were inspecting a battalion and had 'not come to hear a debate of a natural history society'.

It was not long before the Fusiliers got down to more serious business. While Tighe was under orders not to mount another full-scale offensive until further reinforcements arrived, approval was given for smaller operations to keep up morale. An assault would be made on the Lake Victoria port of Bukoba, where the Germans had a powerful radio transmitter maintaining contact with Berlin. The Fusiliers were among the force of 2000 men which embarked from the British side of the lake at Kisumu with artillery and mules in four rusty old ferries on 21 June.

It is remarkable that Bukoba did not become another Tanga. Aiming for a surprise attack under the cover of darkness, the invaders were heard from the shore and exposed by rockets illuminating the night sky. The landing was put off until dawn. Then, ordered by their commander, General James Stewart, to land a few miles to the north, they found themselves at the foot of a sheer cliff between 300 and 400 feet high. Selous wrote dryly: 'Had the Germans brought a machine-gun to the top of the cliff, or even lined [it] with riflemen, they would probably have been able to kill every man in the boats.'

Fortunately, the Germans had considered a landing at this point either impossible or too foolhardy to be undertaken. By mid-morning 'The Old and the Bold', along with units of the Lancashires, had reached the cliff-top without mishap. Skirmishing as they went, they started to advance on Bukoba. Selous, leading his company of around 100 men, was often under fire from unseen enemy. Progress was slow, and by nightfall they were still a mile from the town. Driscoll was all for storming it that night, but Stewart, probably wisely, decided to give his exhausted men a rest. They spent a miserable night, without provisions, bitterly cold and plagued by mosquitoes. But Selous was delighted to find that his constitution could stand up to such a hard day. 'I really was not tired at all.' Meinertzhagen, who was with him, wrote: 'He was full of enthusiasm, and we discussed "birds" until far into the night.'

The next day, Driscoll asked Selous to lead a scouting party to assess the German strength at Bukoba. He advanced with twenty men to a position near the wireless station and had started wondering whether the Germans might not have evacuated, when they were ambushed.

'Down,' I shouted, and my command was obeyed with the utmost alacrity. The bullets whistled past us, but no one was hit, and we then crawled until we were within 600 yards of the wireless installation. But whenever I raised myself above the grass to get a good look round I was fired on . . . and the bullets really whizzed over us.

For some time Selous and his men were pinned down. A Sergeant-Major Bottomly came up and took cover beside him. Then Selous's batman Ramazani touched him and said: 'Master, soldier hit, dead.' Selous had not heard a sound, 'but turning my head I saw poor Bottomly lying on his back, stone dead, with a bullet through his head.'

Meanwhile, artillery had opened up. At last Selous was getting a glimpse of modern war, and its ugliness made a profound impression:

> The shells came screaming and whistling over us. The machine-guns were going too with their wicked rattle, and bullets from snipers' rifles came with an unpleasant sound, sometimes apparently within a few inches of our bodies, which were just then pressed as close to the ground as possible. I thought as I lay there only a yard away from the blood-stained corpse of poor Bottomly . . . that I could recall various half-hours of my life passed amid much pleasanter surroundings. And yet what a small and miserable thing this was, after all, in the way of a battle compared with the titanic combats which have been taking place in Europe.

Eventually the fire lifted, and on scouting ahead again, Selous discovered that Bukoba had been evacuated. The wireless station and arsenal were blown up. But there was to be little reward for the Fusiliers, and Selous was critical of the cattle-truck treatment of the men on the journey back, and of the fact that there was no food or welcome in Nairobi. 'Something might have been done by the townspeople on behalf of our tired and hungry men . . . Not even hot water could be obtained to make tea with.'

The capture of Bukoba may have been, as Charles Miller wrote in his account of the campaign, *Battle for the Bundu*, 'little more than a glorified commando raid'. But it was the first British military success in East Africa, and the last for a long time to come. The Schutztruppe was gaining in numerical strength, while the British were being devastated by disease, the virulent local malaria and dysentery. Sickness would become the biggest problem for the British side as the war progressed, but already many units had been reduced to half-strength.

Although the Fusiliers were among the worst affected, Selous remained in remarkable health and high spirits. His letters now were peppered with boasts about his fitness. To Heatley Noble he wrote:

> I think I am the only one of our officers who has not suffered from either bad diarrhoea, dysentery or fever ... The long marches do not tire me at all, and the men now say that when I fall out no one will be left standing in the battalion. This is, of course, nonsense, but as far as standing fatigue, sun, thirst etc, I think I am really better than most of them.

To Millais, the only one of his friends to whom he wrote on Christian-name terms, he indulged in a little bragging about his bravery: 'I may tell you privately, but keep it to yourself, that Colonel Driscoll was very pleased with my conduct at Bukoba, and told me he had recommended me for promotion and something more.'

Letters from home arrived irregularly, but he was delighted to receive one from Roosevelt: 'That was a first-class little fight at Bukoba ... I congratulate you with all my heart. It is simply first-class to have you a fighting officer in the fighting line.' Selous was even more pleased to be duly promoted to captain, though he acknowledged 'I don't know my drill very well,' and his elevation was in the natural course of events as other officers were being invalided home. Having arrived in East Africa with 1100 men, the Fusiliers were down by the end of 1915 to an active duty list of 700, of whom Selous estimated no more than 400 were up to a twenty-mile march with full kit.

Matters were improved by the arrival in Mombasa at the beginning of 1916 of about 30,000 South African troops, who were brimming with swagger after sweeping the Germans out of South-West Africa. Moreover, command of the British forces had been handed over to General Jan Smuts, who, since the end of the Boer War, had become a convert to the cause of Britain and Empire; Smuts had been one of the shrewdest Boer commanders, and there was hope that with his experience of guerrilla war he would torment Germans as he once had Britons.

Smuts's campaign strategy was another pincer movement. His main force would thrust through the Taveta Gap, where the Schutztruppe was concentrated, while a smaller force – commanded by Stewart and including the Fusiliers – made its way through the second corridor and came up on von Lettow's rear. The offensive started on 5 March, and Taveta was re-occupied. At last a foot-hold had been gained on German territory. All might be won if Stewart's commando struck hard and fast. Unfortunately, Stewart's commando was finding the conditions hard. Selous described them as 'long marches in the very hot sun, in choking clouds of fine lava-dust, churned up by the heavy transport'. Stewart ordered night marches, but it was too late. When the twin head of the pincers met at Moshi on 14 March, von Lettow was clear.

Selous's pride in his condition was understandable. May marked the first anniversary of his arrival in East Africa. He had been at the head of his men in every action, marching with full pack weighing 20 pounds, and was one of fewer than 450 Fusiliers still fit for service. Apart from six days when he was laid up with 'jiggers' – an excruciating complaint caused by insects which burrowed into men's toes and laid eggs there – he had been on active service constantly. His bearing had enhanced his standing in the eyes of all ranks. A trooper wrote later: 'Everybody liked and admired him.' A junior officer recalled: 'He was my hero as a boy and he remains so now. He was the easiest of all men to cheat, but yet no one ever dared to do it. Anything mean or sordid literally shrivelled up in his presence.'

For a middle-aged man it would have been a remarkable accomplishment. For one aged sixty-four it was astonishing. But he was suffering from a most ungallant condition – piles. For some months it was kept under control with ointment, but the long marches caused further inflammation, and a doctor advised him to go home for an operation before he had to be invalided out. In June, a medical board confirmed this opinion.

There is almost no record of Selous's last visit home. Millais tells us that he was laid up for twelve days after the operation and went to Heatherside for a short rest. For Gladys the carnage of the war, and having a son as well as a husband in the army, must have cast a pall over their reunion. There is a poignant photograph, taken shortly before he sailed for East Africa again, of Selous and Freddy. They make a striking portrait in uniform, Selous seated and his son standing behind him. Freddy looks like so many of that tragic First

World War generation, a handsome, smiling cavalier. Aged nineteen, he had graduated from Sandhurst a few months earlier and been posted to the Royal West Surrey regiment.

It was not just Gladys who feared for their son. Selous wrote to Millais: 'If he goes out and gets killed it will break his mother's heart, and mine too if I should live to come home.'

Captain Selous had been back on active service for just a month when, on 27 September 1916, *The Times* announced that he had been awarded the DSO. Citing his 'conspicuous gallantry, resourcefulness and endurance', it was a fitting and crowning honour for his service.

Pleased though he was by the award, Selous was depressed by the state of affairs he found on his return. True, the British had by now occupied much of German East Africa and held the main ports and towns as well as the railways. But Smuts seemed unable to engineer a decisive confrontation. Advances were made against an opponent who simply disappeared into the bush, while exacting a heavy toll through ambushes. Meanwhile, disease continued to eat away at the British force and sap morale. Selous had formed the highest regard for von Lettow – 'a very able and determined man' – and his askaris – 'not only as brave as any Zulus, but splendidly led and well armed'.

On 30 November the Fusiliers were in Tanga, where the British had been routed two years earlier. Selous wrote to a friend: 'We are simply rotting here in this hot ennervating climate and 25 per cent of our 400 men are ill or unfit . . . Another month's campaigning in the rainy season will practically see the end of all the white troops out here.'

He was living in a house at Tanga with his old friend Macmillan, who was not up to active service and worked in the quartermaster's section. Selous filled his time by chasing around the old port with a butterfly net, and giving well-attended lectures on his hunting days. His eccentricities and foibles endeared him to his soldiers, one of whom said: 'He was literally adored by the men.'

Another described him as he appeared in Tanga just before his death:

He wore a Terai grey slouch hat, slightly on the back of his head. Khaki knickerbockers, with no puttees, bare legs, except for his socks, and shirt open at the neck, with a knotted handkerchief round the neck to keep the sun off, with a long stick in his hand. It is impossible to forget the impression he made. He was as straight as a guardsman, with a broad deep chest, with a beautiful healthy look on his face.

Militarily, the situation was that the Germans, retreating southwards from Dar es Salaam, had crossed the Mgeta river, which became the frontline between two exhausted armies. The British were in a pitiful state. Malaria, dysentery and blackwater fever had emaciated every unit. In fact, although down to 300 fit men, the Fusiliers were comparatively robust. Selous wrote to Chapman: 'Of the two fine Rhodesian regiments it is said that only 68 are fit. The North Lancs Regt has wasted to nothing, in spite of many drafts.' The South Africans were just as hard hit. In the last three months of the year, 15,000 Commonwealth troops were invalided home. It seemed that all von Lettow needed to do was sit and wait for the British forces to disintegrate.

But he also had to look to his rear. While his main force was concentrated on the Rufiji river, another sixty miles or so south of the Mgeta, a large British force had landed on the coast still further to the south, at Kilwa. Smuts planned yet another pincer movement – to cross the Mgeta and push the battalion-size Schutztruppe force there back to von Lettow on the Rufiji, while the British southern division would encircle the Germans and hold them fast at last in the trap. The Fusiliers were to be part of the northern thrust, with a fresh force of Nigerians and the South Africans.

Selous's unit was moved up by rail from Dar es Salaam to Morogoro in December. From there they marched for eight days through constant rain and quagmire to Kisaki on the Mgeta river. Conditions were appalling, and the Fusiliers' numbers were further reduced from the 384 who set out to 170. Men were not just falling sick, but dying in considerable numbers. They spent a wet and miserable Christmas at Kisaki, where Selous wrote one of his last letters to Gladys, full of foreboding. It has been lost, and this extract is all that was quoted by Millais:

We are on the eve of an attack on the Germans out here. Our

forces are terribly depleted, principally from sickness. The German forces are sure to be entrenching, and as they still have a number of machine-guns, it may be no child's play attacking their positions, and we may meet with heavy losses.

The drive began on New Year's Day, 1917. The Germans had not in fact entrenched, but in falling back through the dense bush they made life very unpleasant. The Fusiliers, leading the advance, were harassed by snipers and landmines. The advance became a nightmare as they blundered on through swamps and elephant grass as high as a man. On 3 January they ran into a Schutztruppe rearguard which made three bayonet attacks and came to hand-to-hand fighting. On the morning of 4 January it seemed that the British might finally have manoeuvred the enemy into a decisive fight. The Germans were virtually encircled on a series of hills near the village of Behobeho.

As Selous marched forward with his company that morning, he was teased about his fondness for tea. A young officer named Haines passed him and called: 'I shall be back and have tea with you today, sir.'

Selous's men were under orders to cut off the Germans' only road of retreat from Behobeho, but arrived to find them already withdrawing. In an account of the action, General Smuts wrote: 'Selous at once deployed his company, attacked the Germans [who] greatly outnumbered him, and drove them back into the bush.'

Reports of the manner in which he fell are conflicting. The only consistent element is that he was attempting to pursue the enemy when the fatal shot was fired by an askari sniper. One account was given in the *Field* by Selous's friend Denis Lyell, who quoted a soldier present:

We were on a crest line at the time with the Germans in front and on both flanks. We were subjected to heavy enfilade fire, and could not locate the enemy properly owing to the wooded nature of their positions. At this stage Selous went forward down the slope about 15 yards, and was just raising his glasses in order to see (more particularly) where certain snipers were when he received his first wound in the side. He

289

was half-turning towards us when he was shot through the side of the head. He died immediately.

Another version, also credible but quite different, was given to *The Times* by Corporal R. Davis, who was commended for assisting the mortally-wounded Selous.

He was not killed instantaneously, as I fought over him for fully ten minutes. He was shot in the head but this wound was not the cause of his death; this wound was caused by a splinter some half an hour previous and when Captain Selous was asked if he was wounded he stated that it was nothing very much and insisted on going on. He went over the ridges at Beho-Beho and was kneeling near a small tree and was seen after the action had been in progress for about 15 minutes to drop his rifle. I immediately went over to him and stayed with him for fully ten minutes before he received his fatal wound, and then I carried or dragged him to the rear of a small hill and there he died. His boy, Ramizani, who had been with him some considerable years, cried when he saw Captain Selous dead, and stood upright on top of the ridge in face of terrible German machine-gun fire and brought out a tree the black sniper who wounded Captain Selous.

Six other Fusiliers fell during this engagement. That afternoon, after word of Selous's death had spread through the British ranks, the men who were closest to him came up for a burial service. It was an appropriate spot for his grave; uninhabited bushland, populated by a few species of animals, including elephant, and numerous species of birds. A clearing was made and graves dug for Selous and the other dead Fusiliers. His body was sewn up in a blanket, and simple wooden crosses made for each grave. There is no record of what was said, but Haines, who had joked with Selous a few hours earlier about tea-drinking, said it was 'one of the most impressive services I have ever attended'.

Years later the bodies of the other dead were exhumed and reburied but Selous's remains were left. In place of the simple wooden cross, a concrete slab and tablet were laid over the grave with the inscription: 'Captain F.C. Selous DSO 25 Royal Fusiliers, killed in action 4.1.17.' The area became a wildlife sanctuary, and was incorporated in a large patch of territory around the Rufiji river which was later declared the Selous Game Reserve.

A legend had formed around Selous's name in East Africa. He was the most celebrated casualty of the campaign, and men who had never met him now joined in paying tribute. Among them was von Lettow, who wrote that Selous 'was well known among the Germans, on account of his charming manner and exciting stories'. It seemed apposite that this simple but noble man had ended a rich, full life by dying in combat.

In Europe, too, there was a sense that amid the toll of the trenches, his was a death which amounted to more than just another futile sacrifice. Sir Ralph Williams wrote in *The Times*: 'I can think of no death more fitting: going forth at the age of 64 to fight for his king on the veld which he loved so well, and where his name was held in such abundant honour.' Robert Baden-Powell said: 'He was the finest scout of our time.' King George V wrote a personal letter to Gladys, expressing appreciation for Selous's contribution to the war. *The Times* obituary ran to more than twenty-four inches, while the headlines in the *Pall Mall Gazette* ran: 'Famous Hunter Killed; Capt Selous Falls in Africa; An Adventurous Life; Many Hair-breadth Escapes.'

One friend, H. A. Bryden, expressed in the *Field* a common regret that Selous had not been more honoured in his lifetime: 'If ever a man deserved knighthood, it was F. C. Selous.'

Gladys's replies to the many letters she received have been lost, apart from one to Keltie, with whom Selous had corresponded irregularly but warmly for many years:

> Thank you very much for your most kind letter to me in my great sorrow. I feel that for him it has been a fine ending to a wonderful life – full to the brim right up to the end – but for me the sorrow and loss – and for my boys so sad, just at a time when they need a father's help and advice. The fine tributes of the world and his many friends will in time help and comfort me a great deal and I am very proud of them.

Perhaps most eloquently, Millais quoted Robert Louis Stevenson's 'Requiem':

Here he lies where he longed to be . . .
the hunter home from the hill.

Epilogue

The tributes were heartfelt, but too many others were dying in 1917 for Selous to stay long in the public consciousness. In the next few years, however, two gestures were made towards his memory. One came to nothing, but the other endured.

The first was a proposal by a fellow officer who wrote urging *The Times* 'to agitate' for a part of East Africa to be named after Selous. Rhodes had Rhodesia, why not name the country north of the Rufiji river 'Selousia'? A brief debate in the letters column was sensibly brought to a conclusion when Sir Harry Johnston wrote that the idea of giving European names to geographical features in Africa was not a good one, and that, anyway, Selous's connection with East Africa was slight, compared with Southern Africa.

The second idea, for a Selous memorial, was raised at the end of the war, and rapidly gained public support. A committee was formed, which included Rider Haggard, Smuts, Roosevelt and Jameson. The subscribers – among them Otto Beit, Lady Dorothy Stanley, Sir Alfred Sharpe, Rider Haggard, Smuts and Roosevelt (but not Jameson) – were generous, and the appeal raised almost £2500. W. R. Colton RA was commissioned to produce a bust, which was duly unveiled at the Natural History Museum in South Kensington on 10 June 1920, where it remains. More than £1500 was left over from the appeal fund, and this was used to set up the Selous Memorial Scholarship at Rugby School, primarily for the sons of officers killed in action.

The war ground on through 1917, marked in Europe by Passchendaele, and in East Africa by von Lettow's continued elusiveness. As Smuts pursued, so the Schutztruppe melted further south. By the end of the year, von Lettow had withdrawn across the Rovuma river into Mozambique, and German East Africa was declared a British protectorate. But von Lettow had lost none of his audacity. Even as the Kaiser's spent forces in Europe were finally crumbling before the Allied advance in September 1918, the

293

Schutztruppe crossed back into East Africa and then, astonishingly, wheeled westwards to drive into Northern Rhodesia. It was von Lettow's last gesture of defiance. On 13 November, two days after the European armistice, he received orders to cease fire, and on 25 November 155 Germans and 1156 askaris surrendered to a King's African Rifles battalion in Abercorn.

In the months after Selous's death, Gladys managed to keep herself busy by, among other things, cutting out all the obituaries and tributes to him which appeared in the press and pasting them into a book. Meanwhile, Freddy had been gazetted to the Royal East Surrey Regiment, and attached to the Royal Flying Corps, which was still an army unit. Popular and brave, Freddy Selous was still aged only nineteen when he won the Military Cross and the Italian Silver Medal for Valour, and was promoted to the rank of captain.

Then, two days after the first anniversary of Selous's death, occurred the second great catastrophe of Gladys's life. In aerial combat over German lines, Freddy's frail flying machine broke up in mid-air. The fuselage plunged to earth, and he was killed instantly. His commanding officer wrote to Gladys: 'He was beloved by officers and men alike. In fact, his popularity extended to a far greater area than his own aerodrome. In the short time that I have known him I have been struck with the courage and keenness of your son.'

It was as if some malevolent influence followed the family name. Selous's brother, Edmund, noted that every member who had gone off to war had been killed. The effect of this second terrible blow on Gladys can only be imagined. She never spoke of Freddy, and seems to have tried to erase all evidence of him at home. While Heather-side was kept as Selous had left it, so that his portrait, guns, trophies and the framed illustrations from his books which were hung on the walls, made it seem almost like a shrine to his memory, there was nothing of Freddy to be seen.

Her second son would be lost to her as well, although not through war. Harold Selous left Radley College for officer training, and was commissioned just before the armistice. But after reading modern history at Cambridge, he joined the Colonial Service and went to Nyasaland. Like his father, he fell in love with Africa, and, apart from a few brief visits to England, he remained there until his death in 1954.

Gladys's spirit survived these pains. She remained an attractive and vivacious woman, although often alone in the great rambling house at Heatherside. One of her nieces recalled: 'She had friends, went abroad at intervals (mainly to ski) but often she was a wealthy widow alone. In spite of upbringing she was no church-goer, she was not "clubbable" and did not throw herself into public works. I think she must have had many lonely days.' Gladys did, however, live in some style, with servants who included a team of maids, an exceptionally cantankerous gardener named Renton, and a chauffeur, Pratt, who drove her about in a gleaming Chrysler. The grounds of Heatherside, with its splendid dahlias – for which Gladys took personal responsibility – were opened to the public once a year.

One regular companion of her later years was Percy Molteno, a member of a prominent Cape family, who had been involved with Selous in the South African Conciliation Committee during the Boer War. Molteno was married, but his wife never accompanied him to Heatherside, and resented the attention he paid Gladys. She seems to have indulged, rather than encouraged, these visits, but he was clearly in love with her.

Gladys died in hospital at Guildford in 1951, aged seventy-seven. Harold returned from Nyasaland to settle her estate. He survived her by only three years, and with his death, childless, Selous's line was ended.

By the 1970s, the name Selous had passed into history. Then it reappeared in a new and baleful guise. Thrown on to the defensive by African nationalist guerrillas, the authorities in the rebel white state of Rhodesia decided in 1973 to establish a counter-insurgency force. From this initiative emerged the Selous Scouts, what the Rhodesians called a 'pseudo-terrorist group'. This meant merely that its members assimilated the environment of the enemy, but in the dying days of white Rhodesia, and the increasing brutality of the bush war, the description became grimly apposite to the methods of the Selous Scouts. Massacres, supposedly of guerrillas but in fact including a high proportion of women and children, were carried out on nationalist camps in Mozambique, notably at Nyadzonya. 'Dirty tricks' at home against black civilian opponents of Ian Smith's regime, and the actions of individual Scouts who were plainly psychopathic killers, further tarnished the unit's name. In the end, it was later noted by Smith's intelligence chief, Ken Flower, 'the Scouts frequently operated without authority or beyond recall, and in the latter stages of the war their activities became so questionable that they were the only Rhodesian unit to be disbanded with obloquy.'

It is sad and inappropriate that this notorious group should have been the basis on which the name of Selous has been most widely known in recent times. Africa has often brought out in white people the worst in man. He it ennobled. And despite many misjudgments, his own fondest hope, that a prosperous multi-racial partnership should evolve in the territory between the Limpopo and Zambesi rivers, still survives, despite the upheavals of the past two decades.

Bibliography

MANUSCRIPT COLLECTIONS

(a)   The Zimbabwe National Archives, Harare. This is the most important collection of material on Selous's life, containing his journals and diaries, letters to his mother and private papers. It also houses the correspondence and papers of many contemporaries, and much material relating to the British South Africa Company.

(b)   The Rhodes House Library, Oxford. The archives of the Rhodes Paper, indispensable for study of the British South Africa Company.

(c)   The Royal Geographical Society, London.

(d)   The British Natural History Museum, London.

(e)   The Brenthurst Library, Johannesburg.

PUBLISHED WORKS

Baldwin, William Charles, *African Hunting and Adventure* (1863)
Baines, Thomas, *The Gold Regions of South-East Africa* (1877)
Bent, J. T., *The Ruined Cities of Mashonaland* (1892)
Blake, Robert, *A History of Rhodesia* (1977)
Bulpin, T. V., *To the Banks of the Zambezi* (1965)
Cary, Robert, *A Time to Die* (1968)
Cary, Robert, *Charter Royal* (1970)
Cattrick, Alan, *Spoor of Blood* (1959)
Coillard, François, *On the Threshold of Central Africa* (1897)
Colvin, Ian, *The Life of Jameson* (1922)
Cumming, Roualeyn Gordon, *A Hunter's Life in South Africa* (1850)
Darter, Adrian, *The Pioneers of Mashonaland* (1914)
Finaughty, William, *The Recollections of William Finaughty, Elephant Hunter* (1916)
Gale, W. D., *Zambezi Sunrise* (1958)
Hole, Hugh Marshall, *The Making of Rhodesia* (1926)
Hole, Hugh Marshall, *The Passing of the Black Kings* (1932)
Jeal, Tim, *Livingstone* (1973)
Johnson, Frank, *Great Days* (1940)
Kerr, Walter Montagu, *The Far Interior* (1886)
Lockhart, J. G., and Woodhouse, C. W., *Rhodes* (1963)
Longford, Elizabeth, *Jameson's Raid* (1982)

Mason, Philip, *The Birth of a Dilemma* (1958)
Millais, J. G., *The Life of Frederick Courtenay Selous* (1918)
Miller, Charles, *Battle for the Bundu* (1974)
Newitt, M. D. D., *Portuguese Settlement on the Zambezi* (1973)
Pakenham, Thomas, *The Boer War* (1979)
Patterson, Lieutenant-Colonel J. H., *The Man-eaters of Tsavo* (1907)
Pearson, Hesketh, *Labby – The Life of Henry Labouchère* (1936)
Pease, Sir Alfred, *The Book of the Lion* (1913)
Ranger, Terence, *Revolt in Southern Rhodesia* (1967)
Roberts, Brian, *Cecil Rhodes – Flawed Colossus* (1987)
Robinson, R., and Gallagher, J., *Africa and the Victorians* (1961)
Roosevelt, Theodore, *African Game Trails* (1910)
Selous, F. C., *A Hunter's Wanderings in Africa* (1881)
Selous, F. C., *Travel and Adventure in South-East Africa* (1893)
Selous, F. C., *Sunshine and Storm in Rhodesia* (1896)
Selous, F. C., *Sport and Travel East and West* (1900)
Selous, F. C., *Recent Hunting Trips in British North America* (1907)
Selous, F. C., *African Nature Notes and Reminiscences* (1908)
Selous, F. C., Millais, J. G., and Chapman, Abel, *The Gun at Home and Abroad – The Big Game of Africa and Europe* (1914)
Stokes, E., and Brown, R. (eds), *The Zambesian Past – Studies in Central African History* (1966)
Sykes, Frank W., *With Plumer in Matabeleland* (1897)
Tabler, E. C., *The Far Interior* (1955)
Tabler, E. C. (ed.), *Trade and Travel in Early Barotseland (The Diaries of George Westbeech)* (1963)
Tabler, E. C., *Pioneers of Rhodesia* (1966)
Tabler, E. C. (ed.), *To the Victoria Falls via Matabeleland (The Diaries of Major Henry Stabb)* (1967)
Tawse-Jollie, E., *The Real Rhodesia* (1924)
Wallis, J. P. R. (ed.), *The Southern African Diaries of Thomas Leask* (1954)
Williams, Basil, *Cecil Rhodes* (1921)
Willis, W. A., and Collingridge, L. T., *The Downfall of Lobengula* (1894)
Wilson, Derek, *White Gold, the Story of African Ivory* (1976)

BOOKS ALSO CONSULTED

Anderson, E. N., *The Social and Political Conflict in Prussia 1850–64* (1956)
Baker, Sir Herbert, *Rhodes by his Architect* (1934)
A Biographical Dictionary of Jersey (1948)
Burnham, F. R., *Scouting on Two Continents* (1927)
Churchill, Randolph, *Men, Mines and Animals in South Africa* (1892)
Cloete, Stuart, *African Portraits* (1946)

Fitzpatrick, Sir Percy, *The Transvaal from Within* (1899)
Hall, Richard, *Stanley – An Adventurer Explored* (1974)
Howard, Michael, *The Franco-Prussian War* (1961)
Kruger, Rayne, *Goodbye Dolly Grey* (1959)
Lord, John, *Duty, Honour, Empire: Life of Richard Meinertzhagen* (1971)
Morris, Donald R., *The Washing of Spears* (1966)
Roberts, Brian, *The History of the Kimberley Club* (1976)
Simpson, J. B. S., *Rugby Since Arnold* (1967)
Thomas, Thomas Morgan, *Eleven Years in Central South Africa* (1873)
Whelan, Townsend (ed.), *Hunting Big Game*, Vol. 1 (1946)

ARTICLES

'Mashunaland and the Mashunas', F. C. Selous, *Fortnightly Review*,
  mid-1889
'F. C. Selous – A Character Sketch', *The Review of Reviews*, March
  1893
'The Shooting of the Envoys', F. C. Selous, *African Review*, 1894
'Game Preservation in Africa', F. C. Selous, *African World Annual*,
  1910
'My Most Exciting Adventure', F. C. Selous, *African World Journal*,
  1917
'Taps for the Great Selous', F. R. Burnham, *Boone & Crockett Club
  Annual*, 1929
'A Note Concerning the late Mr Allan Quatermain' (introduction to a
  bibliography of H. R. Haggard's works), J. E. Scott, 1947
'Selous and His Road', Bertha Selous Philips and Elizabeth Walsh,
  African World Annual, Vol. 47, 1951
'Twin of the Twentieth Century' (reminiscences of James John Selous
  in claiming to be the son of F. C. Selous), *Concord*, July 1954
'The Rewriting of African History During the Scramble', Terence
  Ranger, 1963
'Selous – A Reassessment', R. Blair, *Rhodesiana No. 17*, 1967
Proceedings of the Royal Geographical Society, 1881, 1883, 1888, 1893,
  1895
Proceedings of the Royal Colonial Institute, 1892–3, 1894
Proceedings of the Manchester Geographical Society, 1893
African Review, 10 Feb. 1894, 15 Dec. 1894, 19 Jan. 1895
African World Annual, 1910, 1913, 1917, 1918
The Field, Oct. 1875, 16 Dec. 1911, 15 June 1912, 24 Oct. 1918
The Meteor (Rugby School magazine), 7 Feb. 1917
Pall Mall Gazette, 6 Jan. 1917
The Scout, 3 Feb. 1917
South Africa, 25 Dec. 1897, 5 Feb. 1898, 5 Mar. 1898, 13 Jan. 1918

The Times, 16 Feb. 1894, 21 Feb. 1894, 24 Nov. 1899, 31 Oct. 1899, 8 Jan. 1917, 22 Jan. 1917, 30 Apr. 1917
Transvaal Advertiser, 22 Nov. 1888

Index

INDEX

305

INDEX

306

INDEX

INDEX

INDEX

312

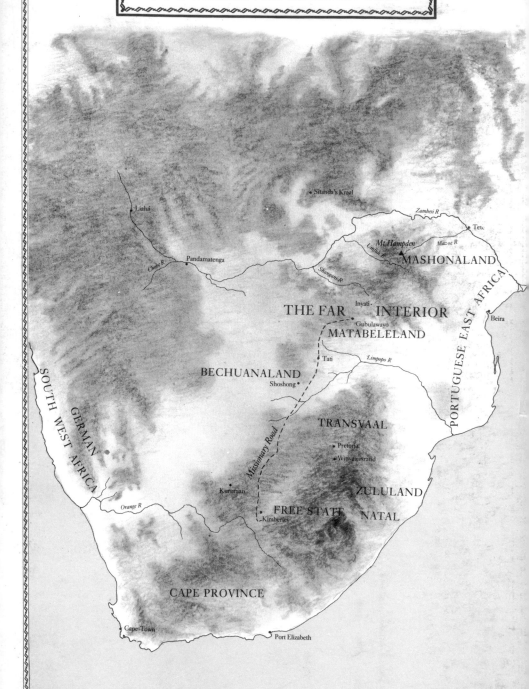

SOUTHERN AFRICA IN 1889